Transformations of Romanticism in Yeats, Eliot, and Stevens

Transformations of Romanticism in Yeats, Eliot, and Stevens

GEORGE BORNSTEIN

The University of Chicago Press

CHICAGO AND LONDON

THE UNIVERSITY OF CHICAGO PRESS, CHICAGO 60637
THE UNIVERSITY OF CHICAGO PRESS, LTD., LONDON
©1976 by The University of Chicago. All rights reserved
Published 1976
Printed in the United States of America
80 79 78 77 76   9 8 7 6 5 4 3 2 1

PS 324
B69

Library of Congress Cataloging in Publication Data
will be found at the end of this book.

For Benjy

Contents

One of the irrelevancies is the romantic. It looks like something completely contemptible in the light of literary intellectualism and cynicism. The romantic, however, has a way of renewing itself. It can be said of the romantic, just as it can be said of the imagination, that it can never effectively touch the same thing twice in the same way. It is partly because the romantic will not be what has been romantic in the past that it is preposterous to think of confining poetry hereafter to the revelation of reality. The whole effort of the imagination is toward the production of the romantic. When, therefore, the romantic is in abeyance, when it is discredited, it remains true that there is always an unknown romantic and that the imagination will not be forever denied. . . . To collect and collate these ideas of disparate things may seem to pass beyond the romantic to the fantastic. I hope, however, that you will agree that if each one of these ideas is valid separately, or more or less valid, it is permissible to have brought them together as a collective source of suppositions . . . relevant to the difficulties of the imagination in a truth-loving time.

Wallace Stevens, *Opus Posthumous*

Preface

This book explores the obsessive relation to British romanticism of three major poets of our century—Yeats, Eliot, and Stevens. Their copious commentaries upon that relation open important approaches to their work and raise broader issues of literary history and poetic theory. The book systematically argues that the growing critical recognition of romanticism's importance to modernism should apply to overtly anti-romantic Eliot as well as to pro-romantic Yeats and Stevens. The best way to see such importance seems to me to alter our way of analyzing poems to emphasize more rigorously their mental action. By that I mean paying more attention to the acts of mind of the speaker as he utters the poem than to the content of his statements. While Stevens' famous reference to "the poem of the act of the mind," like Blake's similar phrases, has served as touchstone before, this book develops it more comprehensively as a central approach to the radical continuity of nineteenth- and twentieth-century poetry.

Chapter 1 provides a theoretical groundwork in two ways. Its first part uses two poems by Stevens, "Of Modern Poetry" and "Man and Bottle," to propound the nature of mental action in Yeats, Eliot, and Stevens and, through them, the relation of modernism to romanticism. While my examples come principally from those three poets, similar instances from other moderns will occur readily to the informed reader. The elements of romanticism most useful for understanding modernism include theories like creative imagination, forms like the Greater Romantic Lyric, and particular manipulations of imagery, speaker, and rhetorical strategy. The high stature of Yeats, Eliot, and Stevens implicates reappraisal of their work with reconsideration of the governing context of modernist criticism, for which their poetry became a prime example and Eliot's prose a prime mover. Accordingly, the second part of the chapter reviews first the rise of anti-romantic criticism in our century and then the more recent works resisting and correcting that trend.

Each of the remaining chapters deals at length with a single poet and comprises two parts: one establishes the centrality of romanticism to the writer's chief aesthetic concerns and the other demonstrates its relevance to his poetry in terms of mental action. While briefly noticing echoes, sources, and parallels, I have emphasized the dynamic nature of each poet's relation to his literary heritage. Typically, poets of this era began writing under the sway of debased, turn-of-the-century romanticism, freed themselves by an anti-romantic reaction, and then later reconciled themselves with their predecessors. The basic pattern allows for enormous diversity. Yeats, who understood romanticism most deeply, began as an adherent of Shelley and Blake, reacted particularly violently against Shelley, and eventually created a poetry of mental action that heightened vision, lessened external nature, and assigned near-independence to images; he is both last of the old romantics and first of the new. Eliot, after his early and superficial romantic phase, became a leading anti-romantic theorist even while covertly resuscitating high romantic modes and developing a poetry whose true theme is his alternate fascination with his own imagination and his fear of it. Stevens, after an initial attraction and then repulsion, eventually won through to what he called "new romanticism" and succeeded in a radical provisionalizing of romantic acts of mind that satisfied both the violence and the vitality of his imagination. As literary historians, these writers seek less to see romanticism steadily and whole than creatively to misinterpret it to find what will suffice; at their best as poets, they seek not to repeat but to transform romanticism into the poetry of our climate.

The role of Eliot in this study deserves special explanation. I see the underlying tension of his work as the conflict between the fear and fostering of explosive powers within the psyche often associated with imagination. In prose he externalized such daemonic forces and projected them most often upon the romantics, while in poetry he sought to snare the eruptions in a framework of order. More even than with most poets, Eliot's prose takes its meaning from his own needs (as he himself acknowledged). The enthusiastic elaboration of his anti-romantic polemics by a generation of commentators has hindered proper appreciation, not just of high romantic poets, or of modern ones like Yeats and Stevens, but even of overtly anti-romantic moderns like Eliot himself. Against the too-credulous adoption of Eliot's premises I advance an antithetical evaluation of his criticism and its relation to both his own poetry and general post-romantic tradition. My opposition to his criticism does not carry over to his poetry, where my aim is not to devalue but to revalue Eliot. The surprisingly close congruence of his best work to romantic norms reveals clearly the internal strains by which that poetry divides against itself. We are left with an Eliot at once more human and more moving, and perhaps more appealing than the traditional figure to my own generation of readers.

A book like this entails many debts. I am more obliged than mere footnotes can tell to the many fine scholars working in the field and trust that those with whom I explicitly disagree will take my remarks as testimony to the continuing importance of their work rather than as poor recompense for their admirable labors. It is a pleasure to record more personal obligations. Professor Daniel Fader, who over the years has taught me a great deal about the art of writing, read and minutely annotated the entire manuscript with scrupulous care. Professors John Margolis and Stuart McDougal read and made helpful comments on several chapters. My research assistants, Susan Clemens and Elizabeth Bergmann, worked cheerfully and perceptively for long hours. Finally, my wife has managed to tolerate and even to encourage my efforts with her customary support and generosity.

This project was begun under a fellowship from the American Council of Learned Societies and completed under a fellowship and grant from the Horace B. Rackham School of Graduate Studies, University of Michigan. I should like to thank them and my department for practical assistance of the most basic kind.

1

Introduction:
The Poem of the Act
of the Mind

In May 1940, after a decade of defending poetry from hostile challenges, Wallace Stevens published "two theoretic poems" on modern poetry and its historical situation. Together they admirably elucidated the tenets of modernism and exemplified its creative transformation of romantic tradition. The second, and better known, was the programmatic "Of Modern Poetry":

> The poem of the mind in the act of finding
> What will suffice. It has not always had
> To find: the scene was set; it repeated what
> Was in the script.
>   Then the theatre was changed
> To something else. Its past was a souvenir.
> It has to be living, to learn the speech of the place.
> It has to face the men of the time and to meet
> The women of the time. It has to think about war
> And it has to find what will suffice. It has
> To construct a new stage. It has to be on that stage
> And, like an insatiable actor, slowly and
> With meditation, speak words that in the ear,
> In the delicatest ear of the mind, repeat,
> Exactly, that which it wants to hear, at the sound
> Of which, an invisible audience listens,
> Not to the play, but to itself, expressed
> In an emotion as of two people, as of two
> Emotions becoming one. The actor is

A metaphysician in the dark, twanging
An instrument, twanging a wiry string that gives
Sounds passing through sudden rightnesses, wholly
Containing the mind, below which it cannot descend,
Beyond which it has no will to rise.
                                        It must
Be the finding of a satisfaction, and may
Be of a man skating, a woman dancing, a woman
Combing. The poem of the act of the mind.[1]

All poetry is an "act of the mind," but Stevens is right to insist that the phrase particularly fits modern poetry. Since the romantics, acts of mind have themselves been the subject and substance of major poems in a direct way. If Wordsworth and Blake showed "the growth of a poet's mind" to be an appropriate subject for epic, they and their contemporaries adapted it for lyric as well. Whether dependent on Wordsworth's egotistical sublime or Keats' negative capability, romantic poems are less about their ostensible subjects than about a psyche interacting with them. "Frost at Midnight" is about Coleridge's mind, "To a Nightingale" about Keats', and even Shelley's "Mont Blanc" is more about Shelley's mind looking through (not with) his eyes at the mountain than about Mont Blanc itself. Likewise, Yeats' "To the Rose upon the Rood of Time" is about himself rather than the Rose; Stevens' "The Sun This March" is not about the sun; and even Pound's haiku-like "In a Station of the Metro" presents not the Metro but his creative reaction to the faces there. The frequency of locational titles suggests one root of this tradition, the neoclassic topographical or meditative-descriptive poem which the romantics metamorphosed into a kind of lyric that is still with us. Since that sea change, title and setting often simply indicate the place in which an act of mind occurs, and the act itself is the true subject of the poem. "Lines Composed a Few Miles above Tintern Abbey," "The Idea of Order at Key West," or, in a more complicated way, *East Coker* belong to this genre.

Stevens' "Of Modern Poetry" offers a starting point to investigate post-romantic poetry of mental action, for it is at the same time a miniature treatise on modern poetics and a poem exemplifying its own tenets. Within Stevens' frame of insistent value in the opening and closing lines, the poem propounds a theory of literary history, diction, subject, effect, and image comprehensive enough to serve as a definition of modernism in poetry. It first establishes that sense of a sharp break with the past so ubiquitous in modern literature. In terms of the theatrical metaphor governing the poem, a change of "theatre" necessitates a change in "scene" and "script." While Stevens does not fully work out this tripartite distinction, "theatre" apparently refers to our entire cultural complex, "script" to actual words in literary art, and "scene" both to conventions of poetry and to our sense of the world around us. In short, poetry as instrument of modern culture recreates a world for us. The poem then issues a catalog of insistent needs in which a series of "has to"s culminates in a categorical "must."

The catalog opens with the poet's recurrent need to revitalize his language. To face us, poetry must "learn the speech of the place," as poets like Yeats, Eliot, and Stevens himself had done about the time of the First World War. That third major revolution toward common style completed for our time the earlier ones of Dryden against Milton and Wordsworth against the Augustans. War itself is an obligatory subject, not only because poetry has a public as well as a private function but also because, for Stevens and others, war serves as a figure for the task of the poet in language and the imaginative man in reality. Blake's *Marriage of Heaven and Hell* (published 1793), the coda to *Notes toward a Supreme Fiction* (1942), and the fifth section of *East Coker* (1940), for example, all formulate semantic and psychological struggles through martial figures, which are themselves a learning of the speech of those places and times.

For the play of mind performed in appropriate language the poet constructs a new "stage" in both the chronological and spatial senses of the word. He creates a new structure appropriate to the new temporal phase of our culture. Within this new scene the poem becomes an actor speaking not to the sensual ear but, like the piper on Keats' urn, to "the delicatest ear of the mind." While the poem can disquiet as well as satisfy, the audience most wants it to realize for the ear of the mind that supreme fiction of a fully achieved humanity which we each crave. Another word for such centrality is *unity*, whether Yeats' Unity of Being or Eliot's unified sensibility. Here, the unity is expressed alternately as two people or two emotions becoming one; in Stevens' world the event suggests the marriage of imagination and reality as well. For all three poets, the modern stage must display a wedding scene of this sort, and harmony—which Yeats traced back particularly to Dante—is an important concept for them.

In the image of the actor as metaphysical musician, Stevens reasserts the radical humanism of post-romantic poetry. This centering of values in a fully realized humanity continues the romantic tradition of Blake, Shelley, and Keats, from which Coleridge saw Wordsworth ("To William Wordsworth") and himself ("The Eolian Harp") as early formulators sometimes timorously retreating. By this point in the poem Stevens' syntax has characteristically lent a sort of visionary reality to his figures of speech. The repeated and calculated obscurity of reference of the pronoun "its" leads us to visualize a poet as an actor playing a stringed instrument in a darkened theater and to forget that the "actor" originated in a simile for modern poetry in line 12 and that the "sounds" refer us back to the linguistic theses immediately preceding that simile. Stevens has created a romantic image of integration like those specified at the end of his poem, but his honest doubt has led him to provisionalize his own creation by denying its independent actuality. Yet "in the dark" both of the new theater and of collapsed traditional values, the familiar harp or guitar of romantic poetry still twangs out sounds "wholly containing the mind." Stevens' modern poem—here the break with Eliot is evident—descends neither to hell nor natural man, and has no will to rise either to heaven or supernatural man; it is a poem of earth and humanity, more than natural and less than religious, and taking the place of both. At the same time, acts of mind, by which Stevens creates and develops his vision, are the determining field of movement for this poem whose overt subject is modern poetry. The poem becomes an example of its own dicta as the language reveals to us the movements of the poet's mind.

In this poem whose syntax tricks us into vision, the framing lines at the start and finish leave us with a sense of urgency rather than of doubt. More important, they give the poem its final rightness. Modern poems present a state of satisfaction less often than the act of finding it, the grail less often than the quest. Uniting the theatrical metaphors and thematic mutations, the "act" of mind results in a phenomenological poetry where the mental action of finding or, more properly, creating satisfaction becomes the poetic subject. Stevens says "finding" because, like the great romantics, he knows that exercise of negative capability is a necessary prelude to imaginative action. Finding this satisfaction is poetry, and is part of what Stevens means when he says in *The Man with the Blue Guitar* that "Poetry is the subject of the poem." He provides another variant of romantic distinctions between poetry (not necessarily in verse) and poem, closer to Shelley's division than to Coleridge's.

4

So far the poem is illuminating but unsatisfying. It suddenly comes right with Stevens' examples of possible subjects—a man skating, a woman dancing, and a woman combing. What do these have to do with "acts of mind"? Stevens superficially appears to have selected inappropriate subjects for his poetic program, and his subtlety here has misled at least one critic into construing the lines as a license for indifference to subject. But random eclecticism was never Stevens' darling: "Not all objects are equal," we read in *Adagia,*[2] for not all objects call forth a full play of mind or represent an achieved self-harmony. Stevens' three images resemble Yeats' famous "body swayed to music" in suggesting unity, formal motion, and self-sufficiency in the production of ordered beauty. In short, they are Images in the special post-romantic sense.[3] Like a girl singing ("Kubla Khan," "The Solitary Reaper," or "The Idea of Order at Key West"), these Images are overt subjects of poems, but only overt. The proper subject of actual poems of the Romantic Image, or for Stevens' hypothetical ones here, is the poet's relation to his icons of unified being, which have at once the order of art and (unlike Keats' marble men) the motion of life. As in Yeats' "The Circus Animals' Desertion," the images grow in pure mind—finding them is a mental act—but out of common experience. By ending with skater, dancer, and comber, and by improvising such an image in the musician, "Of Modern Poetry" becomes a profound commentary on its overt subject and acts out its true one in a second and climactic way.

For all its typicality, Stevens' poem denies the organizational principles of one variety of modern poetry. Unlike the suppression of links in the chain of Eliot's preconversion work or the ideogrammic method of Pound's post-Imagist poems, "Of Modern Poetry" progresses in an immediately comprehensible way. The abrupt juxtapositions of, say, Prufrock give way to the patterns of a mind involved with its own projection of imaginative action in syntactic coherence. We follow the contours of meditative thought to the verge of vision, and the minor syntactic distortion (in pronoun reference) causes us to concede a kind of reality to what is really only a figure of speech. Stevens shares the romantic emphasis on mind and image of Eliot or Pound, but where typically they seize independence through syntactic disruption, he frees himself through syntactic provisionalizing of his vision.

"Of Modern Poetry" simultaneously departs from romantic lyric (Keats' nightingale is a real bird, Stevens' actor a simile come to life) and yet indicates its affinity to that tradition. Its companion

5

poem of 1940, "Man and Bottle," sketches the peculiar relation of romanticism to modernism more clearly:

> The mind is the great poem of winter, the man,
> Who, to find what will suffice,
> Destroys romantic tenements
> Of rose and ice
>
> In the land of war. More than the man, it is
> A man with the fury of a race of men,
> A light at the centre of many lights,
> A man at the centre of men.
>
> It has to content the reason concerning war,
> It has to persuade that war is part of itself,
> A manner of thinking, a mode
> Of destroying, as the mind destroys,
>
> An aversion, as the world is averted
> From an old delusion, an old affair with the sun,
> An impossible aberration with the moon,
> A grossness of peace.
>
> It is not the snow that is the quill, the page.
> The poem lashes more fiercely than the wind,
> As the mind, to find what will suffice, destroys
> Romantic tenements of rose and ice.
>
> (CP 238–39)

Here, as in Stevens' "Sailing after Lunch" and much other modern poetry, the romantic principle of continual perceptual and creative renewal turns against earlier romantic achievement. Like the fountain (itself a traditional image for mind) that destructively flings up the sacred river to disrupt Coleridge's Xanadu, the mind here "destroys romantic tenements/ Of rose and ice." The parallel between the "sunny pleasure dome with caves of ice" and "romantic tenements of rose and ice" combines with the contrast between war and "grossness of peace," images of sun and moon, erotic nuances, and the word "romantic" itself to extend the analogy between these two poems of imaginative mental action. Precise interpretation of the modern one depends on the meaning of "romantic tenements." Tenements carries both the general sense of a building and the more common and precise sense of outmoded or decrepit housing; the word also suggests its legal overtones of land or real property and perhaps its figurative meaning of a dwelling place for the soul. Throughout his career Stevens uses *romantic* in two senses, both of which derive from his responses to literary romanticism. Positively, the word denotes that imaginative perception on which poetry depends. But without recreation within the pulsations of an artery, perception hardens into the dead weight of outmoded convention. Hence, negatively, *romantic* can also denote derivative structures and attitudes leading us into progressive unreality ("delusion"). Stevens, like so many of his contemporaries, could admire monuments of unaging intellect and yet shuffle off coiled conventions to renew romanticism in modern guise. Destruction of romantic architecture in "Man and Bottle" signals overthrow of limiting convention to recover lost impulses and so gather from winter air a live tradition. The parable has both a personal and a historical application, for it describes not only an individual situation but also the development of poetry in English from healthy early romanticism through its debased descendants of the turn of the century to the modernist revolution. Unlike Eliot, who fixated in a facile anti-romantic theory, Stevens and Yeats went beyond this to create a new romanticism for our time.

Despite its razing of romantic tenements, "Man and Bottle" emerges as a poem recognizably in the romantic tradition. As a kind of reverse "Mont Blanc" or "Ode to the West Wind," it emphasizes internal rather than external destructive power and depends on the correspondence between the two. Its whole point lies in the unstated answer to Shelley's question at the end of "Mont Blanc":

> And what were thou, and earth, and stars, and sea
> If to the human mind's imaginings
> Silence and solitude were vacancy?

Although in his prose Shelley repudiated the power of mind to create in the sense of cause its own existence, he in the same essay ("On Life") approached a Berkeleyan position that "Nothing exists but as it is perceived" and elsewhere emphasized the faculty of "Imagination or mind employed in prophetically imaging forth its objects."[4] The implied answer to the question of "Mont Blanc" is "nothing," for only the human mind images forth a value-laden world. In Shelley's poem the mountain's destructiveness yields to a vision of its beneficence, and its vacancy to fullness. So, too, for Stevens does violence of de-creation precede imaginative action. For poets in the romantic tradition, entry into what Yeats called "the desolation of reality" results in new Xanadus.

Correspondence of Stevens' poem to a romantic premise at once thematic and formal gives us a window on those aspects of romanticism helpful for understanding modern poetry, on those acts of mind that made modern poetry possible. To use it we must scrape off the detritus with which imitative later poets and hostile later critics have encrusted original romantic achievements. Without adding another discrimination to Professor Lovejoy's famous list, and without noting all thematic, formal, and technical affinities between romantic and modern poetry, we can usefully indicate those aspects of romanticism relevant for poetry of the act of the mind in the last two centuries. *Mind* here carries its broadest sense, not as narrow denominator of a few mechanistic intellectual operations but as psyche or complex of creative, perceptual, and organizational powers—in short, what Blake meant by his term *mental*. Equally important, the romantics identified mental action itself as a major subject—whether in Blake's *Jerusalem*, Wordsworth's *Prelude*, Coleridge's conversation poems, Shelley's *Prometheus Unbound*, Keats' "Ode to Psyche," or even Byron's *Childe Harold's Pilgrimage*.

Chief among mental powers, whether as lord (to Blake) or *primum inter pares* (to Wordsworth), is imagination. Students of modern poetry seem to me mistaken in stressing the transcendentalizing function of romantic imagination; for their (and our) purposes, the "humanizing" mode is more important. This mode as a touchstone of romanticism carries two major senses—sympathetic and creative. Creative imagination figures in perception as Blake's fiery chariot, allowing us to surpass the mechanical sensation of the corporeal eye, and can involve both making a world by imaginatively perceiving it and making an alternate structure like a poem. To Coleridge Primary Imagination ("the living Power and prime Agent of all human Perception") creates our world for us, while Secondary Imagination ("differing only in *degree*") creates poems. Fancy, in his famous contrast, plays only with given material ("fixities and definites") and is "no other than a mode of Memory emancipated from the order of time and space."[5] This mode also functions as harmonizer of our other faculties.

Keats best exemplifies the other sense of imagination, the sympathetic. Acknowledging an externally existent world, this mode allows the poet to identify with his object of perception or contemplation; it fuses subject and object through projection of the psyche into the object. Keats' letters offer a trivial instance: "If a Sparrow come before my Window I take part in its existence and pick about the Gravel."[6] His poems offer more splendid examples, like the Nightingale ode, where he forgets his sole self to fuse with the songbird ("already with thee") and then is tolled back to himself by the bell-like "forlorn." Such imaginative projection takes place after exercise of Keatsian Negative Capability ("capable of being in uncertainties, Mysteries, doubts, without any irritable reaching after fact & reason") or Wordsworthian "wise passiveness."[7] The romantics did not usually declare wholly for either the creative or the sympathetic modes of imagination; Shelley's *Defence of Poetry*, for example, contains exaltations of both. Modern poets who identify with romantic tradition, like Stevens and Yeats, use the term *imagination* constantly (usually in its creative sense), while those who do not, like Eliot, generally avoid it.

High valuing of imagination had direct formal implications for poetic structure even beyond the characteristic romantic notion of organic form. Because imagination can sustain its own operation and vision only for limited periods, those periods become charged with significance. For poetry of mental action, presentation of those moments shapes design of entire poems. In lyrics, we get framed ecstatic moments, like Keats' sympathetic union with the nightingale or creative imagining of a scene not on the urn. In epics, we get Wordsworth's spots of significant time and Coleridge's admission that "a poem of any length neither can be, or ought to be, all poetry."[8] For long poems one can circumvent this problem only by "spatializing" the moment, as in Blake's apocalypses, or radical condensation, as in Eliot's *Waste Land*. An alternate device is to employ that old form so popular in our century, the long poem consisting of a sequence of lyrics.

For lyrics themselves, strategies for rendering imaginative intervals, or even moments, resulted in innovations of design that poets have followed ever since. In some poems, structure consists of shifting modes of mental action: a speaker in a landscape progresses from description to vision to evaluation. Meyer Abrams has proposed the label "greater Romantic lyric" for this type of poem and has defined it as an "out-in-out process, in which mind [of a speaker] confronts nature and their interplay constitutes the poem."[9] He cites works already mentioned—"Tintern Abbey," "Frost at Midnight," and "Ode to a Nightingale"—as well as Shelley's "Stanzas Written in Dejection" among his examples. I would modify Abrams' argument by holding that the "in" part of his out-in-out process, the part in which the speaker is caught up in a scene that he at least half creates as well as perceives and in which the subject-object distinction weakens or disappears, is not so much simple meditation as vision, sometimes meditative and often involving displacement in space ("Nightingale") or time

("Tintern Abbey"). Occasionally, the controlling mind plunges back into vision at the end, as in the imagined future of Dorothy. Invented largely by Coleridge out of Augustan tradition running from Denham's "Cooper's Hill" to Bowles' sonnets, the form appears in post-romantic poetry with surprising frequency, often substituting human for natural objects. Famous poems like Arnold's "Dover Beach," Whitman's "Crossing Brooklyn Ferry," Yeats' "The Second Coming," Pound's "Provincia Deserta," and Eliot's "Gerontion" all belong to this surreptitious genre. Stevens' "Of Modern Poetry" is a curious variant, which begins with "modern poetry" as object and then generates its own vision out of syntax and imagery, in accord with an out-in-out pattern.

Psychic dramatization and frequent presence of an auditor in Greater Romantic Lyrics suggest their affinity to dramatic monologues, which Robert Langbaum sees as evolving out of romantic "dramatic lyrics."[10] Although dramatic monologues are spoken at moments of high intensity, they lack the visionary structure of Greater Romantic Lyrics. Sometimes they allow for displacement—as when Browning's Duke or Eliot's Magus slips into memory—but they avoid that immersion in vision characteristic of romantic poems. In fact, many of their speakers can be described fairly as failed visionaries, pathological rather than prophetic, whose speeches exceed their occasions. Yet the very gratuitousness of dramatic monologues[11] alerts us to their status as poems of the act of the mind, for their whole purpose is to display a working mind, and we follow it through its characteristic operations. As the tomb-ordering Bishop and J. Alfred Prufrock jump from object to object, their dissociated sensibilities provide a foil to the form and theme of triumphant vision in their romantic antecedents, while in Pound's early monologues we find minds sometimes in harmony with themselves but at subvisionary integration. The sensibility governing a dramatic monologue is often a manqué version of that governing a Greater Romantic Lyric.

Rendering acts of imaginative mind in appropriate form led to revival of quest as a controlling figure. In its search for "what will suffice," Stevens' "Of Modern Poetry" both continues post-romantic motifs and indicates the decisive romantic innovation in the traditional pattern. The romantics internalized quest romance.[12] Whether in *Alastor* or "La Belle Dame sans Merci," romantic quest involves overcoming neither external obstacles, as in *The Odyssey*, nor allegorical signs for internal ones, as in *The Divine Comedy* or in mythographic versions of Homer, but rather overcoming projected symbols for internal obstacles. Harold

10

Bloom describes the process as first an inward apocalypse and then an "outward turning of the triumphant Imagination," although he recognizes that romanticism tends toward annihilation of such subject-object distinctions in "a transformed ongoing creation of the Imagination."[13] Romantic poet-heroes do not seek nature; instead, they seek their own powers, to which nature often stands as adversary (as in Blake). Whether successful or not, such questers encounter obstacles that figure forth dangers in their own psyches and seek a goal that is a projection of ideal self-realization, or of the world as it would then look. For all their links with French, Celtic, or other sources, Stevens' Crispin and Yeats' Aengus stand clearly in the line of Blake's Milton, Keats' Endymion, or Shelley's *Alastor* youth, while Eliot's Tiresias and Yeats' persona in *A Vision* continue an alternate romantic tradition of using historical material as symbolic psychic projection.

The terms of romantic quest generate a multiple poetic application that recalls medieval fourfold allegory and yet differs from it in significant ways. As opposed to carrying possible tropological, anagogical, and formally allegorical senses that supplement the literal sense, romantic symbols function either as objects for imaginative interaction or as bearers of multiple but less rigidly codified meanings. Thus, the French Revolution in Blake or Prometheus' retraction in Shelley applies to political, individual, and aesthetic processes. In their search to discover archetypes that unify ordinarily disparate experiences by allowing them to be described and perceived in the same terms, romantics at their best tend toward multiple application not readily translatable into other phraseology, as much medieval literature is into theological doctrine, which is one reason romantic scholars so often borrow terminology from their poets. Multiple application in the romantic rather than medieval mode carries over into modern poetry. Yeats' "Sailing to Byzantium" seems at once to be about art, afterlife, and general imaginative experience; Eliot's "Gerontion" combines historical, sexual, and religious meanings in its "After such knowledge, what forgiveness" section; and Stevens' "Man and Bottle" uses war in political, aesthetic, and psychological senses. These poems are polysemous in a romantic manner.

This multiple symbolism alerts us to the true goal of romantic adaptation of religious terminology to secular experience. Although Eliot used the nineteenth-century impetus toward a religion of art as a stick to beat Matthew Arnold, the original romantic notion was to make traditional terminology into an Esperanto of all psychic activity. One burden of Meyer Abrams' recent monumental study is to use "displacement from a supernatural to a natural [I would substitute "imaginative"] frame of reference" to demonstrate "that Romantic thought and literature represented a decisive turn in Western culture."[14] Narrowing that enterprise down to a religion of art was a late nineteenth-century development that ignored original romantic insistence that art, especially poetry, was a paradigm for all mental action. In the *Defence of Poetry* Shelley could maintain that "Language, colour, form, and religious and civil habits of action, are all instruments of poetry" (it is clear that his list could be extended) and that the *Divine Comedy* and *Paradise Lost* had "conferred upon modern mythology a systematic form." Despite Eliot's stubborn rearguard action, that form still endures most often without its doctrinal base; he and romantics from Blake to Stevens read different Dantes.

Organization and direction of romantic imagery supplement the shift from religious to secular application in affecting subsequent poetry. Although nearly all poets use coherent symbolic patterns, Yeats was the first modern poet to exploit them systematically and to propagandize for his technique, which he learned from Blake and Shelley. Therefore he used similar symbols—his tower is one—in a similar manner, in which poems become fully comprehensible "as the years go by and one poem lights up another."[15] This extraordinary degree of symbolic organization, not necessarily wholly conscious to the poet or wholly evident to the new reader, is at once a great strength of romantic poetry and a major obstacle to understanding it. For if such organization lends power, it also demands mastery of a poet's entire work to understand any part of it properly. Although Stevens understood the point well enough to want to call his collected poems "The Whole of Harmonium,"[16] modern criticism largely neglected Yeats' early hint and had to wait for post-World War II defenses of romanticism to discover the extraordinary precision of romantic poetry. Yet this idea of a structure of symbols from various works informing one of them fits well with modern literary theory. Despite Eliot's anti-romanticism, his notion of simultaneous presence and ideal order of past works derives from romantic tenets, and it is no accident that the most prodigious organizer of symbols and genre for our time, Northrop Frye, is an unreconstructed Blakean. Taken one step further, the notion results in comprehending all history as Shelley's "episodes of that cyclic poem written by Time upon the memories of men."[17]

Equally important, the romantics began a change in direction of our "spatial projection of reality." In a brilliant essay Frye contends that:

> The metaphorical structure of Romantic poetry tends to move inside and downward instead of outside and upward, hence the creative world is deep within, and so is heaven or the place of the presence of God. Blake's Orc and Shelley's Prometheus are Titans imprisoned underneath experience; the Gardens of Adonis are down in *Endymion,* whereas they are up in *The Faerie Queene* and *Comus;* in *Prometheus Unbound* everything that aids mankind comes from below, associated with volcanoes and fountains. . . . In pre-Romantic poetry heaven is the order of grace, and grace is normally thought of as descending from above into the soul. In the Romantic construct there is a center where inward and outward manifestations of a common motion and spirit are unified, where the ego is identified as itself because it is also identified with something which is not itself. In Blake this world at the deep center is Jerusalem. . . .[18]

Although I think Frye overstates the case (his argument would in effect force us to extend to other exceptions the label "pre-Romantic," which he applies to awkward passages in Wordsworth), his contention is largely true. Equally important are his correlation of spatial projection with the human mind as model and his closing suggestion that modernism did not create a third framework of imagery, so that even its anti-romantic strain "had no resources for becoming anything more than a post-Romantic movement."[19] Frye gives only one modern example, from Auden, but many others abound. Thus, among our poets, the gravediggers of "Under Ben Bulben" thrust buried men back down into the human mind; Stevens writes a final soliloquy of the interior paramour; and Prufrock lingers in chambers of the sea.

Most of the poems we have been discussing have identifiable speakers, but romantic manipulation of organized imagery made possible a second type of poetry of mind, a psychodrama in which the poem's contents become projections of psychic activity. In Shelley's *Prometheus Unbound* the entire poem is a projection for us of a paradigmatic psyche, of which "characters" like Prometheus, Jupiter, and Demogorgon are but parts.[20] As Shelley pointed out in the preface, his imagery was "drawn from the operations of the human mind." Yeats adapted this strategy for *The Wanderings of Oisin,* while to the extent that Eliot misses the goal (as stated in his own note to line 218) of having all *Waste Land* speakers somehow merge into Tiresias, his poem becomes a psychodrama of failed integration. *The Waste Land* is to *Prometheus Unbound* or *Jerusalem* what "Prufrock" is to the Greater Romantic Lyric—a projection of a figure of less unified and less fully active sensibility.

In lyric the technique results in "speakers" who are neither characters nor personae but themselves projections of mental principles. Some of Blake's Pickering Manuscript poems, like "The Golden Net," fit this description. Among moderns, Stevens' interior paramour and angel of reality adapt romantic procedure, while in *The Wind Among the Reeds* Yeats carefully explained that he used Aedh, Hanrahan, and Robartes "more as principles of the mind than as actual personages." (*VP* 803) The lyric "Aedh [later, "He"] hears the Cry of the Sedge," for example, is "spoken" by the sacrificial aspect of imagination. Often poems mix their modes: the adventurous portions of *Alastor* belong to psychodrama but the Narrator's interpolations belong to a character (himself). To rephrase Earl Wasserman's interpretation of the poem, it presents a speaker narrating a psychodrama he himself does not understand.[21]

Speakers who embody principles of mind mark an extreme case of "impersonality" in romantic poetry. Contrary to critical rumor, there are far fewer romantic confessional or personal poems than hostile scholars claim. A distinction between poet as poet and poet as man pervades romantic theory. Shelley told the Gisbornes that "the poet & the man are two different natures,"[22] while even Wordsworth insisted that the emotion ensuing after tranquil recollection and contemplation was only *"kindred* to that which was before the subject of contemplation."[23] The apparently autobiographical "Resolution and Independence" grew out of Wordsworth's encounter with an old beggar, whom Wordsworth then *imagined* meeting in the poem plying his former trade of leech gathering. But even if Wordsworth had met the old sailor gathering leeches, the distinction between persona and person would hold as well for romantic as for other poetry. Fortunately, such quaint notions as the poet-persona falling on the thorns of life in "Ode to the West Wind" being Percy Bysshe Shelley the man are no longer in need of refutation. For convenience' sake, we may refer to the speaker of "Ode to the West Wind" as "Shelley," but that is simply a shorthand term to avoid repetition of awkward locutions. Romantic poetry is as "impersonal" as any other, as Yeats and Stevens knew. As manuscripts of *The Waste Land* and new biographical information about Eliot come to light, one wonders in what sense he escaped from personality and emotion more fully than did Shelley.

Why has full realization of the impact of romantic poetry, not just on Yeats, Eliot, and Stevens but on the modernist movement to which they belong, not found its way into literary histories sooner? The answer lies in the anti-romantic bias of Eliot (abetted to a lesser extent by Pound) and its influence on a generation of scholars and critics. In creating a literary theory to justify modern poetry, Eliot read his objections to the late, decadent romanticism that surrounded him back into the early, strong variety. The New Critics and others elaborated his scattered broadsides into a systematic critique, which dropped the romantics (and behind them Spenser and Milton) virtually out of the mainstream of poetic tradition.

II

Canonization of modern poetry in general, and of Eliot in particular, was won at the cost of warping literary history. The great romantics and their admired Milton lost prestige and nearly disappeared from modernist views of "the tradition" except as heretical deviations. The years *entre deux guerres* saw Donne as a Metaphysical Ariel casting out recently unmasked Calibans. Elaborated by influential figures like the New Critics in America and the *Scrutiny* group in England, this view came to dominate curricula in schools and universities, despite some heated opposition. A countermovement began in earnest after the Second World War, but lacking the broad appeal and polemical skill of the anti-romantics—and perhaps also the charismatic personalities—it failed at first to win widespread allegiance even within the academies. Romantic scholars saw their subject whole, but almost no one else did. This split persisted until the late fifties and early sixties, when the achievements of romantic scholarship began to make conventional views impossible to accept. By then, too, the first important postwar studies tracing single aspects of poetic development from the early nineteenth to early twentieth centuries had appeared. But what was needed, and still is, was a reappraisal of modernist poetry from a viewpoint recognizing the centrality of romanticism, for in distorting literary history, criticism had distorted modernism itself.

A mode of criticism and view of literary history eager to deny the latent romanticism within modern poetry derived principally from Eliot's early writings, with some methodological support from those of I. A. Richards. While postponing detailed treatment of Eliot's theses until chapter 3, we can note here that he reacted against the decline of romantic lyricism in the Georgian poets, and the degradation of prophetic stance in writers like Henry Newbolt,[24] by positing a poetry whose speaking voice evinced a unified sensibility of thought and feeling. Since the best analogue in English literary history was the early seventeenth century, Eliot capitalized on the Donne revival by installing him and lesser Metaphysicals as standards for judging other writers. Wit, irony, logical and sensory precision, maturity—these were the characteristics that guaranteed an integrative mind able to amalgamate Spinoza, typewriters, and cooking smells. Particularly damaging to some romantic (and modern) poetry was insistence on wit, which involved "a recognition, implicit in the expression of every experience, of other kinds of experience which are possible, which we find as clearly in the greatest as in poets like Marvell."[25] These values combined congenially with I. A. Richards' affective poetics, which also stressed irony ("bringing in of the opposite"[26]) and located value in ever-greater states of complexity and harmonized balance. Judged by these criteria, though more to Eliot than to Richards, romanticism emerged as an egotistical deviation, infected by crude emotion, a weak grasp on reality, pretentious claims, and uncertain technical skill. Shelley in particular evoked hysterical denunciations from Eliot, while Keats became the most attractive romantic.[27]

American New Critics like Cleanth Brooks and Allen Tate, as well as British critics like F. R. Leavis, absorbed the lessons of Richards and seized upon Eliot's scattered pronouncements to reconstruct English literary tradition into a vast preparation for the modernism they so admired. Two books of the late thirties —Brooks' *Modern Poetry and the Tradition* (1939) and Leavis' *Revaluation* (1936)—illustrate the trend. Both set up a poetic line beginning with the Metaphysicals and emphasize "wit" even in their chapter titles (Brooks' "Wit and High Seriousness" and Leavis' "The Line of Wit"). Both avowedly elaborate Eliot's views, Leavis citing Eliot's critical achievement in the second sentence of his initial chapter. Brooks demotes Milton by barely mentioning him, confining himself to asides like calling Milton's Lucifer "an example of metaphysical wit."[28] Leavis devotes a chapter to demonstrating that Milton "forfeits all possibility of subtle or delicate life in his verse," displays "a guileless unawareness of the subtleties of egotism," and appeals to "minds that have no glimmer of intelligence about contemporary literature."[29] Both exalt Keats, abuse Shelley, and take a mixed view of Wordsworth. Brooks moves on to modern poetry, where he finds Eliot and Yeats the two masters, while Leavis refers readers to his earlier *New Bearings in English Poetry* (1932), which stressed Eliot, Pound, and Hopkins. For both critics, as for so many others of their generation, to defend modernism was to attack romanticism. "The prevailing conception of poetry is still primarily defined for us by the achievement of the Romantic poets," noted Brooks in 1939. "The modern poetry of our time is the first to call that view seriously in question."[30]

The resultant enthusiastic misreadings have been refuted often enough since Richard Harter Fogle's early and devastating critique, "Romantic Bards and Metaphysical Reviewers,"[31] to free us now for a more general look at their causes. What anti-romantic modernists most often wanted in poetry was a complex union of heterogeneous materials inspired by experience in life. Preoccupied with searching for a speaking voice with the tones of Donne, they missed the point of much romantic poetry because they could fathom neither the psychodramatic mode nor the lyrics whose "speakers" were principles of mind. One of the most ironic moments in literature comes in the first act of *Prometheus Unbound*, when Jupiter's Phantom repeats Prometheus' curse and thus mindlessly curses himself. Yet this brilliant presentation of deformed desire witlessly turning back on itself depends on our seeing the poem as psychic projection. We also need to recognize both the speaker's prophetic stance and adaptation of religious rhetoric to see that "I fall upon the thorns of life! I bleed!" does not signify Shelley the man wallowing in self-pity. The habit has a deep hold: even in a well-meaning "Retrospective Introduction" (1965) to *Modern Poetry and the Tradition,* where he indicates a desire to "lay more stress on the extent to which Eliot, Yeats, and the other modern poets built upon the Romantic tradition,"[32] Brooks praises Wordsworth's "A Slumber Did My Spirit Seal" for suggesting "a series of paradoxes worthy of John Donne."[33]

Search for an individualized speaking voice in poems deliberately contrived to avoid one leads to distortion of modern as well as romantic poetry. "If a man is to write lyric poetry he must be shaped by nature and art to some one out of half a dozen traditional poses, and be lover or saint, sage or sensualist, or mere mocker of all life," wrote Yeats.[34] Even in poems not "spoken" by principles of mind, Yeats' search for intense, passionate speech combined with adoption of stock poses to prevent the sort of irony dear to modern inventors of the Donne tradition. They have on

17

occasion invented examples of Metaphysical wit in his work, as in suggesting that "artifice" in "artifice of eternity" carries negative connotations in the Keatsian vein of cold pastoral. Instead of paying attention to the dynamics of vision, the critic is finding doubts in the diction. A similarly skewed emphasis occurs when Leavis confronts the fourth stanza of "Ode on a Grecian Urn." Instead of discussing the end of the stanza as the intensest part of a developing vision, with Keats *imagining* there a scene not even on the urn, he reads the poem as a "daydream" and the lines as showing Keats' ironic awareness of the futility of "getting it both ways":

> The serenity, before the end of the stanza, takes on another quality. . . . That "emptied" is a key-word: we end the stanza contemplating, not the scene of ideally happy life, but the idea of streets that
>
>> for evermore
>> Will silent be,
>
> and of a town to which
>
>> not a soul to tell
>> Why thou art desolate, can e'er return.[35]

Leavis does not so much mistake as reduce the meaning here, for the sorrow of imagination approaching its own exhaustion cuts deeper than the verbal byplay he allows. In 1942 Allen Tate claimed that "Yeats's romanticism will be created by his critics";[36] in retrospect, we can see now that what they created instead was Keats' Metaphysical modernity.

Recent important corrections to modernist orthodoxy have succeeded not just on their own substantial merit but also because acceptance of modern poetry was making embattled defense unnecessary even while advances in romantic scholarship were making anti-romantic prejudice look silly. Consequently, more current books denying a strong link between romanticism and modernism have argued their cases more tactfully. The two most important recent statements have been J. Hillis Miller's *Poets of Reality* (1965) and Monroe K. Spears' *Dionysus and the City: Modernism in Twentieth-Century Poetry* (1970). For all the difference between Miller's implicit affinity with modern French criticism and Spears' roots in American New Criticism, they both seek to separate modernism from romanticism.

On its surface Miller's argument arouses little objection. "My interpretation of these writers questions the assumption that twentieth-century poetry is merely an extension of romanticism," he states. "A new kind of poetry has appeared in our day, a poetry which grows out of romanticism, but goes beyond it."[37] The key word here is "merely": not even the most avid romanticist would want to reduce modernism to a repetition or simple extension of the past. Yet it is possible to argue that modernism is, among other things, a development of and from romanticism, indebted to its forebear in important ways and departing from it in others; at its best, modernism is often a creative transformation of romanticism, not fully comprehensible without it. Miller's conception of the two periods prevents him from doing this. He sees a "double bifurcation" in romanticism, involving splits between two realms (heaven and earth, supernatural and natural) and between subject and object; together, these lead to an attempt "to reach God through the object."[38] This conception omits the whole visionary and apocalyptic strain of romanticism best exemplified by Blake, as Miller admits. His argument, in effect, contrasts modernism with one aspect of romanticism. But even that contrast is questionable, for it is difficult to maintain that distinctions like that between subject and object are more basic to Shelley than, say, to Yeats. Likewise, Miller's notion that nihilism is a possible romantic consequence which modern poets must work through en route to a new poetry of reality neglects the extent to which that working through is a chief ingredient in romanticism itself. Then, too, Miller says little of modern development of characteristic romantic forms and techniques. Concerned with mind, he abstracts philosophic statements from a body of poetry rather than following the mental action through a specific poem. One is left with a sense that in the brief theoretical introduction to his complex book he exaggerates a philosophic distinction into a literary position he does not need to defend.

Monroe Spears, former editor of the New Critical *Sewanee Review*, begins by confronting "the chief historical question, that of the relation of modernism to Romanticism."[39] He wants to save the "modern" Eliot generation from confusion with "contemporary" neo-romantic cohorts of Allen Ginsberg. To do that he first argues against strategies for yoking romanticism to modernism and then sets up four "forms of discontinuity"—metaphysical, aesthetic, rhetorical, and temporal—as hallmarks of poetic modernism. "The great moderns are haunted by the fear of discontinuity and obsessed by the problem of relating past and present," he concludes.[40] So, however, were the great romantics. Of Spears' four discontinuities, only the rhetorical seems unromantic, and even here we have recent efforts by the unlikely pair of Auden and Brooks to trace modern alogical juxtapositions

19

back to Keats' "Ode to a Nightingale" and Wordsworth's Lucy poems.[41]

Spears locates three major varieties of the argument for a romantic view of modernism, which he identifies primarily with Edmund Wilson, Northrop Frye, and Frank Kermode. First, he unfortunately misstates Wilson's position: "Modernism, according to Wilson, was merely a second wave of Symbolism." Wilson in fact saw modernism not simply as a Second Symbolist Coming, but as "its [Symbolism's] fusion or conflict with Naturalism."[42] Nevertheless, Spears properly stresses that Wilson exaggerated the resemblance of Yeats and Eliot to the Symbolists as well as their allegedly escapist tendencies. Symbolism itself remains a minor conduit of reshaped romantic tenets into modernism, though in ways whose intricacy has not yet been fully revealed. Against Frye's Blakean view of romanticism[43] Spears scores fewer points. To argue that "Romanticism as thus defined [that is, by Frye] has nothing to do with the retreat from reality and the connotations of ineffectual dreaminess which are part of the meaning of the word for such critics as Wilson"[44] is simply to say that Frye avoids errors made by earlier critics. Mere repetition does not confer validity on mistaken interpretations. Spears' second charge against Frye is true in part: he holds that the argument lacks "operational validity" because "the innocent reader who approaches Eliot or Pound as he would Wordsworth or Shelley, in the faith that they are all Romantic and therefore to be read in the same way, will soon discover that he has been misled."[45] Yet this is not so fully true as it first sounds. Frye's own successful recreations of imagistic patterns for poets of both periods use the same method with equally valuable results, while his theory of archetypes applies to the whole of literature. One aim of the present book is to provide alternate techniques, such as interpreting "Gerontion" or "The Second Coming" as Greater Romantic Lyrics. Finally, Spears treats Kermode's thesis which finds "the essence of modernism in a special poetics of the Image."[46] Here Spears is illuminating, although he confuses Kermode's avowed antipathy to the "noxious historical myth of Symbolism"[47] with his admiration for a poetics of the Image. Kermode uses a refutation of Symbolist literary history to combat Eliot's view of English literary tradition, but he wants to reinstate Milton partly in terms of Images.[48] That is, Kermode rejects anti-romantic modernist myths of literary history and establishes an important congruence between modern and romantic poetry.

Although Spears emphasizes the work of a Canadian, Frye, and an Englishman, Kermode, two Americans, Harold Bloom and Robert Langbaum, also belong at the forefront of numerous critics recently arguing for continuities between the romantic and modern poetic revolutions.[49] Before examining those four revisionists more closely, we may pause over Stephen Spender's transitional *The Struggle of the Modern* (1963). Himself a distinguished poet of the second modernist generation, Spender elaborates a provocative thesis:

> We are confronted with the paradox that although there has been a reaction against the Romantics and back towards the poets who preceded them, nevertheless, the same poet-critics who made this revolt have taken over the subjective view of the imagination which was Romantic.[50]

He argues that the modern "revolution in method, in technique" carried a romantic emphasis on imagination at its theoretic core. In seeing this, Spender has half-liberated himself from anti-romantic literary mythology, although he still views romantic metaphor as "vague" and Shelley's collected works as "a wild, exotic, and unweeded garden." Even so, Spender thinks "The Romantics are of our modern world, and modern poetry comes out of their situation."[51]

In his remarkable chapter "A Short History of the Pers. Pron. 1st Sing. Nom." Spender comes as close to describing a poetry of mind of the last two centuries as his view of romanticism will allow. He sees that in modern reinvention of reality "the mode of perceiving itself becomes an object of perception"[52] and focuses on the role of the "I" in poetry. Claiming that "it is the Romantics who are nearest to the moderns," Spender approaches definition of a central impulse in romantic poetry; only the introduction of "feelings" at the end of this sentence indicates that his analysis is about to go wrong: "The Romantic 'I,' reacting against the exalted but limited and transparent intellectual 'I' of the eighteenth-century élite, projects the 'I' from which art has never quite escaped since—the seductive artistic 'I' which suggests that what is art for the artists, might become life for the spectator and reader living out Romantic feelings." As his use of the reductive catch-word "feelings" portends, Spender immediately trivializes his insight: "Every reader is free to imagine himself to some extent a potential Byron, Keats, Shelley or Dylan Thomas not in writing his Romantic poetry, but in taking over his feelings and behaviour, sharing his self-destruction, loving his women, drinking his drinks."[53] Had he gone on to elaborate the analogy between psychic integration of a poet-persona in literature and a fully realized humanity of a reader in life, Spender would have forged a strong connection between romanticism and modernism as poetry of mind. Instead, he leaves us as armchair voyeurs of bohemian life.

By evaluating the main line of romanticism in Blakean terms, Northrop Frye and Harold Bloom avoid Spender's limitations. Frye's rehabilitation of quest romance, with exposure of its attendant imagistic patterns, has rescued a sizable tract of poetry for serious criticism. That achievement began with his revolutionary study of Blake, *Fearful Symmetry* (1947), whose "whole purpose" was "to establish Blake as a typical poet and his thinking as typically poetic thinking."[54] In arguing for the centrality of Blake, Frye overthrew tacit academic connivance at the Eliotic position that Blake was a poet of queer genius suffering from "the crankiness, the eccentricity, which frequently affects writers outside of the Latin [and, presumably, Metaphysical] traditions."[55] Redirecting critical emphasis from Blake's lyrics to his prophetic books, Frye legitimized the prophetic stance on which so many romantic poems depend. Basic to exfoliation of his theories in *Anatomy of Criticism* (1957) and elsewhere is his contention for Blakean imagination as mythopoetic norm.

Most brilliant of critics decisively influenced by Frye is Harold Bloom, who has provided both a Blakean reading of romantic poetry in *The Visionary Company* (1961) and suggestive comparisons with modernism both there and in his studies of individual poets. Throughout, Bloom's guiding principles have been acceptance of Blake's identification of imagination with the real man and insistence that "the theory of poetry is the theory of life."[56] What concerns us more than the controversial particulars of his interpretations is his recent collection of essays, *The Ringers in the Tower: Studies in Romantic Tradition* (1971), the closest extant approach to a survey of romantic literature of the last two centuries. Although he mentions Pound and Eliot only in passing gibes, Bloom uses his notion of internalized quest to trace convincingly an ongoing post-romantic literary tradition whose chief English antecedents are Spenser, Shakespeare, and Milton. In Britain the line runs from the romantics themselves through Tennyson, Hallam, Browning's "Childe Roland," Ruskin, and Pater to Lawrence and Yeats, while in America Emerson and Whitman prepare the

way for moderns like Stevens and contemporaries like A. R. Am-
mons.

A new theory of poetic influence accompanies this recontruction
of the canon. Bloom's *Yeats* (1970) and my own *Yeats and Shelley*
(1970) independently evolved the pattern of a later poet's use of
creative misinterpretation of an admired precursor: initial
identification with him, swerve into independence, and final
(though partial) reconciliation. Here we pass beyond traditional
histories of literature to a conception that parallelisms of idea or
image are valuable not merely as explicatory aids but more impor-
tantly as signs of a poet putting the past to creative use in achieving his own poetic identity. In *Ringers in the Tower* Bloom an-
nounces that his "major subject is poetic influence (perhaps rather
poetic misprison), conceived as an anxiety principle or variety of
melancholy, particularly in regard to the relation between poets in
the Romantic tradition."[57] This seed has generated Bloom's
strange and wonderful sequence beginning with *The Anxiety of
Influence* (1973), one of the major works of critical mythography in
our century, with its eclectic proliferation of Greek terms and abstruse psychobiography. Bloom's thesis describes his own relation
to his own critical precursors—Blake and Shelley, Nietzsche and
Freud—with astonishing clarity. I do not think that it fully fits
even the strong poets he legitimately chooses, for despite its
enormous erudition the book belongs to mythology in the best
sense rather than to literary scholarship. While we often come to
similar conclusions, Bloom and I arrive by antithetical
methodologies and foci. Although I do not subscribe to Bloom's
multiple uses of the term *anxiety*, to some of his more recondite
terminology, or to his moving and terrible doubts about the value
of poetry and historical status of romanticism, I do support his
dynamic conception of literary history. Pro-romantic Yeats and
Stevens, as well as anti-romantic Eliot, all used romanticism to
formulate their own poetic strategies and stances, whether in
quietly borrowing ore from loaded rifts or noisily labeling part of
the romantic treasure trove as fool's gold. They sometimes projected onto romantic poets obstacles they feared within themselves and then attacked their own hypostatized flaws. Perhaps for
all self-conscious poets, literary history becomes a quest for poetic
identity.

Working from different assumptions than the neo-Blakeans,
Frank Kermode also forced a reassessment of recent literary history in his *Romantic Image* (1957). He locates continuity between

romantic, symbolist, and modern poets in "these two beliefs—in the Image as a radiant truth out of space and time, and in the necessary isolation or estrangement of men who can perceive it," both of which he sees as "thoroughly Romantic" and "true for critics and poets who are militantly anti-Romantic."[58] By *romantic,* Kermode means high valuation of image-making mental powers and substitution of organic for mechanical conceptions of art. The Image itself seeks to reconcile opposites such as action and contemplation, and takes for its most frequent emblem "the beauty of a woman, and particularly of a woman in movement."[59] Although Kermode does not mention them, Stevens' woman dancing in "Of Modern Poetry" is the archetypal figure, while the woman combing or man skating in that poem are possible alternates.

Kermode's useful insights need modification in two ways. First, in his urge to discredit Eliot's version of literary history, Kermode too simply conflates Pound's *image* and *vortex* or Eliot's symbolism with the Romantic Image itself, either in earlier writers or in moderns like Yeats and Stevens. By allowing more for development within the tradition, and by distinguishing between the relative richness of Yeats' reinterpretation and the relative poverty of Pound's, he could still have challenged anti-Miltonic literary history while rescuing romantic moderns from a literary guilt-by-association. Second, most poems in this genre present not simply the Romantic Image itself but the poet's struggle to create it: they are poems of mind in the act of creating the Image. Kermode comes close to sensing this in contending that in "Among School Children" Yeats "involves us in the children and their work, in the poet's self-deceptive pose, before he shows us how all this is related to the bronze and the marble, the dancer and the tree" because of a desire "to speak of his own part in the process of perception-creation."[60] The first six stanzas of the poem present not just autobiographical background but crucial steps toward vision in a modified Greater Romantic Lyric, and presentation of process rather than result of vision is the realized goal of the poem. We need to shift the focus of analysis from the Image itself to the mental action that creates and sustains the Image in the poem.

The last of our revisionists, Robert Langbaum, began such an exploration in his *The Poetry of Experience,*[61] which appeared the same year as Kermode's book. In his introductory chapter on "Romanticism as a Modern Tradition," Langbaum parried stock charges of sentimentality, inflated diction, and formlessness in romantic poetry and argued that "the essential idea of romanticism . . . is . . . the doctrine of experience—the doctrine that the imaginative apprehension gained through immediate experience is primary and certain, whereas the analytic reflection that follows is secondary and problematical. The poetry of the nineteenth and twentieth centuries can thus be seen in connection as a poetry of experience."[62] By emphasizing Victorian dramatic monologues Langbaum charted a direct English route from romanticism to modernism, bypassing the usual French detour of Symbolism. The monologues of Browning and Tennyson provided a native continuity between dramatic lyrics of Wordsworth, Keats, or Shelley on the one hand and Pound, Eliot, and Yeats on the other. Likewise, by treating experience itself rather than pure Images, Langbaum provided a counterweight to Kermode's analysis.

In postulating "a form imitating not nature or an order of ideas about nature but the structure of experience itself," Langbaum very nearly defined a poetry of the act of mind, primarily in terms of nineteenth-century examples. He swerved away from it in two main ways, both of them shifts to affective modes of criticism. First, in extending Joyce's term *epiphany* to the "climax of a dramatic action"[63] he emphasized not the pattern of visionary experience but "disequilibrium between the moment of insight, which is certain, and the problematical idea we abstract from it." This is a valid concern, as the last stanza of the Nightingale ode attests, but it leads away from consideration of the whole shape of experience. Correspondingly, he sees dramatic monologues as "a poetry of sympathy"[64] in which the reader's disequilibrium between sympathy and judgment guarantees that the poem imitates not life but human experience. Langbaum's illuminating thesis justifies his switch to affective aspects of dramatic monologues, but displaces his concern from sequential revelation of the speaker's acts of mind as subjects of the poems to the reader's evaluative assessment of the speaker's account of himself.

Looking at modernism in terms of acts of mind causes us to revalue the place of romanticism in literary history and to alter the terms in which we discuss poetry of the last two centuries. Centrality of imagination leads to continuities of both form and technique. Forms such as the Greater Romantic Lyric or dramatic monologue complement psychodramas or poems in which the "speaker" is a principle of mind. Both strategies project reality in similar spatial patterns of imagery and often involve internalized quest, multiple application, displacement of religious imagery to secular experience, and pursuit of the Romantic Image. The re-

25

maining chapters of this book examine in turn the work of three major modern poets, first defining their conceptions of romanticism (often creative misinterpretations) and then establishing the relationship of their own poetry to romantic tradition. We begin with a self-proclaimed last romantic, Yeats, progress through the overtly anti-romantic Eliot, and conclude with the new romanticism of Stevens.

2

The Last Romanticism of W. B. Yeats

Our greatest modern poet repeatedly and accurately labeled himself a romantic. The declarations come not just in the famous and often misunderstood lines from "Coole Park and Ballylee, 1931" but throughout his work. The recently published rough draft for his autobiography, made fifteen years before that poem, includes five separate pledges of allegiance. "I was a romantic in all," he recalls early on, and he repeats the phrase later: "I had, a romantic in all, a cult of passion."[1] Throughout his prose and poetry, Yeats tirelessly links himself to romantic forerunners, both by explicit avowal and by continual implicit testimony of his own poetry. One might expect such clear evidence to have shaped not only higher criticism of Yeats but also modern criticism and literary history generally, yet such has not happened. Only recently have Yeats studies moved beyond an early and influential error that "Yeats's romanticism will be created by his critics" toward a proper placing of Yeats himself in romantic tradition.[2] The first part of this chapter argues that Yeats' concept of romanticism, his construal of romantic heroes as incarnations of passionate mood or as principles of mind, and his interpretation of specific romantics display psychological doctrines and mental actions making the poet's quest for images the paradigmatic imaginative act. The second part applies those conclusions to a reading of the mature poetry, particularly to the surprising number of Greater Romantic Lyrics.

In his Introduction to *The Oxford Book of Modern Verse* (1936),[3]

Yeats saw clearly the connection between romantic and modern. Here, as in his pioneering essay on Shelley or his brilliant and at times bizarre commentary on Blake, he was decades ahead of modern scholarship. After acknowledging the "revolutionary importance" of Pater's sanction for allowing poems to arise out of their own rhythm, Yeats listed five avowed points of the early modern revolt against Victorian poetry. Except for condemnation of Browning's "psychological curiosity," they agree with standard literary histories both of Yeats' tragic generation and of the following one—rejection of irrelevant description of nature, scientific and moral discursiveness, political eloquence, and poetical diction. In retrospect, however, even this comprehensive reaction did not seem deep enough. In a crucial later passage of his essay, Yeats identifies a more basic opposition and singles out romanticism as its harbinger:

> When my generation denounced scientific humanitarian preoc-
> cupation, psychological curiosity, rhetoric, we had not found
> what ailed Victorian literature. The Elizabethans had all these
> things, especially rhetoric. . . . The mischief began at the end of
> the seventeenth century when man became passive before a
> mechanized nature; that lasted to our own day with the excep-
> tion of a brief period between Smart's *Song of David* and the
> death of Byron, wherein imprisoned man beat upon the door.
> Or I may dismiss all that ancient history and say it began when
> Stendhal described a masterpiece as a "mirror dawdling down a
> lane."[4]

The brief period between Smart's *Song of David* in 1763 and Byron's death in 1824 is, of course, the romantic one, the age of writers whom Yeats in the same essay terms "the first romantic poets, Blake, Coleridge, Shelley. . . ." Like Eliot and many other moderns, Yeats locates a cataclysmic shift in sensibility in the seventeenth century, but unlike his American rival he elevates romanticism into a heroic though abortive countermovement. Yeats here is thinking of Descartes as (in Boileau's phrase) slitting poetry's throat by divorcing inner from outer, subject from object, thought from action, and of Newton and Locke as codifying mechanical principles of nature and correspondingly associative ones of mind. Throughout his life Yeats favored organic metaphors for mind and art popularized by the romantics, and a creative role for mind that followed the poetry of Shelley and Blake. For this he eventually discovered a philosophic anchor in Berkeley and idealist philosophy more secure than his early

28

theosophy. "The romantic movement seems related to the idealist philosophy; the naturalistic movement, Stendhal's mirror dawdling down a lane, to Locke's mechanical philosophy," he wrote in his 1932 essay on Berkeley. "When I speak of the romantic movement I think more of Manfred, more of Shelley's Prometheus . . . [than of] the fakir-like pedlar in *The Excursion*."[5] That cunning juxtaposition of Manfred and Prometheus, the indomitable though failed quester and the successful transformer of self and world, reminds us that both heroes are emblems of imaginative activity asserting human autonomy from the tyranny of material illusion. Yeats had little sympathy for Wordsworth's mode of naturalized imagination, despite their common concern with autobiographical self-recognition and the dynamics of memory.

To reject the romantic struggle was to accept the mimetic naturalism of Stendhal, which made art—and the artist—into a mirror rather than a lamp. Yeats feared that such an approach would leave "man helpless before the contents of his own mind" and fretted over its impact even on writers like Pound and Joyce.[6] Just as Stevens a decade later described mind as "a violence from within that protects us from a violence without . . . the imagination pressing back against the pressure of reality,"[7] so did Yeats in his essay on Berkeley declare that "something compels me to reject whatever—to borrow a metaphor of Coleridge's—drives mind into the quicksilver."[8] Both Yeats and Stevens write out of philosophic positions contrary to technologically accepted epistemologies of their day: like the great romantics Stevens insists that "reality" is not the external scene but the life that is lived in it; and Yeats in poems like "The Tower" holds that man creates his own universe.

Yeats' life became a continual quest for mental action to defeat mimetic passivity. The metaphor of beating on the door in the *Oxford Book* links the effort to Blake, to whom Yeats attached a similar phrase in "An Acre of Grass," written the same year:

> Myself must I remake
> Till I am Timon and Lear
> Or that William Blake
> Who beat upon the wall
> Till Truth obeyed his call. . . .[9]

The wall here is both sense perception and nature, for in romantic tradition the two fuse: we create what we see, and we see what we are. Consequently, the modes of "imagination" and "mind" Yeats dismisses in the previous stanza ("Neither loose imagination,/ Nor the mill of the mind/ Consuming its rag and bone,/ Can make the truth known") are those faculties cut off by a mechanized nature. The imagination is "loose" because deprived of strong sensory perception in an enfeebled body; correspondingly, the mind has become a "mill," with full Blakean overtones of logic and mechanism, at best parasitically processing the past experiences of the heart.[10] The "truth" is the world perceived by those faculties rejuvenated by "frenzy"—by the breaking up of stale patterns of perception and the recombination of mind and imagination into "an old man's eagle mind." Yeats desperately hopes for the confidence with which Blake, returning tottering from the gates of death, knew that the real man lives forever, and like all the romantics he does not champion mere unbridled emotion.

So far we have been listening to the late Yeats, who returned to an ardent though individual romanticism after a middle-aged lag in enthusiasm. Yet the romantic theme of mind's necessary activity against an otherwise merely material outer world sounds throughout his career, as does a nearly pathological anxiety that without imagination mind will degenerate into a sterile analogue of a meaningless, mechanized nature. The great writers of the early nineteenth century provided both rationale and example for the young Irishman writing at its close. In his review of an exhibition by William Morris and others in 1890, he wrote: "The movement most characteristic of the literature and art and to some small extent of the thoughts, too, of our century has been romanticism . . . freedom of the spirit and imagination of man in literature."[11]

That freeing of imagination and spirit had been won at high cost, however, and young Yeats saw himself as rescuer of romantic tradition from its own defects. In his retrospective account of the crucial years between 1887 and 1891, he formulated a précis of his own relation to literary history: "If Chaucer's personages had disengaged themselves from Chaucer's crowd, forgot their common goal and shrine, and after sundry magnifications became each in turn the centre of some Elizabethan play, and had after split into their elements and so given birth to romantic poetry, must I reverse the cinematograph?" (*Auto* 193) The middle-aged memoirist writing that remark exaggerates his own early self-consciousness of departure from the great romantics, for in the eighties and nineties he identified himself with them more closely than he later liked to admit. As always with the later Yeats, his remarks on romantic subjectivity fit his own early poetry better than that of his precursors and reveal that distortion which, more than sources or influences, comprises literary history. Still, Yeats' paradigm of a movement from Chaucer's unified society through Elizabethan unified individuals to romantic single elements does illuminate his early poetic view.[12] He applies the remark himself by recalling his early drive to write an Irish *Prometheus Unbound,* with Oisin or Fion instead of Prometheus and (Christian) Cro-Patrick or (pagan) Ben Bulben in place of the Caucasus, which culminated in *The Wanderings of Oisin* (1889). But what did he mean by the gnomic phrase "split into their elements"? He interpreted the shift from medieval to Renaissance as individuation, in which Elizabethan individuals replace Chaucerian "personages," who derive their identity from group aims and relations, particularly common religious devotion. In contrast, Yeats saw his favorite Shakespearean characters, like Hamlet, Lear, or Timon, as heroic, isolated figures impressing themselves upon us by their own magnified personalities. By splitting even those personalities into "elements," romanticism both purified art and divorced it from common life.

To Yeats romantic figures were often either great symbols of passion and mood or else embodiments of subtle principles of mind, emblems of great emotions or actors in an internal psychodrama. He copied both techniques in his own poems. *The Wind Among the Reeds* (1899) alerted readers in a note that speakers like Aedh, Hanrahan, and Robartes were used "more as principles of the mind than as actual personages" (*VP* 803) and went on to identify them as aspects of imagination. More frequently, however, he followed the alternate strategy. On 19 May 1893 he lectured to the National Literary Society in Dublin on the shift from Elizabethan drama to romantic lyric:

> When the time was ripe the English spirit cast up that lyrical outburst of which Byron, Shelley, and Keats were the most characteristic writers. Character, no longer loved for its own sake, or as an expression of the general bustle of life, became merely the mask for some mood or passion, as in Byron's "Manfred" and his "Don Juan." In other words, the poets began to write but little of individual men and women, but rather of great types, great symbols of passion and mood, like Alastor, Don Juan, Manfred, Ahasuerus, Prometheus, and Isabella of the Basil Pot. When they tried, as in Byron's plays, to display character for its own sake they failed. (*Uncoll* 270–71)

Yeats here mingles genuine insight with his need to find in the past what would suffice him as poet in the present. Ignoring the

Wordsworthian option of the common man as hero or the real display of character in plays like Shelley's *Cenci* (which he increasingly disliked), Yeats traces in romanticism lineaments of his own work and dilemmas of the nineties and after. Like his image of Byron the feckless dramatist, Yeats himself never really succeeded in creating rounded characters in his plays; his dramas succeed best when his heroes or heroines become such symbols of passion or mood as Cuchulain in the *Four Plays for Dancers* or Swineherd and Queen in *A Full Moon in March*. Even his Countess Cathleen, created the year before his lecture, represents a perhaps fanatic compassion rather than character for its own sake. "The Circus Animals' Desertion" (1939), with its retrospective formulation of "character isolated by a deed," aptly describes these masks for mood and passion on the stage. Similarly, Yeats' early poetry casts up continual surrogates for romantic types like "Alastor" (as he persistently miscalled the nameless hero of Shelley's poem)—Fergus, the Wandering Aengus, or even Oisin, to name but a few. Although he sometimes mixed the terms, he propounded a distinction between character and personality ("Character is the ash of personality"[13]) and sought to purge accidentals of character from the core of personality. His audience, like the late paradigm of Greek boys and girls adding character to the personality of Pythagorean plummet-measured faces, would flesh out his abstractions with their own passionate response.

Logically extended, these romantic principles led to making the poet himself into his own hero and his poetic quest into the archetypal imaginative act. This extrapolation underlay Yeats' attraction to idealist philosophy, which he associated with romanticism; as Denis Donoghue has shrewdly surmised, "In the idealist tradition the contemplation of one's own mind is bound to be the exemplary act."[14] When he turned to such dramatization in his early poetry, Yeats portrayed himself in the act of directly contemplating his own mind less often than in the guise of those same romantic types of passion or mood that he elsewhere sought to depict, most often as a Shelleyan seeker of Intellectual Beauty. In *Reveries* he recalled the outset of his career: "I was about to learn that if a man is to write lyric poetry he must be shaped by nature and art to some one out of half a dozen traditional poses, and be lover or saint, sage or sensualist, or mere mocker of all life." (*Auto* 87) It was a lesson he never forgot. Even the verisimilitude of such late poems as "Among School Children," where Yeats does contemplate his own acts of mind, should not obscure from us his self-presentation as archetype rather than individual. When composing "A General Introduction for My Work" in 1937, he returned to the romantics to illustrate the distinction between man and poet and to the concepts of his 1893 lecture:

> Even when the poet seems most himself, when he is . . . Shelley
> 'a nerve o'er which do creep the else unfelt oppressions of this
> earth,' or Byron when 'the soul wears out the breast' as 'the
> sword outwears its sheath,' he is never the bundle of accident
> and incoherence that sits down to breakfast; he has been reborn
> as an idea, something intended, complete . . . he is more type
> than man, more passion than type. (*E&I* 509)

Separation of a personal from a poetic self has become commonplace in modern criticism, but more to expose the intentional fallacy or to counteract excessive biographical reduction than to explore rebirth into coherence and concentration. Neglect of these alternate principles of self-portrayal and mental action, which Yeats derived from the romantics, has caused endless trouble. To study them further we must turn to the impact of specific romantics on Yeats.

To Yeats, Shelley and Blake were not just the two most important romantics but the two most important of all poets for his own work. While continually echoing their phrases, he derived his characteristic modes and stances from them, both directly and indirectly through their impact on intervening writers like Hallam, early Browning and Tennyson, the Rossettis, Swinburne, and Morris. Most important of all, they furnished him with alternate poetic identities, with dramatizations of a poetic role he could carry over into his own art, and with paradigms of mental action he could render there. Enthusiasm for them repeatedly discharged itself in searching commentaries, of which the most important are the culmination of his "four years' work upon the 'Prophetic Books' of William Blake" (*Auto* 161) with Edwin Ellis in their three-volume edition *The Works of William Blake: Poetic, Symbolic, and Critical* (1893), his essay "The Philosophy of Shelley's Poetry" (1900), and the portraits in *A Vision* (1925; rev. 1937), where Shelley appears in Yeats' own phase 17.

Pondering his relation to his two chief precursors led to an astute recognition of deeper affinity to Shelley than to Blake. A speculation on the late Victorian tendency to make art into a substitute for religion catalyzed this self-revelation:

> [Shelley] had shared our curiosities, our political problems, our
> conviction that, despite all experience to the contrary, love is

enough; and unlike Blake, isolated by an arbitrary symbolism, he seemed to sum up all that was metaphysical in English poetry. When in middle life I looked back I found that he and not Blake, whom I had studied more and with more approval, had shaped my life. (*E&I* 424)

The remark illuminates Yeats' late warping of Shelley and his lifelong distortion of Blake. In his youth he had so identified himself with Shelley that he had to repudiate him to find his own maturity, and in the process he created a surrogate ancestor in Blake. For if Yeats saw Shelley as the archetypal poet, with more violence he made Blake into the archetypal mystic seer. He began his 1896 review of Richard Garnett's *William Blake* with just such a distinction: "Just as Shelley is the example from which most men fashion their conception of the poetic temperament, Blake is, to the bulk of students, the most representative of seers, the one in whom the flame is most pure and most continual." (*Uncoll* 400) Yeats found himself among "most men"; three years earlier he had thought Blake not only a great poet but "a mystic also" (*Uncoll* 282) and it was as "mystic" that Blake beckoned him. In fact, a frenzy to correlate the connections among Blake, Swedenborg, Boehme, and the Cabbala had kindled Yeats' original desire to collaborate with Ellis on their monumental edition. (*Auto* 161) During his most Shelleyan phase, Yeats fashioned Blake into a literary battering ram with which to break out of the dead-end of the nineties and through to the twentieth century. As his parallel doubts about Shelley's mysticism and his own early poetry grew, Yeats began to think that like Blake he needed a system of antinomies to attain a full vision. While Blake thus sanctioned Yeats' betrayal of Shelley (whose skeptical dialectic Yeats persistently neglected), he could not take his place, for Blake was not a mystic at all and Yeats the man was, or at least he really believed that a spiritual world existed independently of humanity and would therefore have been branded a Deist by Blake. His salvation was that in his poetry the poet repudiated the mystic, as the swordsman the saint, although not without vacillation.

Shelley and Blake attracted Yeats because they were the most apocalyptic romantic poets, just as Yeats himself was the most apocalyptic of our great moderns. *Apocalypse* literally means an uncovering; hence, it is easily associated with prophecy, and in Christian tradition with burning away the material world preparatory to the Last Judgment. As Meyer Abrams has pointed out, Christian psychobiographers like Augustine internalize apocalypse, in accord with Luke 17:20-21: "And when he was demanded of the Pharisees, when the kingdom of God should come, he answered them and said, The kingdom of God cometh not with observation: Neither shall they say, Lo here! or lo there! for, behold, the kingdom of God is within you."[15] Romanticism tends to displace Christian internal apocalypse to a secular framework, usually with imagination as redeemer. Blake and Shelley wanted to strip away veils of mental illusion, associated with material nature, to reveal a world transformed by imaginative perception. They were poets of psychic transformation, both in theme and in form. So was Yeats. In the eighties and nineties he was so much a Shelleyan that to continue growing he invented a viable personal alternative that he forcibly embodied in Blake. Before 1900 Yeats was a Shelleyan poet, according to his partial although not inaccurate reading of his predecessor; after that, he still sometimes shared Shelley's true qualities (particularly a visionary skepticism) even while condemning those inner inadequacies that he externalized in Shelley. But Yeats never was a true Blakean poet, although he extrapolated much of his intellectual system from an amalgam of Blake, Boehme, and occult sources.

In his poetry Shelley adopted the prophetic stance of a visionary, not a mystic, and to his credit Yeats continually saw that.[16] He responded in particular to two notes in Shelley's visionary song, one of which—a devotion to Intellectual Beauty—his ear genuinely perceived, and the other of which—evocation of images—it half created. The resultant Shelley looked remarkably like the early Yeats, and Yeats found that he could describe both himself and his model in the same terms. For this he turned especially to the *Defence of Poetry*, from which he quoted passages like that describing poets as legislators or prophets (*E&I* 67), and to earlier commentaries like those of Hallam and Browning. His visionary Shelley climaxed Victorian "subjective" interpretations, which used Shelley as contrast to "objective" poets. Hallam's influence cut deepest: "When I began to write I avowed for my principles those of Arthur Hallam in his essay upon Tennyson," recalled Yeats in 1913. (*E&I* 347) That essay praised imagination and the image-making powers of mind that enabled Keats and Shelley to adhere to imaginative truth because they "lived in a world of images."[17] Characteristically, Yeats interpreted Hallam's phrase literally in accord with his own psychic research, and he combined it with Hallam's sketch of the subjective poet as a solitary outcast working out subtle emotions for a literary elite.

It is time to end the critical superstition that Yeats somehow mistitled his discourse on "The Philosophy of Shelley's Poetry." In fact, he knew better than his critics what he was doing, and his reasons go deeper than the overt associations of his two subtitles, "His Ruling Ideas" with philosophy and "His Ruling Symbols" with poetry. He designed the essay to vindicate the entire romantic enterprise, above all the mental action by which inspired men beat upon the door of mechanical nature. Hence, he began by asserting that "the imagination has some way of lighting on the truth that the reason has not" and displaced religious diction to a partly secular context by citing his belief in *Prometheus Unbound* as "a sacred book." (*E&I* 65) The philosophy of Shelley's poetry pivoted on the distinction between nature and Intellectual Beauty, while the poetry itself depended on systematic exploitation of symbolic imagery. Yeats saw Shelley's ruling idea as "his vision of the divine order, the Intellectual Beauty" (*E&I* 67) and his works as portraying a quest for it. That quest was partly internal, for Yeats identified Julian (of *Julian and Maddalo*) with Shelley himself in citing the rhetorical question, "Where is the love, beauty, and truth we seek/ But in our mind?" (*E&I* 70)

I should like to go beyond my account in *Yeats and Shelley* of the many congruencies between their poetry—including Yeats' identification of the Rose with Intellectual Beauty; his attachment to it of multiple meanings; his masking himself first as the questing *Alastor* youth, then as Prince Athanase in his tower, and finally as Ahasuerus; and his adaptation of Shelley's systematic use of celestial (sun, moon, and star) and terrestrial (cave, water, and tower) imagery—to a crucial further element for understanding Yeats' full relation to romanticism. In his two essays on Shelley, Yeats elaborated an account of the origins of images that grows out of romantic theory and becomes both dominant theme and controlling form for many of his own mature poems. With the receptivity of Wordsworthian wise passiveness, and freedom from irritable reason of Keatsian negative capability, imagination delivers its images "when the body is still and the reason silent." (*E&I* 65) These images can simply arise from the subconscious but they can also be evoked by "a form of meditation which permits an image or symbol to generate itself, and the images and symbols so generated build themselves up into coherent structures." (*E&I* 422) Variations or meditations on the mental act of calling up such self-generated (or, as Yeats liked to say, "self-begotten") images form the subject of such famous Yeatsian poems as "Among School Children" or "In Memory of Major Robert Gregory," to name but two. To receive these images mind entered the state

Yeats named *revery,* for which he quoted Shelley's definition: "Those who are subject to the state called reverie, feel as if their nature were resolved into the surrounding universe or as if the surrounding universe were resolved into their being." (*E&I* 79-80) He wondered whether Shelley had "lit on that memory of Nature the visionaries claim for the foundation of their knowledge." (*E&I* 74) Here Yeats capitalized Nature to distinguish this storehouse of images from the material nature of the naturalists. The same spiritus mundi turns up as source of the vision of the rough beast in "The Second Coming." Such ancient symbols free subjective art from "the barrenness and shallowness of a too conscious arrangement" (*E&I* 87) and guarantee "abundance and depth" in a world of massed images. Much of this theory follows romantic doctrine, or at least romantic hints, in accord with one of Shelley's definitions of imagination—"mind employed in prophetically imaging forth its objects."[18] What is noteworthy is the rarity of sympathetic imagination in Yeats, who instead occupied himself almost wholly with the creative side. He systematized romantic traditions of mental action and its preconditions, and made the creation of images both cause and subject of his own poetry to an unprecedented degree. Even more than Shelley's, his caves and (in some aspects) towers become settings for mind descending within the psyche toward those illuminations that poets before the romantics would have approached by an upward and outward movement.

Yet however hard he tried to conflate himself with Shelley, Yeats wisely doubted his precursor's mysticism and, more arbitrarily, his foreign mythology. After 1900 Yeats' massive shift in sensibility capitalized on these early reservations to force a temporary but thorough devaluation. While in "The Philosophy of Shelley's Poetry" he reluctantly confessed Shelley's lack of magical lore and balanced incessant doubts by approvingly quoting Mary's misleading praise of "mystic ideality" tingeing *The Sensitive Plant* (*E&I* 73), by the time of "*Prometheus Unbound*" (1932) he could bluntly state that "Shelley was not a mystic" and continue with an accusation more true of early Yeats than of his sometime idol: "His system of thought was constructed by his logical faculty to satisfy desire, not a symbolical revelation received after the suspension of all desire." (*E&I* 421-22) Furthermore, Shelley had not grounded his system in nationality and folklore. Believing that art should centaurlike grow out of rich local tradition, Yeats after *Oisin* regularly lamented Shelley's cosmopolitan eclecticism of setting and mythology. In sympathetic moods he "mourned the richness or reality lost to Shelley's *Prometheus Unbound* because he had not discovered in England or Ireland his Caucasus," while in hostile moments he denounced "an air of rootless fantasy." (*E&I* 350, 74) This claim is not wholly silly, for both peasant and poetic traditions opposed themselves to the bourgeois materialism of a mechanized nature that Yeats hated and that did, ironically, infect the young Shelley's most extended venture into folk mythology, *Queen Mab*. But in fact Shelley, with his strong grasp on reality and deep classical learning, could with equal felicity rework Greek mythology or even invent his own more safely than Yeats, who coveted strong regional ties as a ballast to the balloon of the mind.

The "movement downwards upon life" that Yeats mentioned to Florence Farr in 1906[19] led away from the Shelley who had shaped his life. Now Shelley's pure art of Intellectual Beauty appeared as half of an antithesis balanced by the earthier work of Dickens or Burns. Like an alchemical geneticist he aimed to unite "a Shelley and a Dickens in the one body."[20] An antinomial vision of paired opposites replaced his earlier Intellectual vision—fair and foul, good and evil, mind and body—for "all things fall into a series of antinomies in human experience."[21] His career became a heroic attempt to remedy Shelley's defects, which were not so much Shelley's as early Yeats'. For he had so identified himself with Shelley that only a violent repudiation could free him as poet. His increasingly violent attacks on Shelley screened an acute and devastating self-critique. In "The Philosophy of Shelley's Poetry" he had distinguished Blake's poetic genius from Shelley's as glad worship of the sun compared to melancholy desire for the Evening Star:

> It was therefore natural that Blake, who was always praising energy, and all exalted overflowing of oneself, and who thought art an impassioned labour to keep men from doubt and despondency, and woman's love an evil, when it would trammel man's will, should see the poetic genius not in a woman star but in the Sun. . . . In ancient times, it seems to me that Blake, who for all his protest was glad to be alive, and ever spoke of his gladness, would have worshipped in some chapel of the Sun, but that Shelley, who hated life because he sought 'more in life than any understood,' would have wandered, lost in a ceaseless reverie, in some chapel of the Star of infinite desire. (*E&I* 93-94)

To read that passage is to realize Yeats' schizophrenia about his two poetic masters, for the first sentence (except for the sun) accurately describes, in terms of Blake, Yeats' best mature art, and the second, in terms of Shelley, a hatred of life often true of his worst. Although the description is truer of Blake than of Shelley, Yeats never saw either poet plain, but rather in relation to his own aspiration and achievement.

Not only did the gladness he took from Blake correct the melancholy he derived from Shelley, but Blake's vision of contending contraries helped his own development of antinomial vision and of sufficient images. "My mind had been full of Blake from boyhood up and I saw the world as a conflict—Spectre and Emanation—and could distinguish between a contrary and a negation," he recalled in *A Vision*. " 'Contraries are positive', wrote Blake, 'a negation is not a contrary.' " (*Vision* 72) Although Yeats could not always distinguish a contrary from a negation in terms Blake would have accepted, his own interpretation of Blake's precept did move him downwards upon life. Besides allowing for "earthier" elements, it transvalued the romantic cult of the moment, which Yeats had acquired partly at the instigation of Walter Pater. He repeatedly cited Blake's remark that the artist does his work within the pulsation of an artery. Both in *A Vision* and in the later poetry, the ecstatic moment became the nexus of unification: "I had an unshakeable conviction . . . that invisible gates would open as they opened for Blake, as they opened for Swedenborg, as they opened for Boehme," he confessed. (*Auto* 254) This vision persists as late as "Under Ben Bulben," where Yeats describes images of the quattrocento as a preparation for those of Blake and others:

> . . . forms that are or seem
> When sleepers wake and yet still dream,
> And when it's vanished still declare,
> With only bed and bedstead there,
> That heavens had opened.
>
> (*VP* 639)

Yeats rewrote Blake by interpreting such transfigurations as incompatible with human life and associating them with an independently existing spiritual world, but their Blakean ancestry is clear.

Blake exemplified above all romantic mental action with nature as antagonist. Romanticism began with Blake's early *Poetic Sketches:* "The poems mark an epoch in English literature, for they were the first opening of the long-sealed well of romantic poetry; they, and not the works of Cowper and Thompson and Chatterton, being the true heralds of our modern poetry of nature and enthusiasm."²² As Blake developed he heralded another type of modern poetry, which sees nature as antagonist. "No matter how enthusiastically he commended enthusiasm, alike of love and of hate, he ever intended the mind to be master over all," Yeats observed in the same essay. Recognition of Blake's warfare between mind and nature distinguishes the solidest parts of Yeats and Ellis' edition. Their explication of the Prophetic Books further confirmed the value of systematic imagery. Combining those qualities with praise of Imagination, resistance to undue dominance by reason, and reliance on symbols, Blake appeared almost as an alternate Shelley, to whom Yeats could impute his own mysticism with more apparent although little actual justification.²³

But even Blake had his limits, and Yeats carefully guarded against transferring to him the autocracy by which Shelley both shaped and complicated his poetic life. Commentators have made too much of the charge that "the limitation of his view was from the very intensity of his vision; he was a too literal realist of imagination, as others are of nature" (*E&I* 119) for Yeats' remark applies only to Blake's critique of the fine arts, as the context makes clear. It is possible that Yeats might have expanded his doubts to Blake's poetry²⁴ and life, transforming Blake into brother of that company in part II of "The Tower" whose mistaken action, based on moonlit rather than blended truths, brings catastrophe. More certainly, he transferred his qualms about Shelley's "rootless" mythology to Blake's, as usual masking a defense of his own art:

> He spoke confusedly and obscurely because he spoke of things for whose speaking he could find no models in the world about him. He was a symbolist who had to invent his symbols; and his counties of England, with their correspondence to tribes of Israel, and his mountains and rivers, with their correspondence to parts of a man's body, are arbitrary. . . . He was a man crying out for a mythology, and trying to make one because he could not find one to his hand. Had he been a Catholic of Dante's time he would have been well content with Mary and the angels; or had he been a scholar of our time he would have taken his symbols . . . from Norse mythology; or . . . Welsh mythology . . . or have gone to Ireland . . . and have been less obscure because a traditional mythology stood on the threshold of his meaning and on the margin of his sacred darkness. If Enitharmon had been named Freia, or Gwydeon, or Dana, and made live in Ancient Norway, or Ancient Wales, or Ancient Ireland. . . . (*E&I* 114)

This is partly true; Blake's individual mythology does make his prophetic books difficult at first. Nor does a recent scholar's accurate restatement of Blake's own view—that he would have invented a system of his own in any case to avoid being enslaved by another man's and to liberate his own imagination—help much, for Yeats directs his remarks as much to the elements of the system as to the system itself. He would respond truly that Blake here shows symptoms of the lack of Unity of Culture afflicting his own time and affecting even a great artist. In fact, some of Blake's elements do derive from traditional mythology, both Protestant and perennial. But the point is that Yeats' proposed remedies do not work: reliance on Freia, Gwydeon, or Dana would not make Blake more intelligible. Precisely how a modern poet could build a satisfactory mythology satisfactorily clear to a large number of readers was never adequately solved by the modernist generation.

Yeats' lifelong distortions of Shelley and Blake fall into two categories: early distortions that made Shelley and Blake more like Yeats, and a later group designed to liberate him from them. His late strictures so violate both his own earlier views and the apparent facts that they suggest a need for distortion in both cases. A look at the *Vision* portraits clarifies and confirms Yeats' intentions. By assigning Shelley to his own phase in *A Vision* and Blake to the preceding one, Yeats could externalize in them both his best hopes and worst fears for himself as poet, while tacitly conceding his greater kinship with Shelley. Both romantics appear in highly antithetical (subjective) phases. A glance at the tables for true and false faculties in Blake's phase 16 (The Positive Man) confirms its relevance to Yeats. Creative Mind ("which in the most *antithetical* phases were better described as imagination"[25]) can take its true form of Vehemence or its false one of Opinionated Will, as does Yeats' own imagination in his later poetry. Likewise, the Mask (or anti-self, often used as a persona) has a true form of Illusion and a false one of Delusion, which are the two aspects of Yeats' tower-dwelling students of images. While artists of this phase can collapse into an "incapable idealism" that sees one side as all white and the other as all black, at their best

> they produce the comedy of Aretino and of Rabelais or the mythology of Blake, and discover symbolism to express the overflowing and bursting of the mind. There is always an element of frenzy, and almost always a delight in certain glowing or shining images of concentrated force: in the smith's forge; in the heart; in the human form in its most vigorous development. . . . (*Vision* 138-39)

This extraordinary insight links the "frenzy" Yeats prays for to accomplish a Blakean self-transformation in "An Acre of Grass" to the fires of Golgonooza and Byzantium. The struggle to find a mask of Illusion rather than Delusion and an imagination vehement rather than opinionated in order to combine symbols into a mythology expressive of the overflowing of the mind comes close to defining a poet of mental action like Yeats, but not so close as the ensuing description of Shelley.

Exposition of phase 17, the Daimonic Man, centers on attainment of Unity of Being in life and art through images, with Shelley and Dante as chief examples and Yeats' own career as undersong. The poet must find his true Mask (Simplification through Intensity) and avoid his false (Dispersal) to create figures of "intellectual or sexual passion" like Athanase, Ahasuerus, and so many personae of Yeats' own poetry. Such a poet must confront his destiny or environment (which Yeats calls Body of Fate and identifies as Loss for this phase) with his intellect to fashion "the Mask as Image, some woman perhaps" rather than hoping for utopian conquest of loss and succumbing to inevitable paranoia at its failure. Yeats attributes this disaster to Shelley in terms that better fit his own early verse: "He lacked the Vision of Evil, could not conceive of the world as a continual conflict, so, though great poet he certainly was, he was not of the greatest kind." Yeats himself had learned to form his own Vision of Evil from Blake's contraries, although he could have deduced it from an undistorted Shelley as well. We can hear his fears of his own late poetic temptation even more clearly when he warns that antithetical men can mistake automatonism for poetical invention and use it "to evade hatred, or rather to hide it from their own eyes; perhaps all at some time or other, in moments of fatigue, give themselves up to fantastic, constructed images, or to an almost mechanical laughter." The twin dangers of self-deception and arbitrary images underlie some of Yeats' own lapses in the 1930s, such as his strident marching songs. Similarly, his description of Shelley's political activity as "out of phase" and contrary to his true solitary Masks echoes Yeats' misgiving about his own "dreams of converting the world." Even more than that of Blake, this sketch of Shelley suggests the dangers and triumphs possible to a Yeatsian poet of mental action both as writer and as man.

Romanticism affected Yeats so radically that he could not permanently throw off a sensibility by turns Shelleyan and Blakean, although in antagonistic periods he could condemn in his models tacit projections of his own faults. By the end of his life he returned to a genuine although guarded admiration for both. The testamentary "Under Ben Bulben" begins by invoking Shelley's Witch of Atlas and progresses to an image of Blake preparing a rest for the people of God. Although Yeats saw romanticism primarily in terms of Shelley and Blake, he studied and commented on Keats, Byron, Wordsworth, and Coleridge as well, often in ways directly relevant to his own work. They became either precedents to legitimize his own doctrines or foils to show the proper character of an imaginative poet.

Of the four, Keats appears most often, frequently in tandem with Shelley. Yeats' reaction to Keats follows the familiar pattern of intial literary attraction, then rejection based partly on his new psychological theories, and finally a reconciliation—with Keats, a very mild one. He began by making Keats and Shelley into Dioscuri of aestheticism under the aegis of Hallam: "Keats and Shelley, unlike Wordsworth, intermixed into their poetry no elements from the general thought, but wrote out of the impression made by the world upon their delicate senses."[26] Besides delicate senses and freedom from popular morality, Yeats found in Keats support for his early concept of romantic character projection. He invoked Isabella of the Basil Pot in particular as a symbol of passion or mood, like Athanase. (*Uncoll* 271) In general he saw Keats as a shadow Shelley, but sometimes he reversed their roles, claiming for example that *The Eve of St. Agnes* showed Keats tapping the strength of living folklore in contrast to Shelley's desiccated mythology. (*Uncoll* 287)

Keats' use of concrete detail became at once his strength and his weakness to Yeats. Positively, he could easily picture Keats' poetic world. Negatively, Keats' fidelity to natural objects weakened the symbolic interconnections of his work. He appeared as a fragmentary Blake: "Keats . . . is as much a symbolist as a Blake or a Wagner; but he is a fragmentary symbolist, for while he evokes in his persons and his landscapes an infinite emotion, a perfected emotion, a part of the Divine Essence, he does not set his symbols in the great procession as Blake would have him." (*E&I* 149-50) Yeats consistently responded to Keatsian pictorial ability but just as doggedly missed the dialectic of sympathetic imagination that informs his best work. Thus, Keats appeared static. In one of Yeats' plentiful theoretic dichotomies, Keats in 1913 served as archetypal poet for a kind of vision ("the intense realization of a state of ecstatic emotion symbolized in a definite imagined region," *Letters* 583) that Yeats was already leaving behind in favor of "self-portraiture."

Dramatic self-portraiture presented the tension between self and anti-self. The notorious lines on Keats in "Ego Dominus Tuus" (written in 1915) depend on the psychological theories adumbrated in *Per Amica Silentia Lunae* (1918), which used the poem as introduction, and developed further in *A Vision*. When Hic argues that "No one denies to Keats love of the world;/ Remember his deliberate happiness," Ille responds:

> His art is happy, but who knows his mind?
> I see a schoolboy when I think of him,
> With face and nose pressed to a sweet-shop window,
> For certainly he sank into his grave
> His senses and his heart unsatisfied,
> And made—being poor, ailing and ignorant,
> Shut out from all the luxury of the world,
> The coarse-bred son of a livery-stable keeper—
> Luxuriant song.
>
> (*VP* 370)

It is a spectacular misfire. The causes become clearer when we read the gloss in *Per Amica* on the poem's contrast of Keats and Dante: "All happy art seems to me that hollow image, but when its lineaments express also the poverty or the exasperation that set its maker to the work, we call it tragic art. Keats but gave us his dream of luxury; but while reading Dante we never long escape the conflict, partly because the verses are at moments a mirror of his history. . . ."[27] Yeats wants to find in Keats' lyrics the struggle for imaginative self-creation in the role of poet. But the place to look for that is in the mythological poems, principally the *Hyperions*, from which Yeats borrowed a line ("but I am here alone") for *A Full Moon in March*.[28] Yeats misinterprets lyrics like the Nightingale ode because their mode of sympathetic imagination operating on natural objects is foreign to him. His poems rarely display sympathetic imagination at all, and the use of natural objects as goal of imaginative aspiration repelled him. Nature was to be demechanized by being turned into symbol. Keats' great achievement in naturalizing imagination, culminating in the Autumn ode, passed Yeats by, and for him Keats remained among the "great lesser writers." (*Auto* 273)

If Keats served many uses, Byron served two: like all the romantics, he created heroic, isolated figures emblematic of passion and mood, and more than the others he sought a style of personal speech adaptable to Yeats' own poetic development. Besides wearing his ties in Byronic fashion (*Auto* 83), young Yeats responded to

Manfred and Don Juan as he did to "Alastor," Athanase, or Isabella: especially Manfred seemed to him a projection of heroic drives and an embodiment of personality rather than character.[29] Yeats marshaled such heroes to resist the modernism that threatened to leave mind helpless before its own contents. Byron offered a surrogate for Ahasuerus as well, in the allusion to Homer as "blind old Man of Scio's rocky isle," which Yeats quoted in his autobiography.[30] Yet Byron had not achieved his poetic aims, and himself illustrated the gap between man and poet. (*Letters* 467) He had, however, at least tried for the "syntax and vocabulary of common personal speech" that Yeats in 1924 saw his own poetry as adopting: "Byron, unlike the Elizabethans though he always tries for it, constantly allows it to die out in some mind-created construction, but is I think the one great English poet—though one can hardly call him great except in purpose and manhood— who sought it constantly," he told H. J. C. Grierson. (*Letters* 710) At first glance the style of, say, *Don Juan* seems antipodal to the great style of Yeats' maturity. The point is not that he imitated Byron but that he needed something of Byron's relaxed raciness to break out of his early rhetoric of the nineties. Like Pound and other moderns, he found his great barrier reef for that voyage in the one romantic most concerned with common diction, Wordsworth.

Unlike his volatile changes toward other romantics, Yeats with only rare exceptions persistently denigrated Wordsworth. This romantic was doomed to be a perpetual foil to the virtues of the others in the world of Yeats' criticism. Stimulated by his father, who "abhorred Wordsworth" (*Auto* 88), Yeats at first contrasted Wordsworth's dross with the purer imagistic ore of Keats and Shelley as seen by Hallam. Wordsworth had "condescended to moral maxims, or some received philosophy, a multitude of things that even common sense could understand" (*E&I* 348) and thus betrayed his own genius. As "the one great poet who, after brief blossom, was cut and sawn into planks of obvious utility" (*Auto* 235), Wordsworth forsook his original poetic vision by growing ever more prosaic and didactic. Preoccupied with self-transformation and the continued creation of images, Yeats saw Wordsworth as a ruined hulk warning of the rocks. He insisted that Wordsworth served a discipline he had not created, until growing automatonism robbed his work of dramatic dialectic.[31] By 1919 he decided that Wordsworth, like Shelley, lacked a Vision of Evil; under the influence of Rousseau, he had resolved to dwell upon good only and so could not attain Unity of Being. Although

45

Yeats could always admire outcasts like the Pedlar of *The Excursion,* he missed in that work the architectonic unity of imagery he so prized in *Prometheus Unbound* and the Prophetic Books.[32]

Just as Wordsworth could not help Yeats philosophically or imagistically, neither could he help him stylistically. Wordsworth to him lacked both the nervous, intellectual speech he imputed to his aestheticized Shelley or Keats and the earthier common speech he sought afterward. Unlike Byron's syntax, Wordsworth's lacked "natural momentum." (*Letters* 710) He had sacrificed passion to propriety, whereas Yeats wanted speech both "normal" and "passionate." "I discovered some twenty years ago," he wrote in 1937, "that I must seek, not as Wordsworth thought, words in common use, but a powerful and passionate syntax." (*E&I* 521-22) Yeats seldom found that passion in either Wordsworth's verse or his vision. With Wordsworth, he feared, "poetry gave up the right to consider all things in the world as a dictionary of types and symbols and began to call itself a critic of life and an interpreter of things as they are." (*E&I* 192)

Although Yeats could not accept Wordsworth's version of nature any more than he could Keats', a persistent undertone of affinity runs throughout his critique. Yeats and Wordsworth had more in common than he liked to admit: chiefly, they are the greatest poets of autobiographical self-confrontation in their centuries. Both exploit memory in striking juxtapositions of past and present, and both have written great poems of lament for lost visions. As Yeats pondered his own potential respectability after the age of fifty, his mind turned to Wordsworth, and he concluded the "Anima Hominis" section of *Per Amica* with one of those great flashes of self-insight that distinguish his best prose:

> A poet, when he is growing old, will ask himself if he cannot keep his mask and his vision without new bitterness, new disappointment. . . . Surely, he may think, now that I have found vision and mask I need not suffer any longer. He will buy perhaps some small old house, where, like Ariosto, he can dig his garden, and think that in the return of birds and leaves, or moon and sun, and in the evening flight of the rooks he may discover rhythm and pattern like those in sleep and so never awake out of vision. Then he will remember Wordsworth withering into eighty years, honoured and empty-witted, and climb to some waste room and find, forgotten there by youth, some bitter crust. (*Mythologies* 342)

This is the temptation of quiet which Yeats was still resisting twenty years later in "An Acre of Grass." There he invokes frenzy,

here "new bitterness, new disappointment." More than any of the
first romantics Yeats insists that vision depends on continuing
and new loss, as Harold Bloom has reminded us.[33] To Yeats,
Wordsworth destroyed his ongoing capacity for poetic experience
and could only look back on a lost happiness or else console himself with philosophic maxims. In *Per Amica* Yeats makes aged
Wordsworth into a grotesque reminder of what he feared that he
himself might become.

Yeats turned another potential candidate for romantic scarecrow
into a positive example of mental action. Perhaps because Coleridge never meant enough to young Yeats to warrant serious later
distortion, in maturity Yeats exempted him from the slings and
arrows with which he bombarded Blake, Shelley, or Keats. With
each change in the Yeatsian poetic Coleridge took on new virtues,
particularly in "Kubla Khan" and "The Ancient Mariner." In the
nineties those poems were purely aesthetic after Hallam's fashion,
while by 1916 "Kubla Khan" had become favorable to the spoken
voice, imperfect only by individual words so rich in association
that they made dramatization of the speaker difficult.[34] In both
periods he found in his predecessor a formulation of his own
thoughts on sexual love, "the desire of the man which is for the
woman, and the desire of the woman which is for the desire of the
man, as Coleridge said." (*VPlays* 1283) References to Coleridge
only became frequent in the 1930s, when Yeats correlated Berkeley, Swift, and Burke with the philosophy and politics of Coleridge at Highgate.[35]

Recognition of the creative role that Coleridge assigned to mind
in confrontation with nature prompted Yeats' late admiration. As
we have seen, he found the Coleridgean metaphor of resisting
whatever would drive mind into the quicksilver an apt riposte to
Stendhal's description of a masterpiece as a mirror dawdling down
a lane. Likewise, he invoked Coleridge on Juliet's Nurse and Hamlet to contrast creation of a character by observation or passive
sense-impression and by self-dramatization or active imagination. (*E&I* 410) In a rare clear section of the murky second book of
A Vision he adopted Coleridge's definition of reason as his own
definition of mind: "an organ bearing the same relation to its
spiritual object, the universal, the eternal, the necessary, as the
eye bears to material and contingent phenomena. But then it must
be added that it is an organ identical with its appropriate objects."
(*Vision* 187) The definition clarifies Yeats' incessant use of the
phrase "the mind's eye." What the mind sees, however, are not
the universal and eternal directly, but images or forms of them,

and Yeats' life and art became a quest for those images. He sought either to conjure them up within his psyche as in "The Magi" or to select them from Nature, as in "Coole Park and Ballylee, 1931." This for him was romantic use of mind, instead of the naturalistic mode in which the eye simply reflects "material and contingent phenomena."

Yeats' innate balance of credulity with scepticism and his lifelong commitment to poetry made the true subject of his work as much his relation to images as images themselves. He became a student of mental action, as much concerned with process as object, and his poetry continuously records the dynamics he learned. Hence, he is often closer to Shelley or to Keats and Wordsworth, whose great subject is their personal relation to visions deriving from imaginative actions, than to Blake, the romantic most concerned with elaborating the vision itself. The subject of "Sailing to Byzantium" is not the golden bird any more than the subject of "Ode to a Nightingale" is the nightingale. Fear that absorption into vision would lead him "to chaunt a tongue men do not know" afflicted Yeats as early as "To the Rose upon the Rood of Time," and he usually sought instead to stand as poet on the border dividing two worlds, where Janus-like he could look both ways. Sometimes he strayed into the world of pure images but never into that mechanized nature which he saw the romantics as resisting.

We need a full grasp of Yeatsian romanticism to understand his most famous declaration of affinity, in "Coole Park and Ballylee, 1931." The first three stanzas embody one romantic way of looking at nature, in which mind transforms it into symbolic emblems.[36] Couched in a seductive rhetorical question, identification of water with "the generated soul" in line 8 shocks us by its casual abruptness, although it seems clear enough in its context and was anticipated thirty years before when Yeats identified water as Shelley's great symbol of existence. But the two stanzas on Lady Gregory so break the romantic complexities of the first three that the opening of the last stanza startles us as much as the conclusion of the first:

> We were the last romantics—chose for theme
> Traditional sanctity and loveliness;
> Whatever's written in what poets name
> The book of the people; whatever most can bless
> The mind of man or elevate a rhyme;
> But all is changed, that high horse riderless,
> Though mounted in that saddle Homer rode
> Where the swan drifts upon a darkening flood.
>
> (*VP* 491-92)

48

Discrepancy between opening declaration—"we were the last romantics"—and what follows has misled even some excellent critics into deprecating his avowal: Harold Bloom dismisses it sardonically, and Richard Ellmann empties it of all meaning while suggesting its opposite.[37] If Yeats had not removed the original penultimate stanza, now known independently as "The Choice," preparation for this stanza would have been clearer,[38] since Yeats attributed broken lives to the romantics even while allowing them occasional self-completion in their work. But the real difficulty lies in the appositives advanced in Shelleyan series:
—traditional sanctity and loveliness
—whatever's written in what poets name the book of the people
—whatever most can bless the mind of man or elevate a rhyme.
These not only seem an odd definition of romanticism, but the second directly contradicts a favorite Yeatsian charge that his two chief romantics, Shelley and Blake, *lacked* folklore and popular mythology. The series is, I think, not static but progressive, with the third clause climaxing the previous two: to be a romantic was to choose what blessed the human mind, something identical with what elevates poetry—in short, imagination. Yeats saw two historical supports for this—traditional forms of high culture and traditional folklore, both of which he defended as valid forms of imagination in opposition to growing dominance of middle-class civilization with its mechanical idea of nature. He had amalgamated similar ideas forty years earlier in "To Ireland in the Coming Times," where he pleaded for compatibility of literary nationalism, Intellectual Beauty, and druidic mythology. There, he was not arguing for chauvinism or superstition. Here, he is not defending, say, Christian religious rites or poltergeists, but the imaginative mental action that his poem, like Stevens' "On Modern Poetry," both praises and exemplifies. Yet in combining quasi-religious devotion ("sanctity") and art ("loveliness") with folklore and with imagination as both mental faculty ("mind") and literary theme ("rhyme"), Yeats implicitly claims that as a last romantic he completed the work of the first by grounding it more firmly in cultural forms and national life. How far Yeats' own art deserves to be seen as a continuation of romantic tradition forms our next subject.

II

In the second half of "The Tower" Yeats—as persona—paces on the battlements of his tower, stares at the landscape, and sends imagination forth to encounter it. That series of actions dramatically places him in a central romantic line of symbol, theme, and form; like Thoor, Ballylee, itself the poem becomes an elaborate stage set for Yeats to sport upon in his role as modern romantic. The tower as symbol derives partly from Shelley, as Yeats acknowledged in the related "Blood and the Moon": "And Shelley had his towers, thought's crowned powers he called them once."[39] Yeats adopted both the symbol itself and the notion of varying it from poem to poem from his precursor. Correspondingly, "The Tower" seizes upon the high romantic theme of mind encountering the world through imagination. And finally, the second part of "The Tower"—and indeed the whole poem, for the underlying pattern would hold even without the overt triple division—is a Greater Romantic Lyric, in which poetic movement follows a special course of imaginative mental action. Yeats discovered his great mature subject in his relation to what "The Tower" calls "images and memories," and a characteristic means of developing it in the Greater Romantic Lyric. I mean first to examine that traditional mode before establishing Yeats' creative reworking of it in "The Tower" and other mature poems. After that, a look at Yeats' early poetry will reveal the roots of both that group and other works of his maturity with which this chapter closes. In focusing primarily on later poems I do not mean to scant Yeats' early romanticism but simply assume that subject to be sufficiently established already.[40] My concern here is to demonstrate something different: that many of Yeats' greatest mature poems creatively develop out of romantic themes and modes.

In the Greater Romantic Lyric, Coleridge, Wordsworth, Keats, and to a lesser extent Shelley evolved a structure suitable to their individual conceptions of mental action: in Abrams' definition, "an out-in-out process in which mind confronts nature and their interplay constitutes the poem." The first poem in the new genre, Coleridge's "Eolian Harp," illustrates the pattern: a particular speaker begins by describing the landscape around the cottage with detached affection (out), progresses through an increasingly rapt meditation in which he identifies more and more with his own revery (in), and then breaks off imaginative involvement to return to the original scene in a new mentality (out). While Abrams' interest in the doctrine of such poems causes him to describe the "in" phase as a "meditation" through which the speaker "achieves an insight, faces up to a tragic loss, comes to a moral decision, or resolves an emotional problem,"[41] I would substitute "vision" for "meditation" to emphasize the poem's structure as determined by shifting mental modes from observation to increasingly active imagination and then to its subsidence in an interpretive conclusion. In these terms, the poem's structure is description-vision-evaluation. "The Eolian Harp," for example, moves from Coleridge describing his cottage to his imagining first a fairy world, which in turn modulates into projection of a more general world of "the one Life within us and abroad"; he then imagines himself in a noontime revery on a sunny hillside and finally rises to highest imaginative intensity in envisioning "all of animated nature" as organic harps swept by an Intellectual breeze. He then breaks off the vision and returns to the cottage, where faith, memory, and reason conspire to repudiate his imaginative power for having challenged Christian orthodoxy. Seen doctrinally, the poem "comes to a moral decision"; seen psychologically, it moves through different faculties in a searching presentation of genesis, fulfillment, and exhaustion of imagination.

Like all Greater Romantic Lyrics, "The Eolian Harp" is a poem of the act of the mind. But the genre provides a structure, not a straitjacket, and admits a variety of actions within its basic tripartite pattern. Four representative poems serve as reference points for mapping the grounds on which Yeats built his tower vision—Coleridge's "Frost at Midnight," Wordsworth's "Tintern Abbey," and Keats' "Ode to a Nightingale" and "Ode on a Grecian Urn." Situation, use of memory, and two structural innovations point our attention in "Frost at Midnight," which is in effect a Prayer for My Son. Like Yeats' "A Prayer for My Daughter," a variant on the pattern whose combination of the Atlantic with "Gregory's wood and one bare hill" recalls Coleridge's "sea, hill, and wood," the poem invokes growth in a future environment favorable to imagination for the poet's child, in contrast to the father's own experience. Coleridge's poem opens with a favorite Yeatsian situation—a man meditating at midnight inside his rural home, as in "All Souls' Night" or the more generally nocturnal "In Memory of Major Robert Gregory," two more of Yeats' Greater Romantic Lyrics. Unlike "Eolian Harp," this poem shifts into memory for its first "in" section, where Coleridge creates an image of his past self in remembering dreams prompted by a grate in childhood. Structurally, the vision comes in two parts punctuated by a return to the present, here a brief address to his "Dear Babe," before imagining a future of Hartley's communion with "lovely shapes and sounds intelligible." As Yeats will later sometimes do, Coleridge ends within his vision in impressive rhetoric.

"Tintern Abbey" follows "Frost at Midnight" in offering two visions, making the pattern out-in-out and then back in again, and stresses memory as much as imagination. As in "Coole Park, 1929" (a structurally simpler Greater Romantic Lyric) and "The Wild Swans at Coole" (which in its original stanzaic order tried to be a Greater Romantic Lyric as far as its theme of failed imagination would permit), dynamism derives from confrontation with a place important to the speaker in the past. Wordsworth first describes the scene, then imagines a near past when he remembered it and a further past when he first encountered it, comes back to the present, and then imagines a future for Dorothy. His diction rather than his technique of using memory to prepare for imaginative action claims our attention here. He speaks of animated mental images—"the picture of the mind," "beauteous forms," and being "laid asleep in body and become a living soul"—just as Coleridge calls on "flitting phantasies" and "shapings of the unregenerate mind." Although Yeats would have hated the poem's praise of Nature, he habitually used similar phrases,[42] most notably "the mind's eye," and interpreted romantic references to images, phantoms, and other shapes more literally than their creators did. The point is not that he borrowed terms from, say, Wordsworth, but that a drive to render similar mental action causes related phraseology among writers in this genre.

Keats' two odes return to a normative three-part pattern with obvious links to Yeats' later work but also those differences of stance that made Yeats cleave more unto Shelley. Unlike Yeats, Keats remains in the present tense, for his poems depict an ongoing struggle to transform current experience rather than to invoke memory. "Ode to a Nightingale" speaks a parable of sympathetic imagination—first bodily quiescence, then imaginative projection into the nightingale ("already with thee"), and final collapse of the vision with a bell-like *forlorn* "to toll me back from thee to my sole self." This Keatsian out-in-out pattern of interaction with a natural object remained alien to Yeats, who created visions apart from nature. In the Byzantium poems, his desire to reincarnate himself in a golden bird of art both recalls and "corrects" Keats' limitation of merger within natural rather than aesthetic boundaries. But even while divorcing human life from cold pastoral, Keats did allow his imagination to interact with art. In "Ode on a Grecian Urn" he first describes the urn (out), then enters into his vision to imagine a town not actually on the urn (in) at his highest intensity, and then withdraws again to a more distanced perspective (out). That is, he substitutes an art work for an actual landscape to prompt his Greater Romantic Lyric, as Wordsworth did in "Elegaic Stanzas" on Peele Castle. Yeats does not, although poems like "A Bronze Head" or "The Municipal Gallery Revisited" display similar devices. Most strikingly, his imagining of the halfway house in "Lapis Lazuli" parallels Keats' image of the Grecian town—neither exists in the artistic object, but only in the poet's mind. Yeats took from Keats as much as he could without changing from creative to sympathetic imagination.

The romantics channeled so much creative energy into the new genre because it followed the shape of imaginative experience. More than displaying the results of imaginative creation, it allowed the following through of a mind moving from description or ordinary perception to vision and then back again. Abrams has quoted Coleridge on the return upon itself as a device making for wholeness: "The common end of all *narrative*, nay, of *all*, Poems . . . is to convert a *series* into a *Whole:* to make those events, which in real or imagined History move on in a *strait* Line, assume to our Understandings a *circular* motion—the snake with it's Tail in its Mouth" [*sic*].⁴³ Experience thus assumes the shape of *ouroboros*, the tail-eating snake. Equally important, it becomes a cycle and harmonizes with the cyclic quality that haunts romantic thought about both societies and individuals. Often this cycle takes a special shape: vision breaks off at its intensest moment and the poet returns to his ordinary state, whether in "Frost at Midnight," "Grecian Urn," or "Nightingale." Inability to sustain imagination in the poems matches our experience in life. Wordsworth minimized the discrepancy and drew new strength from his experience, while Keats stressed the discontinuity. At his most extreme a Keatsian poet is not sure which state is real, the imaginative or the ordinary, and is plagued by doubt and questioning, often ending the poem with an interrogative ("Do I wake or sleep?"). Yet despite the persona's questions, these poems ratify vision de facto, for in all of them vision is more important than natural landscape. The poems exist to present the visions, and interest centers on acts of mind, not narrative description of nature. Significance springs only from mind—the landscapes possess no meaning in themselves but only that meaning which the poet gives them by his own mental processes. The banks of the Wye interest us only because of Wordsworth's experiences there, Stevens' Key West could be any other place, and we do not know at all from the poem precisely where Keats encounters his nightingale.

Yeats wrote Greater Romantic Lyrics only in his maturity, when he had cast off the derivative romanticism of the nineties and was creating a modern variety. The form suited the intermittent pulsations of his own imagination, and its circular shape harmonized with his antinomies and gyres. By moving into and then out of vision he could hold reality and justice, actual and ideal in a single poem. Likewise, doubts generated by discontinuity between states matched his own vacillations. The structure itself functioned thematically: it incarnated the process of using mind to discover images, which Yeats saw as the master theme of romanticism. Yet he did not simply repeat his predecessors. Instead, he heightened the importance of vision over nature even further, diminishing description of external scene and preserving only as much of nature as imagination needed. For him vision became a literal summoning of images in nature's spite. In effect, he crossed visionary autonomy from Blake and Shelley with poetic structure from Wordsworth, Coleridge, and Keats, and he infused both stance and form with his own sensibility. The resultant hybrids included many of his best poems between 1918 and 1929.

"The Tower" (VP 409) makes the form an arena for a romantic grappling with the despondency of aging. Unlike Wordsworth, the poet still has both flaming imagination and fervent sense. For Blake, those would have been enough,[44] but Yeats here fears waning of emotion, the third term he introduced into his exposition of Blake. His temptation is abstract argument, for his years demand the philosophic mind, which he conquers through vision. The first five lines of part II present an orthodox beginning for a Greater Romantic Lyric—a speaker looks at a landscape and "send[s] imagination forth" to encounter it. The next line signals a Yeatsian innovation, in calling "images and memories" from the landscape. Were the speaker Keats, he would identify with objects in the scene; were he Wordsworth, he would summon images and memories of his past self. Since he is Yeats, he calls up images and memories mostly of others. With their arrival the "in" part of the lyric begins.

These images divide the great symbols of passion and mood Yeats admired in the romantics into paired creator and follower—Mrs. French and her serving man, blind poet Raftery and the man drowned in Cloone bog, and Yeats' own characters of old juggler and tricked Hanrahan. Despite his Shelleyan situation on the tower, Yeats here repudiates his youthful Intellectual vision of ascent to the ideal that he had founded upon Shelley. Mrs. French's servant, the drowned man, and Hanrahan all carry over ideal moonlit visions into the actual world ("the prosaic light of day") and so end in disaster. Opposed to that, Yeats now wants moon and sunlight to "seem/ One inextricable beam" encompassing antinomies into which all things fall without kindling a mad lust to live only by the moon.

The vision builds to its climax in Yeats' questioning of those images of passion—did they too rage against old age as he does? Just here, in line 101, we suddenly realize what Yeats has done. He has called up the images literally and they stand in front of him:

> But I have found an answer in those eyes
> That are impatient to be gone;
> Go therefore; but leave Hanrahan. . . .

We understand that Wordsworth imagines his past self near Tintern Abbey, or that Keats imagines himself with the nightingale; but what are we to understand by Yeats addressing images here as though they were present? We can make sense of this in two ways: first, he has slipped into revery and these images "in the Great Memory stored" (line 85) have now entered his individual consciousness. If we do not believe in the Great Memory, then we can say that he has called up images from his own conscious or subconscious memory (Yeats knew a fair amount about the characters in this poem), or else simply created them outright, and in the intensity of his vision addresses them as if they were present, which they are in the mind.

Whatever explanation we choose, the speaker modulates out of vision in questioning Hanrahan, his own creation. His second question signals the change: "Does the imagination dwell the most/ Upon a woman won or woman lost?" The "you" in the following line refers more to Yeats himself than to Hanrahan, for this is another of Yeats' continual self-reproaches about his failed relation to Maud Gonne. The lines of the poem,

> If on the lost, admit you turned aside
> From a great labyrinth out of pride,
> Cowardice, some silly over-subtle thought
> Or anything called conscience once

parallel the mixture of pride, timidity, oversubtlety, and conscience in a passage about Maud in the original draft of his autobiography:

And in all that followed I was careful to touch [her] as one might a sister. If she was to come to me, it must be from no temporary passionate impulse, but with the approval of her conscience.

> Many a time since then, as I lay awake at night, have I accused
> myself of acting, not as I thought from a high scruple, but from a
> dread of moral responsibility, and my thoughts have gone
> round and round, as do miserable thoughts, coming to no solu-
> tion. (*Memoirs* 133)

That love, explicitly linked by Yeats to his early romanticism,
signifies the same mistake made by the servant, drowned man,
and even Hanrahan, yet its memory is so strong that even the
memory reduces him to their condition. With realization in the
poem that passion still remembers what was so fugitive, Yeats'
obstinate questionings cease. Yet in making this tangent to the
Intimations ode he veers off into his own orbit, for he refuses the
Wordsworthian comfort of the philosophic mind and, spurred by
the renewed sense of loss on which his poetry depends, makes his
will in triumph of imagination. Exaltation carries over into the
third section, until it subsides again in the closing lines and leaves
the poet where he began, though with a difference.

The images summoned in this poem provide one gauge for
Yeats' claim to have corrected romanticism by fastening its visions
to a national landscape, and thus reinvigorating them. Unlike
Greater Romantic Lyrics of the romantics themselves, "The
Tower" could not be transferred to another setting. Mrs. French,
Raftery and Mary Hines, the bankrupt ancient master of the
house, and others all lived in *this* landscape. Yeats' elevation of
major and minor Irish figures into heroic roles has stirred a large
controversy in which both its defenders and its attackers overstate
their cases. On the one hand, Yeats' allusions to Mary Hines or,
say, to Maeve, do not make his poems any easier for non-Irish
readers (and perhaps not always even for Irish ones); they are, in
fact, obstacles to understanding. On the other hand, critics who
simply condemn the habit, and Yeats' exaggerated claims for it,
miss the point. In "The Tower" he uses them to move away from
romantic subjectivity that made earlier Greater Romantic Lyrics
depend only on the poets' minds and not their environments.
Mrs. French and Raftery, or elsewhere MacGregor Mathers or William Horton, are not immediately meaningful for everybody, but
they do, at least, link private vision to something beyond the poet
himself. In *A Vision* Yeats boasted that he had improved on Blake
by turning historical characters into elements of his mythology
and so made it more accessible. A romantic might respond with
some truth that the representativeness of Wordsworth's or Keats'
minds make them in fact more accessible than Yeats' quirky Celts,

but I think Yeats' own poems do gain both force and a measure of seeming impersonality from his tactic, which the character of his imagination badly needed. Although original romantics may not have required this attachment, Yeats himself clearly did.

Yeats habitually addresses such images as if they were present and often claims that he sees them "in the mind's eye." That phrase takes us back to Hamlet, not thin from eating flies but as visionary prince:

> HAMLET: My father—methinks I see my father.
> HORATIO: O, where, my lord?
> HAMLET: In my mind's eye, Horatio.

Yeats used the expression particularly often from about the time of *Responsibilities* through *The Tower*, when it appears in half a dozen poems and frequently in his prose. He connected it especially to seeing images of human forms, for which the allusion to Hamlet provides a cunning context. In Shakespeare's play Hamlet uses his "mind's eye" to see a mental image of his dead father, but he is shortly to encounter a real ghost. In Yeats' poems speakers summon figures that could be mental images but that also seem, like ghosts, to exist independently. The Shakespearean echo allows us to interpret the images as we choose, with Yeats himself remaining as gnomic as the Delphic oracle.

Because Yeats' chief innovation in the Greater Romantic Lyric was to make vision into a summoning of images, we need to look more closely at these images seen in the mind's eye before turning to more of his poems in that genre. Enough critics have expounded Yeats' complex doctrines of images differently enough times to make anyone wary of opening that particular Pandora's box; here, I mean to restrict my inquiry solely to those in the "mind's eye." They are usually great figures of passion or of mood, like the romantic questers so dear to Yeats. We meet the first as a completed poet figure associated with a tower in a prose account of a tour of the Apennines, which contains a kernel of the kind of visionary experience that Yeats later elaborated in the poetic form of his Greater Romantic Lyrics:

> I was alone amid a visionary, fantastic, impossible scenery. It was sunset and the stormy clouds hung upon mountain after mountain, and far off on one great summit a cloud darker than the rest glimmered with lightning. Away south upon another mountain a mediaeval tower, with no building near nor any sign of life, rose into the clouds. I saw suddenly in the mind's

eye an old man, erect and a little gaunt, standing in the door of the tower, while about him broke a windy light. He was the poet who had at last, because he had done so much for the world's sake, come to share in the dignity of the saint. . . . ("Discoveries" [1906], *E&I* 291)

Yeats goes on to combine the figure with Jesus in an ecstatic rhapsody in which the old man, a mixture of Athanase and Ahasuerus, becomes a prototype of the poet as successful quester and mage. The passage's embryonic doctrine of poet and mask exfoliates later in "Ego Dominus Tuus" (1917), where Hic argues that Dante "made that hollow face of his/ More plain to the mind's eye than any face/ But that of Christ." (*VP* 368) Ille's correction of Hic's oversimple account of how poets create their masks concerns us less than how the masks or images are perceived by observers—in the mind's eye as figures of impassioned questing.

Three other poems in which such images appear to the mind's eye ring changes on the theme of intense desire. In "The Magi" (1914) they are searching again for the divine union of celestial mystery and bestial floor, while in the last section of "Meditations in Time of Civil War" (1923) they are troopers calling for vengeance on the murderers of Jacques Molay. Clearly, the images can represent misdirected as well as admired passion, for Yeats' note to "Meditations" identifies the troopers' cry as "fit symbol for those who labour for hatred, and so for sterility in various kinds." (*VP* 827) A mixed tone pervades the description of William Horton, first image summoned in the Greater Romantic Lyric "All Souls' Night" (1921). Like the early Yeats, Horton had known "that sweet extremity of pride/ That's called platonic love." (*VP* 471) After the death of his lady (Audrey Locke), he fixes "his mind's eye . . . on one sole image," a fusion of both her and God.[45] Despite Yeats' ambivalence toward Horton's (and his own) form of quest, concentrated intensity still makes Horton fit auditor of the poem's "mummy truths."

Besides great figures of passion and mood, the mind's eye could summon figures of self-possessed mastery or symbols from esoteric Yeatsism. To the first group belong Major Robert Gregory and his literary forerunner, the fisherman. In "The Fisherman" Yeats calls up an image of a Connemara man who does not exist but is "a dream" as ideal audience for the cold and passionate poetry he wanted to write. Here Yeats gives us a simple account of his genesis—he simply imagined the man. His accounts of the origin of images were not always so direct, whether in poetry or in prose. The Great Memory that he invoked in "The Tower" and the *Spiritus Mundi* of "The Second Coming" found fuller description in *Per Amica Silentia Lunae*, where Yeats described his own practice of symbolic meditation:

> Before the mind's eye, whether in sleep or waking, came images that one was to discover presently in some book one had never read, and after looking in vain for explanation to the current theory of forgotten personal memory, I came to believe in a Great Memory passing on from generation to generation. But that was not enough, for these images showed intention and choice. . . . The thought was again and again before me that this study had created a contact or mingling with minds who had followed a like study in some other age. . . . Our daily thought was certainly but the line of foam at the shallow edge of a vast luminous sea; Henry More's *Anima Mundi*, Wordsworth's "immortal sea which brought us hither." (*Mythologies* 345-46)

The Great Memory gets into the poetry, but the guardedly expressed (not "I believed" but "the thought was before me") remainder does not, except possibly for the *Spiritus Mundi* of "The Second Coming." The sphinx vision there, like the related one seen by the mind's eye in "The Double Vision of Michael Robartes," will appear in our chronological survey of Yeats' Greater Romantic Lyrics. We have learned enough of the mind's eye and its images to begin.

Yeats wrote eight Greater Romantic Lyrics between 1918 and 1929. They divide into four pairs: "In Memory of Major Robert Gregory" (1918) and "All Souls' Night" (1921) summon images of the dead; "The Second Coming" (1920) and "The Double Vision of Michael Robartes" (1919) conjure images from the Great Memory; "The Tower, II" (1927) and "Meditations in Time of Civil War, VII" (1922) stress the tower top; and "Coole Park, 1929" (1931; written 1929) and "The Crazed Moon" (1932; written 1923) offer landscapes uncommonly symbolic even by Yeats' standards. All relate to romanticism in form and often in theme and symbol as well, as we saw in "The Tower." The earliest of them, "In Memory of Major Robert Gregory," prefigures both the tower symbol and the stanzaic pattern of that poem, for it takes place in the "ancient tower" and uses the same *aabbcddc* rhyme scheme that Yeats derived from Cowley's elegiac ode on William Harvey and based two other romantic poems on—"A Prayer for My Daughter" and "Byzantium." The Coleridgean situation of Yeats' elegy recalls

"Frost at Midnight," while its place in the overall order of Yeats' poems recalls Shelley, for it follows "The Wild Swans at Coole," whose basic image derives from an encounter between poet and swan in *Alastor*.

Mental action in "In Memory of Major Robert Gregory" (*VP* 323) follows the program of description-vision-evaluation, but a brief return to the present divides the vision itself into two parts—one of Lionel Johnson, John Synge, and George Pollexfen, and the other of Robert Gregory himself. Typically for Yeats, the vision reverts to the past, counterpointing the spatial out-in-out with a temporal present-past-present sequence. He begins with a meditative description of his present situation in the tower, whose subdued symbolic suggestion still alerts us for imminent imagination. In the initial vision, images of "discoverers of forgotten truth" and "companions" come to the speaker's mind. All of them are figures of passion or mood: Johnson brooding on sanctity and dreaming of consummation; Synge finding at last an objective correlative to his heart in passionate and simple Aran islanders; and Pollexfen forsaking physical sport for astrological search. A relapse into the present to mention "all things the delighted eye now sees" prepares for the sustained vision of Robert Gregory. Although described as ideal "soldier, scholar, horseman," Gregory appears mostly as artist, particularly if we remember that the eighth stanza, on horsemanship, was added to the poem later at his widow's request. In accomplishing all "perfectly," Gregory resolves the split between active and contemplative, becoming the kind of possible subject for a poem suggested at the end of Stevens' "Of Modern Poetry." The vision culminates in the eleventh stanza where Yeats subordinates Gregory to symbolic ignition of the combustible world. The question "What made us dream that he could comb grey hair?" signals the exhaustion of imagination at its intensest moment and prepares us to shift back "out" into evaluation.

The final stanza deserves more attention than it usually receives. Its first two lines, which return us to the original scene, oppose the wind of nature (not inspiration) to mind and suggest that mind creates its images to counterbalance nature, to resist a violence from without by a violence from within. The speaker then reveals his original plan—not just to call up Synge (whom "manhood tried"), Pollexfen (whom "childhood loved"), or Johnson (whom "boyish intellect approved"), but to *comment* on them "Until imagination brought/ A fitter welcome." Imagination thus redeems the decay implicit in the chronological sequence love-approve-test. Yeats' always erratic punctuation obscures the syntax here. A comma instead of semicolon after "each" in the first two printings[46] makes it culminate the previous sequence—he thought to comment until imagination would enter in. This Yeats has done most fully for Gregory but also in miniature for Johnson, Synge, and Pollexfen, whom he has turned into images of intensity. But, the last two lines suggest, thought of Gregory's death interrupted a lengthier sequence by discharging Yeats' passion ("heart"). This exhaustion of the heart, which recurs as a problem in "The Tower," here marks the end of a remarkable reworking of a romantic mode.

Similar structure holds together the more abstruse "All Souls' Night," written two years later and eventually made into an epilogue for *A Vision*. Again the speaker summons a trio of dead contemporaries—Horton, Florence (Farr) Emery, and MacGregor Mathers, all of whom appear as images of the esoteric students Yeats imitated as Athanase. Since the mental action resembles that of the Gregory elegy,[47] we may focus on the meaning of "the dead." In the earlier poem, the figures were dead in a double sense—they had physically died, and they had become artistic images in the poem, part of the artifice of eternity opposed to time. This Shelleyan association of death with completion or fulfillment, which had informed Yeats' poems of the nineties, spills over into "All Souls' Night," where the ghostly (a deliberate Yeatsian pun) images become fit auditors for Yeats' "mummy truths," both of the poem and of *A Vision*. As creations of imagination they can share Yeats' own imaginative communications. As conclusion to the *Tower* volume, the poem neatly reverses the situation of the initial "Sailing to Byzantium," when Yeats had wanted to be instructed by the spirits; as a result of lessons learned in poems like "The Tower," he can now summon spirits to be instructed by him in imagination's truth. That is, the volume as a whole resurrects flagging passion and harnesses it to imaginative vision. A different kind of action informs the next pair of Yeats' Greater Romantic Lyrics.

Like "The Double Vision of Michael Robartes," Yeats' famous "The Second Coming" calls up impersonal images rather than those fashioned from the poet's past. Yeats ascribes their source to *Spiritus Mundi*, which in a note to another poem from *Michael Robartes and the Dancer* he defines as "a general storehouse of images which have ceased to be a property of any personality or spirit." (*VP* 822) The poem's brevity reveals its structure as a Greater Romantic Lyric clearly:

> Turning and turning in the widening gyre
> The falcon cannot hear the falconer;
> Things fall apart; the centre cannot hold;
> Mere anarchy is loosed upon the world,
> The blood-dimmed tide is loosed, and everywhere
> The ceremony of innocence is drowned;
> The best lack all conviction, while the worst
> Are full of passionate intensity.
>
> Surely some revelation is at hand;
> Surely the Second Coming is at hand.   10
> The Second Coming! Hardly are those words out
> When a vast image out of *Spiritus Mundi*
> Troubles my sight: somewhere in sands of the desert
> A shape with lion body and the head of a man,
> A gaze blank and pitiless as the sun,
> Is moving its slow thighs, while all about it
> Reel shadows of the indignant desert birds.
> The darkness drops again; but now I know
> That twenty centuries of stony sleep
> Were vexed to nightmare by a rocking cradle,   20
> And what rough beast, its hour come round at last,
> Slouches towards Bethlehem to be born?
>
> (*VP* 401-2)

Lines 11 and 18 mark the transitions from description to vision to evaluation. But here Yeats prepares for vision not by passive revery or negative capability but by working himself into a prophetic frenzy. He adopts the stance of seer, and what he describes is not an actual landscape but a metaphoric one: we do not feel that a falcon flies off before his eyes any more than that he literally sees a blood-dimmed tide. Instead, he depicts the state of Europe as if from the top of a mile-high tower, from which he can see as far as the Germans in Russia—whom he mentioned in the original draft.[48] Scholarly quarrels about identity of falcon and falconer —whether Christ and man, nature and spirit, logic and mind —should not be allowed to obscure the emblem's significance, loss of control. It matches the loss of rational control in the speaker's mental action as he moves to a rhetorical crescendo preparatory to vision.

Because the image seen in the mind's eye comes from *Spiritus*

Mundi, Yeats does not have to recall it personally; consequently, he can increase urgency by writing the entire poem in the present tense. The vision section carries over the passionate tone of the quasi description to a displacement only in space and not in time. A here-there(the desert)-here movement matches the familiar out-in-out structure. This vision of antithetical Egyptian Sphinx heralding the end of primary Christianity replaces the erratic falcon with birds once again wheeling in formation. Although Yeats often exults at the end of "scientific, democratic, fact-accumulating, heterogenous civilization,"[49] commentators err in seeing that attitude in the poem. The vision "troubles" the speaker's sight; it is the sphinx whose eye is "blank and pitiless."

With the end of vision the speaker's return to himself completes the doubling action built into the poem by the paired turning of birds, the title itself, and the repeated phrases "turning," "is loosed," "surely," "the Second Coming," and "is at hand." The change reminds us why the Greater Romantic Lyric attracted Yeats so much: its return upon itself suits his true subject, which is more his relation to his vision than the vision itself. Typically, the vision leaves the speaker in a state of partial illumination. Now he knows not only that a nightmarish coming is at hand, but also that it was caused by the rocking cradle of Jesus. This means, I think, not just that the gyres are reciprocal (living each other's life and dying each other's death), but that the new god appears savage because seen through the mental set of Christian civilization and its derivatives. The final question is genuine, not rhetorical; in Yeats' system we know that something is coming but we do not know precisely what, nor can we, for we are bound by the old civilization. Nor does the speaker rejoice, for his phrase "rough beast" suggests horror rather than delight.

"The Second Coming" is romantic in more than form; it is shot through with Blakean and Shelleyan echoes in theme and diction. Behind the poem lurks "Ozymandias," with its picture of a monumental ruin in a desert, while Harold Bloom has identified the source of the center that cannot hold in the Witch of Atlas' rejection of natural love.[50] Likewise, the phrase "stony sleep" comes from Blake's *Book of Urizen*, where it describes Urizen's transitional phase between his Eternal state and his rebirth as fallen man.[51] But reworking of the Last Fury's speech in act 1 of *Prometheus Unbound* dwarfs even those in significance:

> In each human heart terror survives. . . .
> The good want power, but to weep barren tears.

The powerful goodness want: worse need for them.
The wise want love; and those who love want wisdom;
And all best things are thus confused to ill.

(lines 618-28)

The best lack all conviction, while the worst
Are full of passionate intensity.

("The Second Coming")

As many commentators, myself included,[52] have pointed out, Yeats reverses the thrust of Shelley's apocalyptic lines by making them a prelude to another cycle rather than to (possibly temporary) transfiguration. Here, we may note the difference in the mental action of the two speakers. Prometheus frustrates the Fury's plan to torture him with a vision of human suffering by unexpectedly drawing strength from it: "The sights with which thou torturest gird my soul/ With new endurance, till the hour arrives/ When they shall be no types of things which are." A vision of heroic and selfless virtues follows in the songs of the six spirits, preparatory to the poem's later apocalypse of love. In "The Second Coming," however, the comparable lines create a frenzy in the speaker that prepares him for a vision of the rough beast to come, after which he reverts to his original state, having grown in knowledge but not in power. There is a fatalism in the poem that Yeats' *Vision* system often prompted, in which the quest for Unity of Being turns into a quest for knowledge instead, whether the "mummy truths" of "All Souls' Night" or the half-knowledge of "The Second Coming." Against this, Yeats sets ironic self-criticism as in "The Phases of the Moon" or images of Unity of Being like the dancer in "Among School Children."

"The Double Vision of Michael Robartes" (*VP* 382) summons images from *Spiritus Mundi* or the Great Memory and returns us to Yeats' concern with the poet's relation to Unity of Being. In a Greater Romantic Lyric that begins and ends in the ruins of a chapel restored on the Rock of Cashel by Cormac MacCarthy in the twelfth century, Robartes sees "in the mind's eye" two visions —in terms of the system, the first of phase 1 and the second of phase 15. In the second, a girl emblematic of Unity of Being dances between Sphinx (this time a Grecian one, representing knowledge) and Buddha (love). Because all three have overthrown time, like other images in Yeats they seem both dead and alive. In the third movement of the lyric ("out"), Robartes' attention focuses on the girl who outdanced thought. He identifies her with a dream

64

maiden forgotten when awake, one of the Shelleyan ideals of Yeats' youth, whom in later life he preferred to identify with Homer's Helen or Dante's Beatrice. Unlike her, he is caught not between perfect knowledge and perfect love but rather in the human tension between objective thought and subjective images. He faces this predicament both in life and in the two opposing states that form the poem. With vision fled, his gain is knowledge of a personal ideal, not of impersonal forces as in "The Second Coming." Development toward that ideal is the one freedom offered by Yeats' system, although he allows others outside of it. The lyric ends with his romantic "moan" of recognition and equally romantic resolve to render the experience artistically. Like a miniature *Prelude* or *Milton*, "The Double Vision of Michael Robartes" describes an action that is a prelude to poetry.

Yeats' next pair of Greater Romantic Lyrics, "The Tower, II" and "Meditations in Time of Civil War, VII," strikes a middle ground between the personal images of dead friends in "In Memory of Major Robert Gregory" and "All Souls' Night" and the impersonal ones of inhuman extremes in "The Second Coming" and "The Double Vision of Michael Robartes." Both poems make the tower top into a symbolic outpost on the border between self and soul. Yet unlike "The Tower," discussed above, "Meditations"[53] draws its images not from past associations of the landscape but from an analogous event in history—the murder of Jacques Molay, Grand Master of the Templars, which it counterpoints with figures derived from Gustave Moreau's visionary painting "Ladies and Unicorns." They become the ingredients of one of Yeats' most moving struggles against the hatred inherent in the age and in some of his own thought. As he stands on the tower top, images of first the troop of murderers and then the procession of ladies swim "to the mind's eye." In terms of the poem's title, the first represent "Phantoms of Hatred" and the second those "Of the Heart's Fullness." The imagination tries to counter images of hatred with those of fullness, but as even they yield to "an indifferent multitude . . . brazen hawks . . . Nothing but grip of claws" the poem modulates out of vision into its third and final section. There Yeats descends from the tower top, regrets his separation from friends and from public approval, but still resignedly affirms his continued allegiance to "the half-read wisdom of daemonic images." That moment becomes all the more poignant for its frank avowal of human cost.

Although Yeats paired "The Crazed Moon" with "Coole Park,

1929" in *The Winding Stair*, he had written it in 1923, shortly after the other Greater Romantic Lyrics on *Vision* themes. Like them, it can be read in terms of Yeats' system: in a late phase, the moon shines only on moonstruck, disorganized gropers, in contrast to her exuberant children of earlier phases, who danced in order. Further, the later children grow murderous as the gyre approaches conclusion and long maliciously to rend whatever comes in reach. But the poem can also be read more literally, as a Greater Romantic Lyric, an "act of the mind":

> Crazed through much child-bearing
> The moon is staggering in the sky;
> Moon-struck by the despairing
> Glances of her wandering eye
> We grope, and grope in vain,
> For children born of her pain.
>
> Children dazed or dead!
> When she in all her virginal pride
> First trod on the mountain's head
> What stir ran through the countryside
> Where every foot obeyed her glance!
> What manhood led the dance!
>
> Fly-catchers of the moon,
> Our hands are blenched, our fingers seem
> But slender needles of bone;
> Blenched by that malicious dream
> They are spread wide that each
> May rend what comes in reach.
>
> (*VP* 487-88)

The three stanzas reenact the familiar triple pattern, matching out-in-out with present-past-present. The speaker first describes the current state of the old moon, then creates a vision of the moon in virginal pride inspiring both passion ("stir") and order ("dance"), and finally returns to the present with perception of our vain groping's goal—malicious destruction. The landscape here is remarkably insubstantial even for Yeats; one feels as though the speaker were charting a symbolic romantic landscape rather than an actual scene. Polysemously, the moon can refer to a natural object, the twenty-eight phases of *A Vision*, historical development in clock time, or imagination withering from exultance to despair. In his current condition, the speaker's only triumph is to recreate past glory from memory.

Yeats transfers that theme to his favorite Irish setting in the following poem of *The Winding Stair*, "Coole Park, 1929." The poem contributes to the book's running modern adaptation of romanticism, following the Shelleyan tower of "Blood and the Moon" and literary history of "The Nineteenth Century and After" and "Three Movements," picking up the Greater Romantic Lyric form of "The Crazed Moon," and anticipating romantic self-avowal in "Coole Park and Ballylee, 1931" and a romantic holy city of art in "Byzantium." He returns to the Coole-Ballylee region for the national ballast with which he habitually sought to weight romanticism. The landscape's significance derives neither from mere personal experience nor from the arbitrary mythology of *A Vision*, but from its importance to actual historical figures, albeit ones transformed by Yeats' imagination. These historical types, which include younger Yeats himself, become quasi-objective analogues to romantic symbols of passion and mood.

The poem opens with a conventional enough beginning for a Greater Romantic Lyric: in a specific landscape at nightfall, the speaker meditates on a bird's flight and even identifies the surrounding trees as a sycamore and a lime.[54] Although the swallow may pick up the Neoplatonic echoes[55] that Yeats associated with romanticism in general and Shelley in particular, its overt development in the poem follows orthodox romantic use of singing birds to symbolize artists and their works. The ensuing portions champion freedom from oppressive nature, which Yeats always commended in romanticism, in explicating why the speaker fixes his eye on works constructed "in nature's spite."

With the vision of former glory in the second stanza, the speaker reverts to the past. Noble Hyde, meditative Synge, and impetuous Shawe-Taylor and Hugh Lane, with Yeats himself in ironic companionship, become heroic figures whose action indicates the poem's real symbol of passion and mood, Lady Gregory herself. Her character most rouses Yeats' intensity of vision as he moves in the third stanza from remembering the past to creating the powerful image of swallows whirling in formation around her true north. The concluding couplet, with its off-rhyme of "lines" and "withershins" and suggestion both of gyres and of imaginative kairos replacing natural chronos, exhausts his imagination in a momentary blaze.

Superficially, the "here" of the final stanza seems to signal the close of a conventional Greater Romantic Lyric. We expect completion of normative here-there-here, out-in-out, and present-past-present movements. But Yeats plays against our vain anticipation, for "here" turns out to be placed in an imagined future. It is as if Wordsworth's "Tintern Abbey" or Coleridge's "Frost at Midnight" omitted their return to the present which separates their vision of the past from that of the future. Instead, Yeats moves directly from past to future in imagining later travelers, scholars, and poets (or perhaps the ghosts of those mentioned in stanza 2) taking their stand at a ruined Coole and paying tribute to Lady Gregory. By replacing a return to self with a return to vision, Yeats shifts our attention away from the speaker and toward his overt subject. We end in contemplation of Coole rather than of Yeats' relation to it.

In reducing his presence in "Coole Park, 1929," Yeats substituted a second vision for a return back "out," but elsewhere he removed the third section altogether, so that we move from description to vision (with accompanying displacement in time and space) and then stay there. Such poems—the two most famous are "A Prayer for My Daughter" (1919) and "Among School Children" (1927)—have enough in common with the mental action of Greater Romantic Lyrics to be analyzed along with them, but they cannot properly be assigned to that form since they lack the necessary concluding movement. As a result, in them we focus on the visions themselves, which build up to icons of Unity of Being. The poet indicates his relation to them implicitly in the initial section and sometimes later, but he disappears by the end of his poem. (The pattern also appears in lyrics like "On a Political Prisoner," 1920, and recurs as late as "A Bronze Head," 1939.) I will here examine only briefly the earlier of the two famous poems before considering the later one in more detail.

Not surprisingly, "A Prayer for My Daughter" (*VP* 403) originally had a third section, deleted in revision,[56] which imagined a future visit to Coole by Yeats' daughter. That movement would have made the poem parallel to "Coole Park, 1929" in structure. As it now stands, the poem includes only the description of the first twelve lines and then an imaginative revery until the end, all in the same stanzaic form as "In Memory of Major Robert Gregory" and other works. Beginning in a familiar tower setting, Yeats describes natural forces and sleeping child in a way reminiscent of Coleridge's "Frost at Midnight." The Coleridgean echoes continue in the vision of the daughter's thoughts as birds and she as a laurel rooted in "one dear perpetual place," which may recall part of "Ver Perpetuum":

> . . . Deem it a world of Gloom.
> Were it not better hope a nobler doom,
> Proud to believe that with more active powers
>   On rapid many-coloured wing
>   We thro' one bright perpetual Spring
> Shall hover round the fruits and flowers,
> Screen'd by those clouds and cherish'd by those showers![57]

Like Coleridge, Yeats follows gloom with hope. The poem's persistent organicism should not mislead us into thinking that Yeats turns to nature itself; as always, he turns to nature as symbol. Here, natural things stand for "radical innocence" of soul, which discovers in Dantesque fashion that its will is Heaven's will. The poem climaxes with ceremony and custom, which are names for the horn of plenty and the laurel tree, but which also suggest human activity set over against nature. By omitting a final return "out," Yeats succeeds, to modify a phrase of Jon Stallworthy, in writing a prayer for his daughter and not for himself as poet.

The similarly truncated "Among School Children" (*VP* 443) brings to conclusion one form of Yeatsian mental action, mixed with recollections of romanticism. Like "A Prayer for My Daughter," the lyric presents an elderly speaker meditating on childhood. Yeats' note to the "honey of generation" that betrays an infant shape refers us to Porphyry's essay "The Cave of the Nymphs," which had loomed so large in "The Philosophy of Shelley's Poetry." The celebrated antitheses at the start of the final stanza recall Wordsworth's prayer at the close of an excursus on education of children following his account of the Boy of Winander in book 5 of *The Prelude:*

> May books and Nature be their earthly joy!
> And knowledge, rightly honoured with that name—
> Knowledge not purchased by the loss of power!

Yeats, too, seeks knowledge not purchased by loss of power rather than "blear-eyed wisdom out of midnight oil." As always, he counters Wordsworthian naturalism with mental anti-naturalism: to him images of Unity of Being, symbolizing "all heavenly glory" in a typical displacement of religious language, surpass earthly joys of Nature and are the proper subject for books.

Mental action in the poem rewards careful scrutiny. The speaker begins with customary description of a scene, here not a landscape but a schoolroom in which human beings supplant natural objects as stimuli to vision. The following three stanzas express normal enough mental action for an "in" section of a Yeatsian Greater Romantic Lyric. He "dream[s]" of Maud's Ledaean image in youth when she told him of an earlier incident from her childhood. This recollection—and the presence of the young pupils—triggers his powers to create her childhood form, which comes not from memory but from pure imagination, for he had not known her then: "She stands before me as a living child." Already, oxymoronic qualities of images—in this case describing a mental image as living—come into play. After that intense creation the speaker lapses into a more passive kind of vision, in which her present image "floats" into his mind. At this point the poem begins a series of what might be called imaginative reflections on old age, which the present images of the aged poet and his lady have suggested. First comes a picture of a young mother who would be discontent could she see her infant son at the speaker's own age, then a synopsis of Plato's subordination of nature to eternal forms, Aristotle's naturalism, and Pythagoras' mystic theories of artistic measurement, all of which (both philosophers and theories are included) are dismissed as scarecrows, in phraseology recalling stanza II of "Sailing to Byzantium."

From this point starts a progression that rises to the highest imaginative level of the poem in the final stanza. We have had four kinds of mental action—mimetic description, memory, creation of a new image, and metaphoric philosophizing (in Coleridge's terms, Fancy). Yeats now prepares for a new act by rationally distinguishing a mother's animated image of a child from a nun's static one of a saint or God. The point of the distinction, however, is to isolate the quality shared by both images—their heartbreaking effect on humans, in which they resemble a lover's images. Known by passion (lovers), piety (nuns), or affection (mothers),[58] they stand apart from us as images of longing and are self-born because complete and therefore growing out of pure mind (as we learn from "The Circus Animals' Desertion"). Parkinson is surely right in noting the ambiguity of "Presences" and "self-born mockers,"[59] and straightening it out is almost as difficult as deciding who says what to whom at the end of Keats' "Ode on a Grecian Urn." It is simplest to take both as referring to "images," which in more of the poem's prodigal triplicities are known by passion, piety, or affection, symbolize heavenly glory, and mock human enterprise.

Addressed to these images, the astonishing last stanza climaxes the mental action of the poem. It is both account and example of artistic creation. "Labour" collects from previous stanzas meanings of both work and birth pain. "Where" first seems to mean *wherever*, then *not here*, and finally the gymnasts' garden where Unity of Being thrives in the following poem. But images of Unity of Being are created in the mind, not as narrow seeker of "bleareyed wisdom" or studier of images, but as creator of them; this is also where poems like "Among School Children" are created. Like the chestnut tree, the result is indivisible and, like the dancer, it cannot be separated from the dance. The dancer is, of course, the archetypal Romantic Image, kinetically reconciling opposites, as Kermode has shown.[60] Here we are concerned with its role in the poem. In creating the twin images of great-rooted blossomer and body swayed to music, Yeats has burst into a new kind of mental action in the poem: after description, memory, creation of a new image, and poetic philosophy, the speaker concentrates all his faculties into creation of a new kind of image—one of Unity of Being, from which diverse mental and physical components cannot be separated. Tree and dancer become icons for creative mind transfiguring a body, which is itself an icon for poetic creation. "Among School Children" is a poem about mind in the act of finding what will suffice, and what will suffice is active creation of ideal images, not passively received from *Spiritus Mundi* but actively made by mind itself. With this triumph, akin to the inner apocalypses of Shelley and Blake, need for a third or "out" section disappears, and the poem closes in fulfillment of vision.

Yeats' adventures with the Greater Romantic Lyric and related patterns show a sensibility with affinities to Shelley and Blake reworking a poetic form developed principally by Coleridge, Wordsworth, and Keats. The resultant collision exploded the original importance of nature to the form. For Yeats vision became the summoning of images and, in the highest case, active creation of them de novo. He pruned his natural descriptions radically, reducing them to a minimum and exploiting their national associations. This transformed his predecessors' concern with tension between mind and nature to tension between mind and images. That dialectic suited his antinomial correction of the emphasis on ideal beauty in his earlier works; through it, he could reach a poetry of insight and knowledge rather than of longing and complaint. Yet the resultant Greater Romantic Lyrics of mental action form only one branch of Yeats' mature romanticism. To study the others we need first to examine their common root in his early poetic practice. The mental action—sometimes more an inaction—of those youthful Shelleyan and Blakean efforts show both deficiencies that required later remedy and potentialities that made liberation possible. The Rose lyrics and fragments of quest romance offer the best examples.

The static quality that pervades much of Yeats' early verse appears in both "To the Rose upon the Rood of Time" (1892) and "The Secret Rose" (1896). Either could have become a Greater Romantic Lyric of momentary union, but for different reasons both remain static, without developing mental action. As if redacting Shelley's "Hymn to Intellectual Beauty," the poet of "To the Rose" invokes ideal beauty to descend upon him. But he resists a union with the Rose that would generate an out-in-out pattern of relation to vision. Instead, he fears that absorption into the Rose will sever him from sounds of "common things," make him a student of God's words to dead souls, and thus prevent him from being an earthly poet. The poem is persistently oral—it stresses hearing and singing—while Yeats' Greater Romantic Lyrics tend to be predominantly visual. The Rose is to come near, but not too near. This fear of absorption into vision, without return, derives in part from lack of a suitable poetic form and in part from Yeats' early belief in a separate and actually existing spiritual reality, which persists throughout his career but clashes later with a radical humanistic insistence that man has created everything, as in "The Tower." Unlike the similar choice in "Vacillation," Yeats here arrives at his resolution more by refusal of mental action than by working through its processes. A similar dilemma empties "The Secret Rose" of decisive action. More typically, Yeats here actually yearns for absorption into ideal beauty. But, again, he has no means of moving into absorption and then back out. Nor does he yet have an antinomial world view comprehending both real and ideal, foul and fair. Consequently, he remains in separate longing throughout the poem. Were this a Greater Romantic Lyric, Conchubar, Cuchulain, Caoilte, Fergus, and the anonymous folk quester would actually appear to the poet in vision; here, he serially evokes them as already enfolded in the Rose's leaves, but we do not sense that he actually creates or enters into a vision. Early Yeats feels the desire of the moth for the star (an image he quoted from Shelley); he does not yet believe in space flight.

If the Rose poems seldom show dynamic mental structure, they do anticipate a typical device of later and more dramatic poems —direct address to figures in a vision. Yet just as the early poems lack mental action, so do they suffer from corresponding loss in vitality of the summoned images. Sometimes, Yeats speaks directly to the Rose itself, urging it to come near, but the Rose remains more a constructed symbol than an image. That is, it creates only a weak sense of physical presence. But in one poem, "The Rose of Battle," the speaker talks directly to images of dead questers. He calls them "the sad, the lonely, the insatiable," an equally apt description of personae in Yeats' own lyrics closest to his idea of Shelleyan poetry. They palely imitate his admired figures of passion and mood but do not convince us: the poet tells rather than shows us what they are. The device of address to images of the dead works more impressively in later Greater Romantic Lyrics or in the raising of Parnell in "To a Shade" (1913).

Like the later poems, these early ones conscript Shelley's general defense of poetry for Yeats' special kind of visionary art. Sometimes they confess the debt openly, as in "To Ireland in the Coming Times," originally called "Apologia addressed to Ireland in the coming days." (*VP* 137) Here Yeats defends his pursuit of Intellectual Beauty against nationalist charges of escapism by identifying Intellectual Beauty with the spirit of the nation: "The measure of her [the Rose's] flying feet/ Made Ireland's heart begin to beat." The poem proceeds to transfer this Shelleyan argument to Yeats' calling up of images and spirits. Esoteric wisdom enables him to trade gazes with elemental creatures who "huddle from man's pondering mind."[61] They are accessible not to reason but to that imaginative receptivity free from rational or sensory domination. When he revised this poem for the 1925 edition, Yeats made the lines on apprehension evoke memories of Wordsworth's "Tintern Abbey." His

> things discovered in the deep,
> Where only body's laid asleep

recalls the famous Wordsworthian passage where

> we are laid asleep
> In body, and become a living soul.

For Wordsworth, body's sleep allowed the soul to see its divine counterpart within nature; for Yeats, it frees his "mind" (not soul) for esoteric, supranatural revelation. Yeats' drive to authenticate his heterodox vision would have horrified Wordsworth, much as Coleridge horrified himself in "The Eolian Harp." Yeats does work from romantic premises, however, and they underlie not just his summoning of images in his Greater Romantic Lyrics but also his defense of "measured" art as late as "The Statues."

Even in his first poems Yeats followed the romantics in beating on the door of nature, and by the nineties his blows had picked up force. His Rose symbol belonged to an always supranatural and sometimes even anti-natural Intellectual order. A plea for deliverance from nature carries over from lyrics on the Rose to poems like "The Sorrow of Love" (1892). In the original version the girl's appearance destroys dominance of natural sounds that had overpowered "earth's old and weary cry" (*VP* 120) for deliverance and makes them into a mirror of that cry. The argument becomes clearer after the 1925 revisions. There is no need for the defensiveness with which Yeats scholars often approach those revisions; despite Louis MacNeice's influential critique,[62] the revised poem is excellent. It sharpens conflict between nature and mind by making the girl transform a state where nature "had blotted out man's image and his cry" to one where nature "Could but compose man's image and his cry." Contrary to MacNeice, "compose" is not ambiguous: it clearly indicates that nature has changed from conqueror ("blotted out") of vision to mere material for it. MacNeice's facile adoption of Eliotic impersonality as defense against "anarchist individualism which characterized the Romantic Revival"[63] prevents him from seeing this. It is one more example of the bad influence of Eliot's more enthusiastic followers.

One way for mind to dominate nature was to turn it into a work of art. "Coole Park and Ballylee, 1931" did that haphazardly by mining the landscape for emblems, while "The Lover tells of the Rose in his Heart" (1892) calls for more systematic reconstruction. Recoiling from "the wrong of unshapely things," the speaker hungers to change nature into an artifact:

> With the earth and the sky and the water, remade, like
>   a casket of gold
> For my dreams of your image that blossoms a rose in the
>   deeps of my heart.
>
> (VP 143)

This transformation of natural elements into a visual showcase for the image's splendor would replace the opening sounds of natural life hostile to imagination. Appropriately for an art work, the casket contains an image, or, in a Shelleyan series of removes, "my dreams of your image." The golden casket and image set over against nature anticipate the golden bird of Byzantium but fail to create the same sense of animation. The word "blossoms" tries to counteract metallic artifice with organicism, but instead of infusing vitality it lapses into the natural order which the poet longs to escape. We are left with a sense that true vitality belongs to banished and unshapely things. Yeats here has created neither a golden bird nor a great-rooted blossomer.

The poem's overt lack of mental action derives from its speaker, who in 1899 was Aedh. But Aedh is not really a character or persona at all: he is a principle of mind. Yeats' note to *The Wind Among the Reeds* described Aedh, Hanrahan, and Robartes first in magical[64] and then in psychological terms:

> I have used them in this book more as principles of the mind than as actual personages. It is probable that only students of the magical tradition will understand me when I say that "Michael Robartes" is fire reflected in water, and that Hanrahan is fire blown by the wind, and that Aedh, whose name is not merely the Irish form of Hugh, but the Irish for fire, is fire burning by itself. To put it in a different way, Hanrahan is the simplicity of an imagination too changeable to gather permanent possessions, or the adoration of the shepherds; and Michael Robartes is the pride of the imagination brooding upon the greatness of its possessions, or the adoration of the Magi; while Aedh is the myrrh and frankincense that the imagination offers continually before all that it loves. (*VP* 803)

Distinct from Hanrahan's simplifying intensity and Robartes' powerful pride, Aedh represents the sacrificial aspect of imagination. In a poem like "The Lover tells of the Rose in his Heart" there can be no mental action because the speaker is not an integrated character. He is only a fragment of a character, a voice from *Prometheus Unbound* detached from the rest of the play. Far from reversing the cinematograph of literary history in its progression from Chaucerian crowd to Elizabethan heroes to romantic elements, Yeats has carried it one step further. His division of the psyche into separate aspects led eventually to great inner dialogues like "Ego Dominus Tuus" or "A Dialogue of Self and Soul," but it also led him into fragments of quest romance.

Yeats followed *The Wanderings of Oisin,* which he thought of as an Irish *Prometheus Unbound,* with a series of lyrics that behave like fragments of quest romance.[65] Like the romantics, he internalized the quest pattern throughout his work. But sometimes he displaced overt apparatus of romance from larger forms to brief lyrics, as Blake had in parts of the Pickering Manuscript. These are special quests because their "hero" is a principle of mind, whether the sacrificial aspect of imagination like Aedh or a figure of passion and mood like Aengus. They follow a Shelleyan formula of vision of an ideal woman, frustrated search for her, and hint of final union in death. Their goal is Unity of Being, the harmony of our perfected faculties. As in Blake's *Jerusalem* or Shelley's *Prometheus Unbound,* union of male and female principles symbolizes that psychic integration. Apocalypse, or revelation, signals its difference from our ordinary reality; for the same reason, death often serves as conclusion, signifying alternately defeat or measureless consummation. Search for analogy to a transformed state suggested an art work, as in "The Lover tells of the Rose in his Heart" with its golden casket. Often the quester becomes an image in a world of art. This triad of apocalypse-death-art governs one branch of Yeats' poetry and reaches its finest development in the Byzantium poems.

Early lyrics commonly present part of the quest pattern while suggesting the rest. "He [in 1899, "Aedh"] hears the Cry of the Sedge" begins with an echo of Keats' "La Belle Dame sans Merci":

> I wander by the edge
> Of this desolate lake
> Where wind cries in the sedge:
> *Until the axle break*
> *That keeps the stars in their round,*
> *And hands hurl in the deep*
> *The banners of East and West,*
> *And the girdle of light is unbound,*
> *Your breast will not lie by the breast*
> *Of your beloved in sleep.*
>
> (VP 165)

Compare the last stanza of Keats' poem:

> . . . I sojourn here,
> Alone and palely loitering,
> Though the sedge has wither'd from the lake,
> And no birds sing.

Both poems oppose the quest to nature, which appears as withered or desolate and incapable of satisfying imagination. The knight at arms fails partly through exhaustion of sympathetic imagination (reinforced by use of pronouns[66]), partly through false projection of his ideal, and partly through a mistaken attempt to find it in life. Despite appearances, Yeats' poem is less pessimistic. The overt suggestion of failure in fact corresponds to symbolic conditions of success: apocalypse and end of the old life. Breaking of the axle-tree,[67] overthrow of the banners of East and West (space), and unbinding of the girdle of light signify that revelation which will allow union with the ideal lady. In *The Wind Among the Reeds* the speaker was Aedh, whom Yeats used most frequently of his triad of mental principles and identified as the sacrificial aspect of imagination and associated with fire. The poem then becomes a kind of Blakean Last Judgment of the reintegrated psyche symbolized by reunion of the lovers. The title misleads us, for in the poem Aedh hears the cry not of the sedge but of the wind in the sedge, or, in typical romantic fashion, of spirit calling through (not with) nature. Nature cries that union can never take place, the wind that it can because error and creation are burnt up the moment men cease to behold them. As in Blake's *Vision of the Last Judgment*, "the whole creation groans to be delivered."[68]

"The Song of the Wandering Aengus" (1897) is an Irish *Alastor* in miniature. Yeats tied the poem to Irish folk tradition through Aengus (Irish God of Love), legends of the Tribes of Danu, and its original context as "A Mad Song" in the story "Red Hanrahan's Vision." His coy note (*VP* 806) has generated a scholarly search of Lucy Garnett's translations in *Greek Folk Poesy* for sources, but the lyric's real roots are in romantic quest tradition, chiefly Shelley's poem. Here is Yeats':

> I went out to the hazel wood,
> Because a fire was in my head,
> And cut and peeled a hazel wand,
> And hooked a berry to a thread;
> And when white moths were on the wing,
> And moth-like stars were flickering out,
> I dropped the berry in a stream
> And caught a little silver trout.
>
> When I had laid it on the floor
> I went to blow the fire aflame,
> But something rustled on the floor,
> And some one called me by my name:
> It had become a glimmering girl
> With apple blossom in her hair
> Who called me by my name and ran
> And faded through the brightening air.
>
> Though I am old with wandering
> Through hollow lands and hilly lands,
> I will find out where she has gone,
> And kiss her lips and take her hands;
> And walk among long dappled grass,
> And pluck till time and times are done
> The silver apples of the moon,
> The golden apples of the sun.
>
> (*VP* 149-50)

As in *Alastor*, the hero has a vision of an ideal woman by a stream and, after her disappearance, embarks on a vain search for her. Unlike Aedh, Aengus here is not a readily identifiable principle of mind, but rather one of those great figures of passion and mood of whom "Alastor" was always chief for Yeats. Endymion, the Belle Dame's knight-at-arms, and the failed questers of "The Golden Net" and "The Crystal Cabinet" belong to the same company. Just as the youth in *Alastor* "embodies his own imaginations" in "a single image,"[69] so does Aengus find the fire in his head transformed into a glimmering girl. Whether we take the polysemous goal of this quest as a woman, an Irish witch, or Intellectual Beauty, union with her signifies psychic completion.

The poem rejects nature for art as arena for imagination. In the first stanza wood and stream compose a congenial setting. But after the vision of stanza 2, nature in stanza 3 appears blasted, as it does in *Alastor*, whether wasteland of "barren hills and marshy land" in the original version or meaningless repetition of "hollow lands and hilly lands" in the final one. Aengus can imagine completion of his quest only in a metallic garden, a garden of art. The naturalistic silver trout yields to silver lunar apples and golden solar ones, which presumably hang upon a golden bough. Only there, if he can find it, will the visionary unite with his long-sought image. Yet like "La Belle Dame sans Merci," this is basically a poem of pessimism: the speaker has starved so long for his fairy bride that death appears more as defeat than as symbol of consummation. The metallic garden is more a wishful thought than a possible form for his exhausted imagination.

After the turn of the century, Yeats entered an anti-romantic phase in which for over a decade he modernized diction and meter in his poetry while displacing his native romanticism into his dramas. There he continued romantic traditions that had seized him in the nineties and prepared them for his later transformations. *The Shadowy Waters*, begun earlier, continued to obsess him until 1907. In a Shelleyan love quest[70] for Dectora, Forgael finds through imagination an ecstatic union symbolized by death or disappearance and realized in isolation from society. At one point, Forgael nearly metamorphoses into an art work, becoming, at least to Dectora, golden-armed Iollan. The conflict between King Guaire and the poet Seanchan in *The King's Threshold* (1904) redacted part of the argument of Shelley's *Defence of Poetry* in its insistence on the role of art and artists in the state, particularly in its original ending with Seanchan's triumph. *Where There is Nothing* (1902), later revised into *The Unicorn from the Stars* (1908), injected Blakean and Shelleyan drives toward apocalypse into a hero modeled partly on William Morris and partly on Shelley's questers. Yet the play attempted to move Shelleyan vision down into common life. Through collaborating with Lady Gregory on the revisions, Yeats hoped to accomplish his old aim of correcting romanticism by combining its imaginative vision with folk tradition: he wanted "a linking, all Europe over, of the hereditary knowledge of the country-side, now becoming known to us through the work of wanderers and men of learning, with our old lyricism so full of ancient frenzies and hereditary wisdom, a yoking of antiquities, a Marriage of Heaven and Hell." (*VPlays* 713) He began the Cuchulain cycle, which resulted in his greatest figure of passion and mood, and continued experiments with principles of mind as characters, which later culminated in Swineherd and Queen of *A Full Moon in March*. With few exceptions, Yeats' poetic dramas carry the burden of his romanticism from the turn of the century through *Responsibilities*.

"In 1900 everybody got down off his stilts," recalled Yeats in his introduction to *The Oxford Book of Modern Verse* (p. xi). By "stilts" Yeats meant primarily the posed excesses of the nineties, which went back through Pater to aesthetic romanticism. A chief dismounter was Yeats himself, who wanted to descend upon life after his pseudo-Shelleyan idealism. Later he proudly clambered back up on a remodeled romantic pair, as he boasted in "High Talk" (1938), but in this period he was busily withering into truth. Ezra Pound, whom Yeats first met in 1909, helped him fashion more precise and concrete diction. "[Pound] helps me to get back to the definite and the concrete away from modern abstractions," he wrote Lady Gregory in 1913, when Pound was acting as his secretary. "To talk over a poem with him is like getting you to put a sentence into dialect. All becomes clear and natural."[71] The younger generation took its reaction against the nineteenth century even further than Yeats' own, and he absorbed some of its reforms while, at least temporarily, keeping silent about its anti-romanticism. On occasion, he even used that hostility to free himself from domination by Blake or Shelley. In a 1924 footnote to his essay on Blake's illustrations, he confessed:

Some seven or eight years ago I asked my friend Mr. Ezra Pound to point out everything in the language of my poems that he thought an abstraction, and I learned from him how much further the movement against abstraction had gone than my generation had thought possible. Now, in reading these essays,

I am ashamed when I come upon such words as 'corporeal reason,' 'corporeal law,' and think how I must have wasted the keenness of my youthful senses. *(E&I* 145)[72]

Yet Pound's impact turned out to be a coda rather than overture to a new phase of Yeats' anti-romanticism, and he shortly turned back to his original tradition with instruments tuned by the techniques of modernism. He became a great modern poet of romantic mental action and scorned those who seemed to grant imagination a lesser role. Henceforth, he persistently contended that Pound had left man helpless before the contents of his own mind, and that Eliot reduced human beings to straw puppets. "I too have tried to be modern," he wrote.[73]

Along with his Greater Romantic Lyrics, Yeats' other major romantic poems appeared in the magnificent volumes from *The Wild Swans at Coole* (1919) onward. Detailed examination of their vast design would require a separate study, but we can note here their overall relation to romantic ideals before progressing to specific poems. With *The Wild Swans at Coole* Yeats inaugurated his mature romantic subjects and forms in Greater Romantic Lyrics like "In Memory of Major Robert Gregory" and "The Double Vision of Michael Robartes," and in dialogues like "Ego Dominus Tuus" and "The Phases of the Moon." The original 1917 volume, which ended with *At the Hawk's Well,* seemed a frustrated lament on aging. But in removing *Hawk's Well* in 1919 and adding the last seven poems, Yeats made the book move from sorrow in "The Wild Swans at Coole" to new imaginative strength in "The Double Vision of Michael Robartes." His rearrangement of stanzaic order in the title poem during 1917 supports the later changes in the volume as a whole. By placing the current last stanza third, he originally ended the poem on a defeated contrast of continuation of the swans' passion with extinction of the poet's. While a swan in a similar passage of *Alastor*[74] becomes an image of achieved union in contrast to the hero's continuing, unsuccessful quest, Yeats here as in other later works reverses the thrust of his Shelleyan source. Reordering the poem threw stress on the poet's ambiguous awakening in the penultimate line, with its symbolic potential.

Yeats' mature books pern around human relation to images —whether of apprehending, creating, or becoming them—as a means of achieving Unity of Being. That theme dominates *Michael Robartes and the Dancer* (1921), which could nearly be entitled *William Butler Yeats and the Image.* Opening poems on the duties of lovers to offer each other reciprocal images lead to production of images through political action as in "Easter, 1916," apprehension of ominous images of the future as in "The Second Coming," and back to creation of a major image in the tower. I cannot agree with Bloom's contention that "the volume's unifying theme is hatred,"[75] not least because of its closing tribute to the poet's wife. *The Tower* (1928), which develops from "Sailing to Byzantium" to "All Souls' Night" by way of "The Tower" and "Among School Children," adds to the concerns of the previous volume the poet's drive to turn himself into an image, which he learns to do by embracing rather than fleeing personal experience. Its paired volume, *The Winding Stair and Other Poems* (1933), suggests in its title its weaker unity, which in part derives from amalgamating separate books of 1929 and 1932, but from its opening great gazebo through the fires of "Byzantium" to the closing sequences it continually deals with complementary themes. The poems now combined as *From a Full Moon in March* (1935) progressively strip away illusions and images to arrive at "the desolation of reality" of "Meru." *Last Poems*, a botched merger by the publisher of *New Poems* (1938) and other lyrics, works outward again in a progressive assertion of imagination. From its opening address to Rocky Face through its closing "Municipal Gallery Revisited" and "Are You Content?" *New Poems* explores human relation to images as relentlessly as *Michael Robartes and the Dancer*, with the poet continually assimilating himself to his creations in a movement away from the determinism of the opening lyric. Finally, Yeats' manuscript ordering of the remainder of *Last Poems*,[76] beginning with "Under Ben Bulben" and ending with "The Circus Animals' Desertion," enacts a similar movement from images perceived under abstract determinism to those developed from autonomous personal experience. Yeats' Greater Romantic Lyrics clearly exfoliate from the patterned context of his collected lyrics; so, too, do the nine poems (mostly from the 1930s) we shall now consider, not chronologically but as coordinates for a psychic map of Yeats' late poetry.

Yeats' Byzantium poems climax the quest of his early work. They depend on the same triad of apocalypse, death, and art but make each term simultaneously literal and symbolic. These polysemous poems apply equally to history, art, afterlife, and personal psychology. If they seem to describe a historical city (or, rather, two cities, since the first poem is apparently set in the reign of Justinian and the second near the year 1000), they also create a city of art, and if they seem to deal with the soul after death, they also represent transfigured imaginative perception in life. Yeats' *Vision* symbolism helps generate these complexities, for the starlit or moonlit dome presides over either phase 1, bodily absorption into the supernatural, or phase 15, the completed image. What is important is that ordinary human life exists at neither phase. A strong sense of physical presence helps these lyrics to create more convincing multiple meanings than do the Rose poems. They continue Yeats' romantic protest against natural oppression, particularly in the golden bird scorning "common bird or petal," originally "nature's blood and petal." An earlier draft of "Sailing to Byzantium" makes the poet's stance equally explicit: "I fly [from] nature to Byzantium."[77] Like the Wandering Aengus, he yearns for a metallic garden that will suffice imagination.

For all its splendor, "Sailing to Byzantium" (1927, *VP* 407) lacks the decisive mental action of Yeats' Greater Romantic Lyrics. As in "To the Rose upon the Rood of Time," Yeats stands on the border between ordinary life and vision; the poem succeeds chiefly through his more solid construction of both poles rather than by dynamic progress from one to the other. After describing the forsaken country of the young, the speaker invokes the sages and then instead of imaginatively transforming himself into a golden bird he imagines what it would be like to do that—we get, as it were, an imagining of an imagining, rather than an imagining itself. While the country of the young offers body, generation, nature, and life as death in contrast to the soul, intellect, artifice, and death as life of Byzantium, the major difference between states lies in the songs of the matched birds. The natural birds praise whatever is begotten, born, and dies: they celebrate the creature caught in time. Instead, the golden bird sings what is past, passing, or to come: it reveals process rather than creature and thus offers release from the bondage of time.

The special point of view of "Byzantium" (1932, *VP* 497) makes its mental action unique. As several critics have pointed out in other contexts, the speaker stands within Byzantium itself. Historically, he stands in his ideal city; aesthetically, within an art work; eschatologically, in eternity; and psychologically, inside a perceiving mind. This means that the speaker must himself already have become an image; he appropriately has a breathless mouth corresponding to the figure whom he meets, who is likewise more shade than man, more image than shade. It is as though the speaker were one of those achieved images of poets whom Yeats summoned in his Greater Romantic Lyrics, and as though the whole poem were the middle or visionary part of a Greater

Romantic Lyric told from the point of view not of the poet but of a summoned image—a Yeatsian "Ode on a Grecian Urn" told from the point of view of a figure on the urn. For "those images that yet/ Fresh images beget" include such "blood-begotten spirits" as the persona of a poet as man, in process of being reborn as image. As Yeats described the transformation in a prose account of his first literary principle, "he has been reborn as an idea, something intended, complete" and is therefore more passion than type, more type than man. (*E&I* 509) More truly even than the triumvirate of Aedh, Hanrahan, and Robartes, the figures in this poem —speaker, Emperor, floating image, golden bird, and smiths—are principles of mind.

Romantic analogues pervade both poems. As at once historical city and city of art, Byzantium refracts rays from Coleridge's Xanadu, Blake's Golgonooza, and Shelley's Athens, as well as structures in *The Revolt of Islam* and *The Witch of Atlas*. The image of soul clapping its hands and singing recalls Blake's famous description of his brother's soul ascending to heaven, while a draft of "Byzantium" echoed the harlot's curse of "London."[78] Likewise, the bird singing of what is "past, or passing, or to come" follows Ahasuerus who pierces "the Present, and the Past, and the To-Come" in *Hellas*, Los who saw "Past, Present & Future" in *Jerusalem*, and the Bard who sees "Present, Past, & Future" in *Songs of Experience*.[79] The speaker's tribute to the superhuman as "death-in-life and life-in-death" recalls the demon "Night-mare LIFE-IN-DEATH" of *Rime of the Ancient Mariner*. Finally, the golden bird singing to an emperor evokes memories of Keats' nightingale and may even have partly derived from it.[80] Yet as analogues on analogues arise, Yeats' departure from these romantic models looms correspondingly larger, particularly in "Byzantium." Nearly all the analogues develop a central humanistic dialectic in which love and sympathy provide an approach to perfection. But, taken one step further, "Byzantium" leads not so much to fully realized humanity as to dehumanization in the name of the superhuman. The poem's scorn of "the fury and the mire of human veins" can degenerate in other contexts into Yeats' occasional abasement to the coming rough sphinx. As though to thwart that interpretation, Yeats followed "Byzantium" almost immediately with the corrective of "Vacillation" in the arrangement of *The Winding Stair*. Before proceeding to that poem, we may look at three of Yeats' lyrics on the human void to see how they led him back toward the core of romantic vision.

Like Stevens, Yeats found war the most dangerous of those

pressures of reality that threatened to overwhelm imagination. While brooding on war spawned the romantic nationalism of "September, 1913" (which at least balanced low contemporary Paudeens with heroic figures from the past), it also prompted obliteration of the human in "A Meditation in Time of War," composed shortly afterward but not published until 1920:

> For one throb of the artery,
> While on that old grey stone I sat
> Under the old wind-broken tree,
> I knew that One is animate,
> Mankind inanimate phantasy.
> (*VP* 406)

Delineation of vision within a "throb of the artery" derives from Blake's *Milton:*

> For in this Period the Poets Work is Done: and all the Great
> Events of Time start forth & are concievd in such a Period
> Within a Moment: a Pulsation of the Artery.[81]

The two passages epitomize the difference between the two poets, for Blake would have branded Yeats' reduction of mankind to glorify the One a blasphemy against imagination. Had Blake written "A Meditation in Time of War" we could interpret its gray stone and wind-broken tree as ironic symbols of the speaker's bondage. But Yeats means them more straightforwardly, as signs of the bleak havoc feared in the immediately preceding poems "The Second Coming" and "A Prayer for My Daughter." The tree is broken not by a strong romantic wind of inspiration but by a storm of destruction. We are at the antipodes of the humanistic assertion of "The Tower" that man has created lock, stock, and barrel.

This denial of human autonomy and significance appears again in "Two Songs from a Play" (1927). After developing an elaborate mythological parallel among Astraea and Spica, Athena and Dionysus, and Mary and Christ, the first song passionately denounces historical cyclicity:

> Another Troy must rise and set,
> Another lineage feed the crow,
> Another Argo's painted prow
> Drive to a flashier bauble yet.
> (*VP* 437)

Once again, Yeats has reversed his romantic source, the final chorus of Shelley's *Hellas,* which itself echoes Virgil's Fourth

Eclogue.[82] Where Shelley hymns the coming of a possible Golden Age, Yeats rages against the meaninglessness of historical repetition. Reshaping his romantic model with diction like "feed the crow" and "flashier bauble," he reduces Argonautic heroism to empty hedonism. Yet the poem's context once again qualifies its negativism, for "Among School Children" follows four poems later. In the same way, Yeats undercut his own determinism by adding a second stanza to the second poem in 1931: "Whatever flames upon the night/ Man's own resinous heart has fed." The addition contradicts rather than completes the earlier poem, but in locating the source of divine images in the human heart it anticipates "The Circus Animals' Desertion."

In romantic tradition, imagination often asserts itself as a reaction from confrontation with the void. But resurgence depends on honest penetration to the center of emptiness. Yeats reached that point many times, most memorably in "Meru" (1934):

> Civilization is hooped together, brought
> Under a rule, under the semblance of peace
> By manifold illusion; but man's life is thought,
> And he, despite his terror, cannot cease
> Ravening through century after century,
> Ravening, raging, and uprooting that he may come
> Into the desolation of reality:
> Egypt and Greece, good-bye, and good-bye, Rome!
> Hermits upon Mount Meru or Everest,
> Caverned in night under the drifted snow,
> Or where that snow and winter's dreadful blast
> Beat down upon their naked bodies, know
> That day brings round the night, that before dawn
> His glory and his monuments are gone.
>
> (*VP* 563)

Here mind dominates, and its action rather than abstract gyres destroys civilization. In a 1930 diary Yeats linked his insight to Coleridge's: "What has set me writing is Coleridge's proof, which seems to me conclusive, that civilization is driven to its final phase . . . by 'pure thought', 'reason.' " (*Explorations* 316) In the poem mind attacks its own creations, those manifold illusions that hoop civilization together, until at last it stands in "the desolation of reality." The caverned hermits then encounter the utter transitoriness of human achievement. The question is, then what? Were this winter vision Yeats' final position, his poetic career would then stop, as the *Supernatural Songs* do.[83] But his career continued, and a new outburst of imagination followed. For if day brings round destructive night and afterward mind walks barefoot into the dawn of reality, mind will then start to spin those supreme fictions without which man cannot live. As Harold Bloom has rightly remarked, "Despite its Eastern colorings, *Meru* is esoteric only as the central Romantic visions of winter have been esoteric."[84] Yeats here stands with Shelley at Mont Blanc, confronting a snowy mountain and wondering what it and power were "If to the human mind's imaginings/ Silence and solitude were vacancy." Like Stevens' Snow Man, one must have a mind of winter to behold "Nothing that is not there and the nothing that is." But in romantic tradition, mind then pushes back against the pressure of reality in imaginative assertion. With Byzantium or Coole destroyed, it builds new images in nature's spite. "Meru" offers not despair but a limit of contraction.

After rereading his lyric poems in 1932 for the abortive Coole Edition, Yeats made his famous judgment on their theme: "The swordsman throughout repudiates the saint, but not without vacillation. Is that perhaps the sole theme—Usheen and Patrick—'so get you gone Von Hügel though with blessings on your head'?" (*Letters* 798) By "swordsman" he meant the self, world, and fictions, distinct from the soul, eternity, and absolute of the saint.[85] He was thinking of his recently completed poem "Vacillation," which knows that "all things pass away" but whose seventh section rejects in advance the way of Meru's hermits:

> THE SOUL. Seek out reality, leave things that seem.
> THE HEART. What, be a singer born and lack a theme?
> (VP 502)

Like caverned Indian ascetics, Soul wants to turn from transitory human achievement to the One, in accord with the artery-throb in "A Meditation in Time of War" that mankind is inanimate phantasy. Heart counters with the claims of poetry, one form of human achievement. One of Heart's original lines, "No imagery can live in heaven's blue,"[86] approaches Demogorgon's assertion in *Prometheus Unbound* that "the deep truth is imageless." Both those skeptical statements stress images. Like Demogorgon, Heart recognizes a radical incompatibility between human language and the absolute. Not even the highest use of language, to form images, can withstand final illumination. In opting for profane perfection of mankind, "Vacillation" moves outward from winter vision to primary assertion of imagination. It chooses to replace the desolation of reality with the fiction of poetry. In this way the poem can assert that all things pass away and yet that branches of day and night spring from man's "blood-sodden heart." Significantly, Heart voices Yeats' poetic credo. He increasingly came to see heart's emotions as basis for mind's images in a dialectical process within human life.

Not content with abstract argument, the poem creates an image of secular beatitude in its picture of the solitary, fifty-year-old poet sitting in a London teashop:

> While on the shop and street I gazed
> My body of a sudden blazed;
> And twenty minutes more or less
> It seemed, so great my happiness,
> That I was blessèd and could bless.

Again, the lines echo Shelley, this time the description of Emily in *Epipsychidion* as "A lovely soul formed to be blessed and bless" (line 57). Yeats emphasizes his swing away from the absolute by emphasizing body rather than soul. His is not the body of a hermit on Meru, bruised by winter's blast to pleasure soul, but of a man in full self-achievement, for a gratuitous twenty minutes reaching Unity of Being.

These two sections on body and heart answer the poem's opening question, which is more limited than most commentators have indicated. After declaring that a brand or flaming breath (which recalls Shelley's coal of imagination and wind of inspiration) destroys all antinomies of day and night in which man lives, the poet says that body calls the fire death and heart calls it remorse. He then poses his question in terms of their labels: "But if these be right/ What is joy?" The poem proves body and heart's original responses mistaken because they neglect mind, which creates body's blaze in part IV and heart's themes in part VII, in spite of body's decay and heart's remorse. Joy, then, lies in mind's production of images, which mediate between temporal and eternal. In that mediation Yeats usually concentrates on the development of images from life, sometimes taking them as far as their entrance into eternity. Even the Byzantium lyrics with their concern for the artifice of eternity drag the country of the young and gong-tormented sea into the poems, if not into eternity itself. As in Shelley, poetry, "the expression of the imagination,"[87] preserves joy by redeeming from decay the visitations of divinity in man. Although Yeats told Olivia Shakespeare that he began "Vacillation" to shake off his raucous Crazy Jane persona,[88] in *The Winding*

Stair and Other Poems he placed it before the Crazy Jane sequence, as though to indicate that poems like "Crazy Jane Talks with the Bishop" (*VP* 513) adopt its joyful antinomial vision.

Even in their present confused order rather than the one Yeats intended, his *Last Poems* bring his lifelong romanticism to impressive conclusion. Exploring more dangerously than ever before mind's imaginative search for what will suffice, he passionately exposed the source of its completed images in ordinary human experience of the heart. The poems' current arrangement obscures this quest by making "The Gyres" and "Under Ben Bulben" into alpha and omega of the volume, which thus seems to begin and end with knowledge and activity as man's chief solace in a numb nightmare of historical gyres, from which his main duty is to awake. But in fact Yeats intended both poems to inaugurate separate volumes that develop their seeds of imaginative experience while exorcising their accompanying determinism and inhumanity. "The Gyres" can be understood fully only as first step in a process ending with "The Municipal Gallery Revisited" and "Are You Content?" of *New Poems*, and "Under Ben Bulben" as only the first stage toward "The Circus Animals' Desertion." Blakean defiance of nature in "An Acre of Grass" or Shelleyan defense of art in "The Statues" offer important way stations on that journey. But to complete our psychic map of Yeats' late romanticism we need focus here only on three poems, "Long-Legged Fly" (1939), "Lapis Lazuli" (1938), and "The Circus Animals' Desertion" (1939).

"Long-Legged Fly" (*VP* 617) makes civilization depend not on gyres but on human action, and that action depend on what Yeats elsewhere calls "revery" and Keats "negative capability." Caesar's eyes fixed upon nothing and Helen's aimless tinker shuffle indicate that state of freedom from the irritating grasp of fact and reason which precedes imaginative exertion. Man of action, beautiful woman, and artist among them shape history; but while Caesar preserves and Helen destroys a civilization, Michelangelo creates one. His labor differs from theirs not just in its broader claim, but in his transference of revery into his creative act itself. His mind moves like a long-legged fly upon silence not before but during his exertion. Yet all three perform a mental act: it is their minds that move. Like Tom O'Roughly they know that wisdom is a butterfly and not a gloomy bird of prey (or, in Stevens' terminology, that it is gratuitous). The poem itself both offers us their images and explains how they are created.

If "Long-Legged Fly" suggests one relation to romanticism, "Lapis Lazuli," which begins *New Poems'* movement away from "The Gyres," offers many. Like Wordsworth's "Elegiac Stanzas Suggested by a Picture of Peele Castle" or Keats' "Ode on a Grecian Urn," the poem belongs in the tradition of romantic meditations on works of art. Its defense of art against utilitarian challenges remembers Shelley's, while its use of Lear as impassioned figure anticipates the link between Shakespeare's King and Blake in "An Acre of Grass" ten poems later. The poem's cyclic patterns, bardolatry, and particular way of fusing the arts all recall romantic practice. But Yeats comes closest of all to romanticism in the final stanza, where, like Keats before the urn,[89] he imaginatively enters into the artifact he has been regarding:

> Two Chinamen, behind them a third,
> Are carved in lapis lazuli,
> Over them flies a long-legged bird,
> A symbol of longevity;
> The third, doubtless a serving-man,
> Carries a musical instrument.
>
> Every discoloration of the stone,
> Every accidental crack or dent,
> Seems a water-course or an avalanche,
> Or lofty slope where it still snows
> Though doubtless plum or cherry-branch
> Sweetens the little half-way house
> Those Chinamen climb towards, and I
> Delight to imagine them seated there;
> There, on the mountain and the sky,
> On all the tragic scene they stare.
> One asks for mournful melodies;
> Accomplished fingers begin to play.
> Their eyes mid many wrinkles, their eyes,
> Their ancient, glittering eyes, are gay.
>
> (*VP* 566-67)

The mental action in these lines resembles that of the first two parts of a Greater Romantic Lyric. The speaker moves from description of the object toward involvement with it by way of the cracks and dents that seem alternately water-course, avalanche, or lofty slope. Imagining each of the possibilities leads him to wonder whether the shade tree is cherry or plum and then autonomously to imagine the Chinamen's actions on arrival at the half-way house. Like Keats' similar preparatory triplicities ("by river or sea shore,/ Or mountain built") for ensuing imagination of the desolate town in the fourth stanza of "Ode on a Grecian Urn," his vacillations move him from a scene before him into a world created by imagination. That mental act marks mind's high tide in both poems. Yet as always, the late Yeats has "corrected" his romantic paradigm. Keats' imagination exhausts itself in creating its alternate artifact, and the town suddenly turns desolate; consequently, as in the nightingale ode, his final stanza moves back "out" to sorrowful contemplation of vision's separation from reality. In contrast, Yeats ends his poem on a triumphant assertion of imagination, wholly within a vision that incorporates the mournful melodies of art into a mood of tragic gaiety. As in "Among School Children" or "A Prayer for My Daughter," the poem has no need to move back out of vision.

Entrance into artifice is the theme of the Byzantium poems, and "Lapis Lazuli" corrects the bitter wisdom of "Byzantium." Unlike the sages in God's holy fire, or the poet as golden bird, the Chinamen attain a possible vision in this life. Yeats at first saw them as "ascetic, pupil, hard stone, eternal theme of the sensual east,"[90] but in the poem they look out on the "heroic cry in the midst of despair" of Western tragedy rather than on the One of Meru's hermits. The Chinamen contemplate not a gong-tormented sea or meaningless fury and mire, but significant human life, whose pattern and intensity combine the glory of artifice with the vitality of humanity. The speaker himself may have become such an image: he moves from opening vexation to "délight" by the end of the poem. But if he does, he draws his gaiety as image not from the One but from the many who, in changing and passing, may still accomplish great works in nature's spite; the greatest work is to transform the self into an image possessing Unity of Being.

Dramatic metaphors suit this view of mental action. As with the dancer, we cannot know the actor from his role, the man from the image he creates or embodies. "Lapis Lazuli" intensifies the theatrical metaphors that Yeats frequently attached to imagination. This usage has firm roots in romantic doctrine, which habitually deduced the working of imagination from Shakespeare's plays. Thus, Hazlitt and Keats found Shakespeare a master of sympathetic imagination, and Coleridge saw his language as full of secondary imagination. But moderns surpass the first romantics in using drama as metaphor for imagination so often in their poems. Yeats' "Lapis Lazuli" or "The Circus Animals' Desertion" shares this impetus with Stevens' "Of Modern Poetry" or "The Idea of

Order at Key West," while Eliot's only poem including the word "imagination" ("La Figlia che Piange") opens with exhortations like those of a stage director posing an actress. In "Lapis," the actor provides an alternate incarnation to Byzantium's golden bird. He, too, allows the poet to escape into a work of art, but one that surpasses the goldsmith's in vitality. He incorporates antinomies like man and mask, life and art, into himself, whereas the bird represents only half of a series of pairs. The poem itself incorporates many ironies, not least that the speaker is simultaneously author, spectator, and actor of his own drama. Like many romantic ironies, these spring more from situation and mental action than from ambivalent diction.

Whereas "Lapis" takes the first step toward preserving the visionary joy of "The Gyres" while purging its determinism and inhumanity, "The Circus Animals' Desertion" (*VP* 629) forms the far goal of a parallel movement from "Under Ben Bulben." Yeats' late testament begins with superhuman images of completed passion and ends with corresponding human ones of both dead poet and passing horseman, but "The Circus Animals' Desertion" both begins and ends with common experience of the heart out of which such images must begin. Movement of Yeats' manuscript order for the poems recalls that of *The Tower*, which also progressed from initial rejection to acceptance of experience, but the later group ends in the rag-and-bone shop of the heart rather than the mummified mind of "All Souls' Night." Like "Lapis," "Circus Animals" supports its theme, mind's production of images, by theatrical metaphors and even the word "gay" in an early draft,[91] but it moves yet farther downward upon life as source of those images.

Although not a Greater Romantic Lyric, "Circus Animals" adopts the present-past-present structure which Yeats often used in that form. He begins with an account of present difficulties, moves into a revery on images from the past, and then returns to the present with a new perspective. In the first section he thinks that "maybe" he should be satisfied with his heart, while by the third he knows he must. The images from the past of *The Wanderings of Oisin, The Countess Cathleen,* and *On Baile's Strand* which prompt that realization have a meaning beyond both their obvious importance to the poet and their growth out of heart: they cover the period 1889-1904, or Yeats' own early romantic phase. In citing them the aged poet appropriately evokes his own youth, for like Wordsworth in the Intimations ode or "Tintern Abbey" he is writing a poem about loss of youthful power. Typically, his theme

91

is his relation to his vision rather than the vision itself. Unlike Wordsworth, he refuses the comfort of the philosophic mind and instead resolves to repeat the entire process of vision by descending again into heart. In that way he preserves the fresh sense of crucial and continued loss he thought Wordsworth abandoned.

Yeats completes his poem, and his movement downward upon life, in the famous final stanza:

> Those masterful images because complete
> Grew in pure mind, but out of what began?
> A mound of refuse or the sweepings of a street,
> Old kettles, old bottles, and a broken can,
> Old iron, old bones, old rags, that raving slut
> Who keeps the till. Now that my ladder's gone,
> I must lie down where all the ladders start,
> In the foul rag-and-bone shop of the heart.
>
> (*VP* 630)

Interpretation of tone here demands delicacy. Paradoxically, did the poet belabor heart less we would believe his overt contempt for it more. But as old kettles and bottles, a broken can, old iron, bones, and rags, and finally the raving slut join the refuse mound and street sweepings, we begin to think that the poet protests too much and that he almost unwillingly means the opposite of what he says. These are not the accents of true abuse but of raillery, of a poet who can be stiff and proud when on images intent but who has learned that they ultimately begin in heart.

The stanza provides a route to the world of images other than the sea-lanes to Byzantium. Here the poet learns that he can enter into the artifice of eternity not through sages consuming his heart away but through entering into heart's disorderly, disreputable, life-giving experience. The central section exorcises his characteristic sin, leaving the world of humanity behind and transferring his "thought and love" to the images themselves rather than the human passion they symbolize. This sin marred the genuine power of "The Gyres" and "Under Ben Bulben" with indifference to violence and suffering or even exultation in it. They are poems of pride, and unlike Yeats' idealized Parnell a proud man is not always a lovely man. "The Circus Animals' Desertion" does not rejoice in heart—the poet lies down there under compulsion—but it does recognize, as Yeats at his best in poems like "Vacillation" or the second of "Two Songs from a Play" increasingly did, that all ladders start there. And despite that "must," he does have a choice, for he "must" lie down there only if he wants to continue to be a poet achieving images, not just his earlier ones of great passion and mood but his later ones of Unity of Being, fully realized humanity. Like his romantic precursors, Yeats wanted that above all, for that suffices above all.

In centering on the poet's relation to images, Yeats' work does not narrowly treat problems of the poet any more than Wordsworth's *Prelude*, Blake's *Milton*, Shelley's "Ode to the West Wind," or Stevens' *Notes toward a Supreme Fiction* do. Rather, in all these works the poet becomes a figure for imaginative man, poetry for imaginative life, and poem for imaginative work. Only in this sense for Yeats and the others is poetry the subject of the poem. Yeats' career reveals a progressive realization that imagination must find its materials in basic human experience. Often in the nineties his creative distortions of Blake and Shelley led him to repudiate ordinary human life in the name of art. After his intermediary antipathy, he returned to romanticism with renewed awareness of the central humanity on which it depended. The struggle came with difficulty for a poet as proud as Yeats, but ultimately his work teaches us to lie down where all the ladders start in prelude to poetry. As with his admired Dante, the way down is the way up.

When he composed in 1937 the retrospective introduction for his works that now prefaces *Essays and Introductions*, Yeats typically began with self-reproach. His first regret was not defending Pre-Raphaelite and Blakean art against the attacks of Impressionist devotees. The second, and more important, was not defending romantic poetry against the onslaughts of militant modernism: "A little later poets younger than myself, especially the one I knew best, began to curse that romantic subject-matter which English literature seemed to share with all great literature, those traditional metres which seemed to have grown up with the language, and still, though getting much angrier, I was silent." (*E&I* vii-viii) The most influential curser was Eliot, who along with the younger poet Yeats knew best (Pound) fashioned that anti-romantic animus which still haunts the study of literature. Yeats' evasion affected not just his own psyche but the subsequent study of literature in our century. Had he protested, he might have not just preserved us from a generation of facile anti-romanticism but hastened our understanding of the romantic roots of even overtly anti-romantic modernism. For modern poems of the act of the mind belong to a continuing post-romantic tradition. But Yeats kept silent as critic though not as poet, and it is to the rival to whom he left the field that we next turn.

3

The Anti-Romanticism of T. S. Eliot

When delivering the First Annual Yeats Lecture in 1940, modern literature's leading anti-romantic polemicist praised its leading romantic as "the greatest poet of our time."[1] In the same address T. S. Eliot cited Yeats as an exception to the normal rule of literary generations spanning about twenty years. Although he was born twenty-three years after Yeats, Eliot found himself "regarding him, from one point of view, as a contemporary and not a predecessor."[2] By casting off his late Victorian style of the nineties and remaking himself as poet (and man) in the early twentieth century, Yeats seemed a part of the revolutionary modernist generation in poetry.

In paying his graceful tribute to Yeats, Eliot tactfully passed over "aspects of his thought and feeling which to myself are unsympathetic" and which in any case he had abundantly denounced elsewhere. His remarks signal a hard-won though still limited appreciation of a poet he had earlier and variously accused of speaking only of "George Moore and spooks," standing outside both Latin and English tradition, favoring weak diction, having little grasp on reality, living in the "wrong" supernatural world, and succeeding mostly in solipsism.[3] These earlier terms of abuse belong to the litany that Eliot regularly chanted at romantic writers in the years entre deux guerres. For Yeats and Eliot made opposite public uses of romanticism to define their own poetic stances. While Yeats projected himself as the last romantic, Eliot posed as an anti-romantic modern; and whereas Yeats strove to rescue romanticism from its own defects, Eliot worked to purge literature as a whole of the contamination of romanticism. Both these postures exaggerate, for Yeats' rescue meant transformation and Eliot's overt wreckage masked covert salvage. Like the speaker of Stevens' "Man and Bottle," Eliot destroyed romantic tenements only to clear the ground for new pleasure domes. To have been told this in his youth would have horrified him; by old age it might not even have surprised him.

In one important respect the patterns of Eliot's and Yeats' long careers share the same relation to the romantics: a tripartite division of strong initial attraction and identification (a theme little heard of among Eliot's more devout admirers), violent rejection in order to form an independent identity as poet, and final if incomplete reconciliation. But here the parallel ends, for three main reasons. First, Eliot's romantic phase stops with his teens rather than with the onset of middle age. When Yeats was thirty-five he wrote his profound exploration of the philosophy of Shelley's poetry, while Eliot at the same age railed superficially and rather foolishly at its immaturity. The poets who meant to Eliot in young manhood what Blake and Shelley did to Yeats were Donne and the Jacobeans among English writers and Laforgue and Dante among continentals. The romantics remained crucial to Eliot, but crucial as counterexamples and as projections of the flaws of his boyhood and fears of his manhood. Second, Eliot's grasp of romanticism was superficial compared to Yeats'. He never studied Shelley or Blake as intensely as Yeats and never understood them as well. There is little to choose between the two poets' varying references to Byron, Keats, and Wordsworth, except to say that in middle age Eliot admired Keats more and Yeats admired him less. Only Eliot's comments on Coleridge's prose (which the late Yeats also respected) illuminate their subject rather than their author. Throughout, Yeats shows a genuine though skewed apprehension of romanticism, Eliot mostly a mixture of misinformation and distortion. Finally, Eliot did not reconcile himself to the romantics while still primarily a practicing poet. His rapprochement coincided with his emergence as dramatist, Christian sociologist, and institution; in none of these identities did the romantics threaten him, and in some of them Coleridge was a positive help.

Proper understanding of Eliot's literary career begins at its neglected beginning, in his obsession with romantic poets. Not surprisingly, reticent Eliot avoided mentioning this six years' infatuation in his early, polemical reviews and essays attacking romanticism under the banner of modern classicism. But by the mid-1930s, with his own position secure and his stormy personal crises at least temporarily resolved, he could offer his public occasional glimpses into his past. The first and most startling appears in his note "On the Development of Taste" to the first of his Norton lectures at Harvard, published as *The Use of Poetry and the Use of Criticism* in 1933.[4] There Eliot generalized his own history into a theory of three stages of poetic growth—childhood, adolescence, and maturity. In childhood we enjoy rousing ballads and battle poetry. Eliot left this phase behind at the age of twelve and passed two years "with no sort of interest in poetry at all." His adolescent phase began abruptly when he picked up a copy of Fitzgerald's *Omar* at fourteen:

> It was like a *sudden conversion;* the world appeared anew, painted with bright, delicious and painful colours. Thereupon I took the usual adolescent course with Byron, Shelley, Keats, Rossetti, Swinburne.
>
> I take this period to have persisted until my nineteenth or twentieth year. . . . Like the first period of childhood, it is one beyond which I dare say many people never advance; so that such taste for poetry as they retain in later life is only a sentimental memory of the pleasures of youth, and is probably entwined with all our other sentimental retrospective feelings. It is, no doubt, a period of keen enjoyment; but we must not confuse the *intensity* of the poetic experience in adolescence with the intense experience of poetry. At this period, the poem, or the poetry of a single poet, *invades* the youthful consciousness and *assumes complete possession* for a time. We do not really see it as something with an existence outside ourselves; much *as in our youthful experiences of love,* we do not so much see the person as infer the existence of some outside object which sets in motion these new and delightful feelings in which we are *absorbed.* The frequent result is an *outburst* of scribbling which we may call imitation, so long as we are aware of the meaning of the word "imitation" which we employ. It is not deliberate choice of a poet to mimic, but writing under a kind of *daemonic possession* by one poet. (*UPUC* 33–34; italics mine)

In those words the man who did more to deprecate romantic poetry than any other figure in modern English letters confesses his adolescent love of it. We learn few specific details but a great deal about why the whole experience was so important to him both then and afterward. Eliot recalls his encounter with romantic poetry and its derivatives as a kind of obliteration of his conscious ego. His language enacts a struggle between the memory and his current self. Diction like "sudden conversion," "intensity," "invades," "assumes complete possession," "outburst," and "daemonic possession" testifies to an overwhelming event that appeared in retrospect as a kind of forcible seizure of the psyche by outside powers. As though to guard against the Wordsworthian effects of recollecting that emotion, Eliot interjects phrases suggesting his more urbane and mature detachment—"the usual adolescent course," "I dare say," and "scribbling." But the deflating and distancing words are clichés whose banality rings false; even then they showed where the energy had flowed thirty years before. His theory of stages creates a similar defensive effect, for it pigeonholes the encounter in an already obsolete phase on the way to an allegedly deeper understanding. The same tactics occur in miniature four lectures later, when Eliot recalls that "I was intoxicated by Shelley's poetry at the age of fifteen" but "now find it almost unreadable." (*UPUC* 96)

Eliot frankly links his literary passion to the onset of sexuality. "At or about puberty" most children lose all further use for poetry, but "a small minority then find themselves possessed of a craving for poetry which is wholly different from any enjoyment experienced before." (*UPUC* 32-33) Eliot belonged to the responsive minority. Two experiences—onset of sexual drives and breakdown of the ego's walls of self-possession by poetry—converged in his adolescence. They shared a common dynamics: "We do not really see [poetry at this period] as something with an existence outside ourselves; much as in our youthful experience of love. . . ." As this and other passages in Eliot suggest, for him the two fused. He encountered them together and associated both with romantic poetry. For the rest of his life he would condemn romanticism as immature or adolescent, link it to loss of rational control, and chafe particularly at celebrations of illicit sexuality outside the constraints of marriage. His denunciations ring with special urgency during the first decade and a half of his criticism, years of intense personal crises partially resolved by confirmation in the Church of England in 1927 and permanent separation from his wife in 1932. Romanticism then served as foil to the effort at conscious discipline of his life and art, a convenient brown demon upon which to project fears of personal and cultural deviation.

The romantics came to signify so much for Eliot not only because they affected him so violently as reader but because they determined his early poetic efforts as writer. He imitated them not by deliberate choice but through a "daemonic possession" by one romantic at a time. The list in his account of the three stages includes the second romantic generation—Byron, Shelley, and

Keats—and their Victorian followers Rossetti, Swinburne, and FitzGerald. His later comments single out the romantics more precisely.[5] In his essay "Byron" (1937) he called Byron his "first boyhood enthusiasm" and embarrassedly recollected "some verses in the manner of *Don Juan,* tinged with that disillusion and cynicism only possible at the age of sixteen, which appeared in a school periodical."[6] The verses were "A Fable for Feasters," which appeared in *Smith Academy Record* for February 1905. Significantly, Eliot cited his memory of this youthful obsession and performance as an "obstacle" to seeing Byron plain later on. Likewise, in 1942 he wrote: "When we imitated Shelley, it was not so much from a desire to write as he did, as from an invasion of the adolescent self by Shelley, which made Shelley's way, for the time, the only way in which to write." (*OPP* 19) Eliot called this process "the way we learn to write," a "deeper imitation" than mere stylistic analysis could produce. Like Pound in "Histrion," written about the same time, the early Eliot conceived of his creative process as a projection into his psyche by great poets. But unfortunately, he later thought his own haunters less admirable than the Dante or Villon who passed through Pound in "Histrion." If he first learned to write like Byron or Shelley, he would later learn to write unlike them, even if he had to butcher their reputations to remake his own attitudes and art. A mature poet chose his own personae.

When we look at the actual poems Eliot wrote between his fourteenth and twentieth years, we wonder what all the fuss was about. These works in the *Smith Academy Record* and (before his discovery of Laforgue) the *Harvard Advocate* seem the sort of conventional effusions any sensitive and intelligent schoolboy or undergraduate might have produced just after the turn of the century. Their regular meters, tone, and themes belong to the butt end of subjective or aesthetic nineteenth-century traditions. The Byronic "A Fable for Feasters," a Jonsonian lyric ("If Time and Space, as Sages Say"), and a pompous graduation lyric summoning his schoolmates to the twentieth century in accents of Tennyson and Keats, comprise the Smith Academy group.[7] His early Harvard poems were a "Song" and "Before Morning," both of which used nature to develop mood in an obvious nineteenth-century manner; a lyric on "Circe's Palace" with its equally nineteenth-century theme of an enchantress resembling those of Shelley, Keats, and Tennyson; a sonnet "On a Portrait" specifically comparing the lady to an evanescent "lamia"; and a lush "Song" suggesting the reworking of romanticism in fin de siècle aestheticism. Only in the three lyrics of his master's year does the impact of Laforgue signal a break with conventional Anglo-American tradition and hint at Eliot's impending development. His graduation "Ode" reverts to standard praise of "Fair Harvard."

"A Fable for Feasters" justifies Eliot's later description of it as "some verses in the manner of *Don Juan*." Its twelve stanzas of ottava rima recall the form of that poem as its jaunty disrespect recalls the tone. Eliot the Anglican may well have shrunk from the plot in later disparaging the poem's adolescent cynicism. The monks of a monastery live as epicures rather than ascetics until a ghost spoils their Christmas gourmandizing by abducting the abbot up a chimney, upon which the Church designates the abbot à saint and the monks return to abstinence. Easy anti-clericism may have pained Eliot as much as obvious metrical padding in this enjoyable teenage imitation. Comic rhymes like "Mormon" and "poor men," or "puddings" and "good things" culminate in the stanza on the abbot's abduction:

> The Abbot sat as pasted to his chair,
>   His eye became the size of any dollar,
> The ghost then took him roughly by the hair
>   And bade him come with him, in accents hollow.
> The friars could do nought but gape and stare,
>   The spirit pulled him rudely by the collar,
>   And before any one could say 'O jiminy!'
>   The pair had vanisht swiftly up the chimney.
>   (*PWEY* 7)

Inversions, poeticized diction ("dowered," "e'er," " 'tis") and metrical stuffing combine in the valedictory "At Graduation, 1905." Its Tennysonian theme of young men as mariners sailing forth to build the modern century fuses with incongruous echoes of Keats. The lines

> For in the sanctuaries of the soul
> Incense of altar-smoke shall rise to thee
> From spotless fanes of lucid purity
>   (*PWEY* 15)

recall both the fane of the poet's mind in "Ode to Psyche" and veiled Melancholy's sovereign shrine in "Ode to Melancholy" before sinking to their bathetic conclusion, "O school of ours!"[8] After assuring Smith Academy, queen of schools, that she was not meant for death,[9] the poem mimics in its last stanza the rhyme of "farewell" and "bell" from the final stanza of "Ode to a

Nightingale." These allusions both lack the incisive thrust of Eliot's later borrowings and fail to sustain themselves throughout the poem. Were it not for Eliot's later hints, we should take them for products of idle derivation rather than psychic possession.

Eliot's first *Advocate* poems show a surer technique within outmoded convention during his early Harvard years. They feature two themes—the passing of love and the lures of an enchantress—and make nature a mirror of mood. The enchantress is alternately Circe or a lamia, a reducer of men to bestiality or "an immaterial fancy of one's own." (*PWEY* 21) Neither here nor in his Smith Academy poems does Eliot show genuine insight or mastery of romantic modes, or any inkling of their subtle mental action. Rather, he derives from the nineteenth century a poetic diction and general atmosphere. His poems wear shreds and patches from the romantic poets without any of the underlying life. He himself seems to have realized this in his first Laforguean effort of 1909, a "Nocturne" on Romeo and Juliet. There he mocked the diction of both Shakespeare's play and Coleridge's "Kubla Khan" in imagining a hero who "in my best mode oblique/ Rolls toward the moon a frenzied eye profound." (*PWEY* 23) It was an ironic farewell to his earlier romanticism.

Eliot's learning to write from deeper imitation of Shelley, Byron, Keats, and their followers to an extent resembles Yeats' seizure by Shelley and Blake. Both called forth an inevitable counterreaction. If Eliot first became a romantic, he would then have to repudiate his models to achieve his own poetic identity. That is what happened. Byron and Shelley fared worst, while Keats was blamed mostly for dying young. For Eliot, romantic poetry showed the flaws of his own early poems—musical jingling, banality, superficial cynicism, ignorance of Latin tradition, confused thought, and imprecise feeling. He identified romanticism with a permanent adolescence of the spirit and its products as an immature phase of poetic development. But unlike Yeats, he had never understood the romantic poets deeply. His alleged commentaries on them are so wrong—not distorted or partial but simply wrong—that their inapplicability is explainable only partly as literary propaganda against the derivative romanticism he found in the London literary scene. A more personal and poetic need prompted them as well, a need to purge himself of his own adolescence and keep the recurrent forces of its survival at arm's length.

At Harvard during 1909-10 Eliot found means to free himself from romantic domination. Partly he fought old precursors with new ones. In December of 1908 he had read Arthur Symons' *Symbolist Movement in Literature*, which he would later call "one of those [books] which have affected the course of my life."[10] Dedicated to Yeats, Symons' book introduced young Eliot to Laforgue, Verlaine, and Rimbaud, and indirectly led him to Gautier and Baudelaire. Laforgue's idiom and tone in particular catalyzed Eliot's creative outburst of 1910-12, which after the three *Advocate* imitations (one of them subtitled "After J. Laforgue"[11]) included "Portrait of a Lady," "Preludes," "The Love Song of J. Alfred Prufrock," "Rhapsody on a Windy Night," and "La Figlia che Piange." French nineteenth-century writers became for him an equipoise to the English. So, too, did writers discovered in his formal course work. Chief among them were the Elizabethan and Jacobean dramatists of George Pierce Baker's course on Drama in England from the Miracle Plays to the Closing of the Theaters.[12] In his introduction to Pound's *Selected Poems* (1928) Eliot later claimed that "the form in which I began to write, in 1908 or 1909, was directly drawn from the study of Laforgue together with the later Elizabethan drama."[13] That statement belongs to the public myth of Eliot and has been accepted too readily, for by 1909 he had been writing under the tutelage of the romantics for several years. His anti-romantic reaction looked to Laforgue and the playwrights but did not leap like Athena full-grown from a working brain; as though to repudiate a disreputable past, Eliot would have us think it did. Shortly thereafter he plunged into Dante's *Divine Comedy* in the Harvard fashion of learning the language as he went along. Forty years later he would call Dante's poetry "the most persistent and deepest influence upon my own verse."[14] In that eventful year Eliot also sat through William Allen Neilson's English 24, Poets of the Romantic Period, which at least provided him with ammunition for future sniping. Herbert Howarth proposes that Neilson's remarks on Byron's *The Island* may have affected Eliot's *Sweeney Agonistes* as well.[15]

The poetic practice Eliot derived from seventeenth-century English drama, nineteenth-century French poetry, and Dante found its theoretic underpinning in the anti-romanticism of the course most important to his intellectual progress, Irving Babbitt's French 17, Literary Criticism in France with Special Reference to the Nineteenth Century. Forceful, exciting, and bigoted, Babbitt conveyed the New Humanism's classical tenets of reason, order, law, and discipline that Eliot used to slough off his adolescent romanticism. In 1928 Eliot would describe himself as having "begun as a disciple of Mr. Babbitt" (*SE* 429), although by then he found Humanism incomplete compared to Christianity. When Eliot surveyed his own career four years before his death, he named Pound and Babbitt as the two molders of his early criticism. "The influence of Babbitt (with an infusion later of T. E. Hulme and of the more literary essays of Charles Maurras) is apparent in my recurrent theme of Classicism versus Romanticism," he wrote. (*TCC* 17) That opposition surfaced in Babbitt's early *Literature and the American College* (1908), which Eliot commended, and runs throughout his four later books, including *Masters of Modern French Criticism* (1912), which presumably utilized material developed in his seminar. Babbitt campaigned against the dangers of romanticism even more fully in his most famous book, *Rousseau and Romanticism* (1919), which he was already planning the year Eliot studied under him.[16]

Rousseau and Romanticism is a quirky book that unwittingly illustrates Eliot's later definition of a heretic as someone who exaggerates a partial truth into a falsehood. Had Babbitt distinguished genuine from sham romanticism and then blasted the latter, he would have done useful work. Instead, he mischievously conflated Rousseau and the great romantics with their feebler derivatives in a sweeping condemnation of the modern mind as a product of emotional naturalism hostile to civilization. From the resultant farrago of insight, distortion, and apparent inability to construe simple texts, romanticism (in the variety Babbitt indicates he is analyzing) emerges as an emotional naturalism, tainted with egocentricity and hostile to reason, whose glorification of unrestrained imagination projects its longing for Arcadia into the practical world with disastrous results. Romantics value delirium and intoxication for their own sake, flee from center to circumference, and always seek extremes. Against these fulminations, it is futile to recall Wordsworth's definition of imagination as reason in her most exalted mood, Coleridge on balance of faculties in the poet, Blake on need for both Prolific and Devourer, Keats on egotism, or Shelley on poetry as expression of indestructible order and at once center and circumference. Babbitt does not really offer us a critique of romanticism; instead, he propounds his own doctrines of authority, discipline, and the inner check and uses romanticism as foil to justify his own tenets. That is the same use that Eliot made of romanticism and perhaps the deepest lesson learned by the disciple from his master.

Not just Babbitt's general attitude and strategy but many of his specific aberrations find their echo in Eliot. Both, for example, cite

Wordsworth's phrase about "emotion recollected in tranquillity" as his definition of poetry, despite Wordsworth's clear identification of it simply as the "origin" of poetry or as the mood in which successful composition usually began.[17] Both attack Keats' identification of beauty with truth by abstracting it from the context of "Ode on a Grecian Urn," treating it as a philosophic statement, and then forgetting Plato.[18] Particularly heartening to Eliot was Babbitt's identification of Shelley as the poet of adolescence: "the person who is as much taken by Shelley at forty as he was at twenty has, one may surmise, failed to grow up." Eliot tirelessly expressed the same view, for reasons we have already suggested, and likewise adopted his teacher's nastiness toward Blake. But Babbitt's critical bathysphere could descend to depths unreachable even by Eliot, as in his astonishing exclamation on Coleridge's "Ancient Mariner, who, it will be remembered, is relieved of the burden of his transgression by admiring the color of water-snakes!" It will be remembered that relief comes from the Mariner's ability to pray, which derives from his love and blessing toward "God's creatures" who now, unlike the albatross earlier in the poem, impress him by their consequent beauty. Romantic mental action remained forever outside Babbitt's ken.

Eliot's literary principles stayed substantially intact for some time after his master's year. The recently discovered[19] descriptive syllabus for his Oxford University Extension Course of 1916 on "Modern French Literature" could have come straight from Babbitt's classroom. In the meantime Eliot had studied in France and Germany, returned to Harvard for doctoral work, settled in England, met Pound, married Vivien Haigh-Wood, and completed his dissertation on Bradley. He apparently fulminated against romanticism in private and found his first chance to erupt publicly in his six extension lectures. The first one interpreted Rousseau's life as a struggle against authority, aristocracy, and privilege in which he exalted the personal above the typical, feeling above thought, goodness over original sin, and spontaneity over form; his "great faults" were egotism and insincerity. When Eliot denounces romanticism as "excess in any direction" splitting up into escapism and devotion to fact, we may hear in the background Babbitt haranguing his students on scientific utilitarianism and romanticism as the "two main forms of naturalism."[20] The second lecture praised the growing twentieth-century trend toward classicism, which stood for form and restraint in art, discipline and authority in religion, and centralization in government. When Eliot adds original sin, we remember Babbitt muttering of Rousseauian individualists attacking the allied traditions of classicism and Christianity.[21] Subsequent lectures explored in more detail reactions against romanticism in politics, religion, and literature in remarkable anticipation of Eliot's famous triple pledge of allegiance in *For Lancelot Andrewes*. The Oxford extension syllabus was the first, obscure shot in his critical campaign. Within a decade the unknown lecturer would be a major force in Anglo-American letters.

Early canonization of Eliot's criticism helped to hide its limitations, which he felt more keenly than did his enthusiastic followers. First was its ad hoc character. The famous early collections *The Sacred Wood* (1920) and *Selected Essays* (1932; expanded 1950) originated mostly as book reviews by a harassed young bank clerk and embattled young poet, just as the later *Use of Poetry* (1933), *On Poetry and Poets* (1957), and *To Criticize the Critic* (1965) consisted mostly of public lectures by a busy man of letters. Enshrined in impressive volumes, they lost their occasional air and became a new army of unalterable law to two generations of critics eager to codify Eliot's precepts. Their Olympian tone, confident dogmatism, and memorable catchwords made them seem more detached and judicious than they were. Yet despite Eliot's own low opinion of book reviewing[22] and embarrassment at the success of his own slogans, the early essays combine shrewdness and sensibility, while the later lectures gain in detachment what they lose in daring. More damaging was the literary context of the early polemics, which helped Eliot as poet but harmed unwary readers and critics. The distortions of the literary past by which Eliot freed himself to create his own poetry limited rather than liberated readers who adopted them as axioms.

Eliot saw the link between his critical theory and poetic practice as both strength and weakness in his prose, but scholars have been quicker to work out correlations with his poetry than to ponder weaknesses in his criticism. Yet for Eliot the two converged. In 1942 he spoke of "acute embarrassment" at rereading his own prose:

> The critical writings of poets . . . owe a great deal of their interest to the fact that the poet, at the back of his mind, if not as his ostensible purpose, is always trying to defend the kind of poetry he is writing, or to formulate the kind that he wants to write. Especially when he is young, and actively engaged in battling for the kind of poetry which he practises, he sees the

poetry of the past in relation to his own: and his gratitude to those dead poets from whom he has learned, as well as his indifference to those whose aims have been alien to his own, may be exaggerated. He is not so much a judge as an advocate. His knowledge even is likely to be partial: for his studies will have lead him to concentrate on certain authors to the neglect of others. . . . We must return to the scholar for ascertainment of facts, and to the more detached critic for impartial judgment. (*OPP* 17-18)

It was a theme that Eliot expounded at least half a dozen times.[23] In 1961 he specified the early context more precisely:

In my early criticism, both in my general affirmations about poetry and in writing about authors who had influenced me, I was implicitly defending the sort of poetry that I and my friends wrote. . . . I was in reaction, not only against Georgian poetry, but against Georgian criticism. . . . In reviewing my own early criticism, I am struck by the degree to which it was conditioned by the state of literature at the time at which it was written, as well as by the stage of maturity at which I had arrived. (*TCC* 16)

The romantics became chief casualties of Eliot's reaction against Georgians. "Because we have never learned to criticize Keats, Shelley, and Wordsworth (poets of assured though modest merit), Keats, Shelley, and Wordsworth punish us from their graves with the annual scourge of the Georgian Anthology," he complained in 1918.[24] As the most influential writers upon his chief rivals, Keats, Shelley, and Wordsworth became a sort of anti-Trinity for Eliot. He often criticized the triad as a group,[25] although he did not spare Byron and Blake, or even the poetry of Coleridge, whose prose he usually admired. Recently, C. K. Stead has suggested that even the Georgians were more innovative than Eliot allowed, and he has proposed the debased prophetic stance of Imperial poets like William Watson or Henry Newbolt as an equally important foil to modernism.[26] Wherever Eliot looked during those early years in London he saw degenerations of romanticism, and that context joined with his own situation to warp his criticism of the original romantics as well.

If critics have neglected Eliot's own statements on the way a poet's needs distort his view of his precursors, they have seized too readily on the other half of those pronouncements, the relation of Eliot's criticism to his own and other modern work. The usual view runs something like this: Eliot's criticism, perhaps with slight modifications, provides a satisfactory key to his own poetry and to modern poetry in general; furthermore, it revalues literary tradition to reveal the centrality of modernism and eccentricity of romanticism. I have already raised some objections to accepting Eliot's view of poetic tradition. Modern poetry in English is central partly because it is squarely in the line running back to the romantics and, beyond them, to Eliot's other nemesis, Milton, and to Spenser. But what about the parallel contention that his criticism provides an adequate approach to his own and to related modern poetry? Certainly, it points to important elements of diction and meter, to wit, and to broader aspects of world view. But critics err in applying its dicta too readily, for three main reasons. First, moderns like Yeats and Stevens write out of overtly romantic positions; we turn them into modern Metaphysicals only by reducing and distorting their achievement. Second, Eliot himself stands partly in romantic traditions of both theory and practice. His criticism gives us a distorted view of Eliot as well as of literary history. To see this we need to estimate how far his critique of romanticism actually applies to romantic poetry and how much it projects onto romanticism dangers he feared in himself. Then, too, he slips quickly past many features that modern poetry, including his own, shares with romantic—its particular systematic interrelation of imagery, forms like the Greater Romantic Lyric, transvaluation of mythology, internalization of quest patterns, and special polysemous language. Revisionist critics have described Eliot's high valuation of evoking immediate experience, exaltation of Image and of image making over purely rational powers of mind, emotive origin of poetry, and struggle to recombine aesthetic and moral stances as placing him firmly in romantic tradition.[27] Eliot often works through to romantic positions in the name of anti-romanticism. Finally, personal need joined historical circumstance in conditioning Eliot's criticism. His emphasis on wit, irony, discipline, and restraint answers to the needs of his psychic life and of his reaction against his own poetic past perhaps more fully than it defines his actual achievement. These caveats are basic to understanding both his criticism and its relation to modern poetry, including his own.[28]

Eliot's anti-romanticism falls into three chronological phases. For the first two, romanticism served as scapegoat for the sins of his poetic youth and sirens of his early maturity. From his critical debut in 1916-17 through the early 1920s Eliot executed a double mining and sapping operation against romantic poets. Technically, he attacked their meter, diction, and inadequate form, while thematically he bombarded their incoherence, morality, and deviation from proper tradition. The code word was discipline, which he found missing in romantic art and thought. From the mid-1920s until the late 1930s Eliot's growing absorption in religion prompted two additional charges against his predecessors. He now detected in them the origin of that usurpation of religion's role by literature which culminated in Matthew Arnold's concept of culture. Concomitantly, he saw his literary opposition of classicism and romanticism as mirroring the theological distinction between orthodoxy and heresy. Having outlined these objections earlier, Eliot now prominently elaborated them. By the late 1930s, with his poetic career virtually over except for *Four Quartets*, in some ways his most romantic poem, Eliot mellowed. Done with the struggle to form a style and sensibility, he could reconcile himself to the virtues rather than decry the vices of his much-abused predecessors. If he never achieved sweetness and light toward them, he did escape from his earlier dark bitterness.

The campaign against romanticism fit into Eliot's lifelong war against Matthew Arnold. Eliot sought to replace Arnold's ordering of poetic tradition with a new one of his own. Where Arnold deprecated Dryden and Pope as classics of our prose, Eliot rescued them for poetry, and where Arnold made the romantics central, Eliot sought to render them peripheral. "From time to time, every hundred years or so, it is desirable that some critic shall appear to review the past of our literature, and set the poets and the poems in a new order," he declared in 1933. "The valuation of the Romantic poets, in academic circles, is still very largely that which Arnold made." (*UPUC* 108, 110) Although more conciliatory to Arnold in that lecture than earlier, Eliot still made his dissent plain. For much of his criticism had been a point-by-point reversal of Arnold. If Arnold learned to feel from Wordsworth, Eliot heard there only "the still sad music of infirmity," and if Arnold found Shelley an angel, Eliot branded him "almost a blackguard." (*UPUC* 69, 89)

These polarities did not stop Eliot from conscripting Arnold into the anti-romantic ranks by removing his more critical statements from their broader context. The polemical "Introduction" to *The Sacred Wood* (1920) featured Arnold's scruples about romantic writers, whose reputations Eliot had designed his book to subvert. A few introductory sentences led directly to a long quotation from "The Function of Criticism at the Present Time" in which Arnold argued that early nineteenth-century England offered its poets a milieu inferior to classical Greece or Renaissance England. The passage cited by Eliot concluded:

> This prematureness comes from its having proceeded without having its proper data, without sufficient material to work with. In other words, the English poetry of the first quarter of this century, with plenty of energy, plenty of creative force, did not know enough. This makes Byron so empty of matter, Shelley so incoherent, Wordsworth even, profound as he is, yet so wanting in completeness and variety. (*SW* xii)

After that salvo by proxy, Eliot continued in his own voice: "This judgment of the Romantic Generation has not, so far as I know, ever been successfully controverted; and it has not, so far as I know, ever made very much impression on popular opinion." It may be excusable for Arnold in 1864 to have thought that the romantics did not know enough, but less so for Eliot in 1920. It is bizarre by 1933, when Eliot again quoted from that passage in Arnold (*UPUC* 104), for by then he had read John Livingston Lowes' *Road to Xanadu*, reviewed half a dozen books on Blake, and apparently reread a considerable amount of romantic literature to prepare for his Norton lectures at Harvard. Yeats had "controverted" the negative judgment of Shelley back in 1900 in an essay that Eliot may well have known, for he reviewed Yeats' subsequent book of criticism, *The Cutting of an Agate*. Yeats' response to Edward Dowden there reads like a prophetic rebuttal of Eliot: "One cannot help believing him [Shelley], as this scholar I know believes him, a vague thinker, who mixed occasional great poetry with a fantastic rhetoric, unless one compares such passages . . . as describe the liberty he praised, till one has discovered the system of belief that lay behind them."[29] But Eliot did not want to understand Shelley and his contemporaries. He wanted to free himself from their influence and to write a radically different poetry from his own early efforts; to do that, he needed to believe that they "did not know enough." That belief was a negation rather than a contrary of the nineteenth-century critical views he allegedly reversed.

While a running attack on specific poets punctuates *The Sacred Wood* as a whole, the critique of romanticism in general finds an early climax in "A Romantic Aristocrat," originally a review of George Wyndham's *Essays in Romantic Literature*. A historical study of romance, Wyndham's book began with the Middle Ages and only reached the British romantics in its final chapter, which focused on Scott. Wyndham provoked Eliot in two main ways.

First, he distinguished classic from romantic by stipulating that while both aimed at unity, "the Classic world aimed at unity by exclusion, and the [romantic] Middle Ages at unity by comprehension."[30] While open to historical challenge, Wyndham's assertion comes close to describing Eliot's own classicism, which rests on purification of classical and Christian tradition. For all his talk of the mind of Europe, as Eliot jettisons first the romantics and Milton, then Yeats and Lawrence, and then Jewish and pagan "heresies," his own goal does seem more and more a de facto unity by exclusion. Second, Wyndham declared that "our day is also the day of the Romantic Revival."[31] To Eliot, immersed in his early efforts at a classical revival in English verse, those were fighting words.

Eliot responded by damning both Wyndham and romanticism. The dual assault epitomized his lifelong hostility to romantic writers, which mixed critique of their work and thought with ad hominem sallies. After a weak excuse that "posthumous books demand some personal attention to their writers" (*SW* 25), Eliot let fly. Here as elsewhere when directed at romantics, his slings and arrows both contradict his own critical principles and show a clever rhetorical skill. The same critic who two years later praised the Metaphysicals for "amalgamating disparate experience" into new wholes—and implied that moderns might similarly combine love, Spinoza, typewriter clacking, and cooking smells (*SE* 247)—belittled Wyndham for unifying his life and interests:

> We chart the mind of George Wyndham, and the key to its topography is the fact that his literature and his politics and his country life are one and the same thing. They are not in separate compartments, they are one career. Together they made up his world: literature, politics, riding to hounds. In the real world these things have nothing to do with each other. But we cannot believe that George Wyndham lived in the real world. (*SW* 26)

This astonishes. Literature, politics, and country life not only can have a great deal to do with each other, but have had, in British tradition particularly. Yeats' "In Memory of Major Robert Gregory" shows what can be done with their unity even in the twentieth century. By "the real world" here Eliot apparently means "the ordinary man's experience" of his essay on the Metaphysicals, but he accepts one and rejects the other. Further, Eliot's own life shows a struggle toward unity, to be able to say that his literature, politics, and city life (and, later, perhaps religion) are either "one and the same thing" or else near allied. Rhetoric here manipulates our response, for by equating "country life" with "riding to hounds" Eliot trivializes it. Analogously, a hater of poetry might have written "politics, country life, and scribbling sonnets," or a political cynic "literature, country life, and counting votes." The loaded rhetoric supports disparagement of a goal of unity close to Eliot's own. Why, then, the fire and brimstone? Ernest J. Lovell, the only other scholar to consider this problem, has theorized that "Wyndham in fact was everything that Eliot was not"—British, aristocratic, prominent in government, and rich in inherited land.[32] This proposed envy of the aristocrat by the still obscure (although already snobbish) bank clerk offers the start of an answer. Wyndham posed not just an enviable but an attractive though unreachable alternative for Eliot, who was then casting about for a suitable transatlantic identity. His irrational fervor against Wyndham suggests exorcism of an inner temptation as much as flagellation of an outer offense. Eliot in fact did escape from an American to a British identity, and the prevalence of the word *escape* in his early criticism suggests how much the idea haunted him.[33] But for Eliot to escape to Wyndham's unity would have been for him to pursue a catastrophic chimera leading to falsity and pretense. In rejecting Wyndham, he rejected an unattainable form for metamorphosis.

Quoting the implied identification of "romantic" with "fairyland" in Charles Whibley's introductory memoir to Wyndham's book, Eliot seized on unreality in his attack on romanticism. He writ the point large in proscribing romanticism from literature:

> Wyndham was a Romantic; the only cure for Romanticism is to analyse it. What is permanent and good in romanticism is curiosity . . . a curiosity which recognizes that any life, if accurately and profoundly penetrated, is interesting and always strange. Romanticism is a short cut to the strangeness without the reality, and it leads its disciples only back upon themselves. . . . there may be a good deal to be said for Romanticism in life, there is no place for it in letters. (*SW* 31-32)

Eliot's need to purge his poetry of romanticism unites with his need to purge his psyche of an illusory ideal to bring him here to the brink of contradiction. For he concludes by rejecting family, caste, party, and coterie to assert that a man must be "simply and solely himself" in the arts; his closing praise of "the Individual" ends up invoking one romantic ideal in the name of anti-romanticism.

Romantic notions of escape from ordinary personality likewise permeate Eliot's famous "Tradition and the Individual Talent." The essay's partisans have too quickly accepted its anti-romantic claims at face value, for it not only describes romanticism wrongly but reaches romantic conclusions. Toward the end Eliot rejects Wordsworth's "emotion recollected in tranquillity":

> "Emotion recollected in tranquillity" is an inexact formula. For it is neither emotion, nor recollection, nor, without distortion of meaning, tranquillity. It is a concentration, and a new thing resulting from the concentration, of a very great number of experiences which to the practical and active person would not seem to be experiences at all; it is a concentration which does not happen consciously or of deliberation. These experiences are not "recollected," and they finally unite in an atmosphere which is "tranquil" only in that it is a passive attending upon the event. (*SW* 58)

The opaque reference of "it" makes unclear what Eliot thinks "emotion recollected in tranquillity" is a formula for; the context here suggests "the emotion of poetry," while the 1928 preface —where Eliot underscored his attack on the phrase by again repudiating it—seems to define it as poetry in general before, in a non sequitur, describing it more correctly as one poet's account of his own method. (*SW* ix) It may help to recall Wordsworth himself:

> Poetry . . . takes its origin from emotion recollected in tranquillity: the emotion is contemplated till, by a species of re-action, the tranquillity gradually disappears, and an emotion, kindred to that which was before the subject of contemplation, is gradually produced, and does itself actually exist in the mind. In this mood successful composition generally begins, and in a mood similar to this it is carried on; but the emotion, of whatever kind, and in whatever degree, from various causes, is qualified by various pleasures. . . .[34]

Wordsworth has described here the *origin* of poetic composition. After misrepresenting his predecessor's account by taking it as the *result* of composition (or, alternatively, emotion recollected in tranquillity as the entire process), Eliot proceeds to restate approximately Wordsworth's actual position: poetic emotion is a new thing, resulting from a combination of various experiences, and emerges partly without conscious control. Eliot chose to refute Georgian and other pervasive acceptance of "emotion recollected in tranquillity" not by pointing out its proper meaning in

111

Wordsworth but by underscoring its inadequacy as a definition of poetry and then working partway back to Wordsworth's actual beliefs. In the process, Eliot handed the false conflation on to a whole new generation of critics.[35]

Escape, daemonic possession, catalyzed reactions: the violent terms Eliot uses here and elsewhere to describe poetic composition suggest the irrationality he saw at its center. Stead and Bergonzi seem the only critics to have stressed this side of Eliot properly. Bergonzi writes, "he regarded poetic creation as a possibly dangerous and even sacrificial surrender to unknown forces. Thus described, Eliot's poetic seems unexpectedly romantic."[36] This is right as far as it goes. But Eliot's aesthetic lacks the keystone of romantic theory—imagination as stabilizing and synthesizing force. He uses the term seldom; in positive usage, he either drops it casually in passing or, in his one sustained though limited application, contrasts auditory with visual imagination primarily to attack Milton. Negatively, he fears its power. He recognizes imagination as a violence from within but not as a rage for order. He therefore relies on external authority to contain the irrationality of composition: first literary tradition and later religious orthodoxy. These he continually berates the romantics for lacking. Yet even his early concept of tradition accords with theirs. When Eliot invokes the historical sense as "a feeling that the whole of the literature of Europe from Homer and within it the whole of the literature of his own country has a simultaneous existence and composes a simultaneous order" (*SW* 49) that each new poet both builds up and modifies, he parallels Shelley's contention in the *Defence* that all poems are "episodes to that great poem, which all poets, like the co-operating thoughts of one great mind, have built up since the beginning of the world."[37] Likewise, his distinction between man and poet (*SW* 54) recalls standard romantic doctrine. But in attacking romanticism, Eliot almost always so misses the mark that we suspect he is really aiming at his own hypostatized flaws or at influential degenerations of high romanticism. In *The Sacred Wood* his fury at alleged romantic deviations from tradition centered principally on Blake.

Placed just before the final essay on Dante to show by contrast why Dante was a classic and Blake only a poet of genius, Eliot's essay on "Blake" constitutes the first of the extensive critiques he would eventually provide for each of the six major romantics and the only one belonging to his first anti-romantic phase.[38] In revising his review of Charles Gardner's *William Blake the Man* for *The Sacred Wood*, he tempered its original praise of Blake by deleting a favorable introductory paragraph and adding three hostile closing ones. He thus focused less on the "perfectly sane mind" than on the "abnormal intensity and strong passions" mentioned in his deleted opening paragraph.[39] His remaining accolades for Blake follow the diction of intensity with which he regularly described his response to romantic poets. While he concedes "great technical accomplishment" to Blake, what really interests him is Blake's "peculiar honesty, which, in a world too frightened to be honest, is peculiarly terrifying." (SW 151) That word "terrifying" recurs later in the essay:

> He was naked, and saw man naked, and from the centre of his own crystal. To him there was no more reason why Swedenborg should be absurd than Locke. He accepted Swedenborg, and eventually rejected him, for reasons of his own. He approached everything with a mind unclouded by current opinions. There was nothing of the superior person about him. This makes him terrifying. (SW 154-55)

"Terrifying" recalls the violent language in which Eliot described both poetic creation and his own early encounter with the romantic poets.[40] Here, he responds similarly to Blake's honesty of perception, his freedom from comforting but limiting cultural and social supports.

To understand Eliot's shock we need to compare his ensuing account of "the dangers to which the naked man is exposed," chief among them a lack of control manifested in eccentric philosophy. Eliot writes:

> And about Blake's supernatural territories, as about the supposed ideas that dwell there, we cannot help commenting on a certain meanness of culture. They illustrate the crankiness, the eccentricity, which frequently affects writers outside of the Latin tradition. . . . Had [Blake's gifts] been controlled by a respect for impersonal reason, for common sense, for the objectivity of science, it would have been better for him. What his genius required, and what it sadly lacked, was a framework of accepted and traditional ideas which would have prevented him from indulging in a philosophy of his own, and concentrated his attention upon the problems of the poet. . . . The concentration resulting from a framework of mythology and theology and philosophy is one of the reasons why Dante is a classic, and Blake only a poet of genius. The fault is perhaps not with Blake himself, but with the environment. (SW 157-58)

Much of this is nonsense, equivalent to Eliot's censure of Blake for not having split up point of view in his long poems into various

113

personalities, when that is exactly what Blake had done. Part of it is true, for Eliot, as Yeats, saw the poetic advantage of a living tradition of accepted symbols and ideas like that available to Dante (although Eliot both underestimated Blake's traditional qualities more than Yeats had and proposed an even less satisfactory alternative). More important than both are the implications for Eliot's own situation: he fears that emulating Blake's honesty would lead to loss of control, and he looks to the framework of Latin tradition to save him from that delirium of the brave. His account projects his own peril not just as poet but, apparently, also as man. The year after the Blake essay Eliot suffered a nervous breakdown resulting at least partly from the intolerable strain of his marriage and personal life and partly from a long-standing mental malady.[41] Blake's honesty terrified Eliot partly because he could not practice it himself, and as both poet and man he reached out to the ordering restraints of Latin tradition, which for him meant classical and Christian orthodoxy. To Blake, this would have been a betrayal of imagination, and perhaps it was.

Eliot's uncollected prose of the years surrounding *The Sacred Wood* supports the fear and distrust of romanticism exhibited there. In 1919 he used his review of Frederick E. Pierce's *Currents and Eddies in the English Romantic Generation* to attack chaos and lack of discipline. "It [Pierce's book] exhibits the Romantic Period as a period of intellectual chaos; it leads us to speculate whether the age, as an age, can ever exert much influence upon any age to come; and it provokes the suspicion that our own age may be similarly chaotic and ineffectual," he wrote. "The period 1788-1832 was a period hungry for novelty."[42] Romanticism becomes an analogue for a contemporary fear and its shortcoming an externalization of contemporary risks, including Eliot's own. The romantics failed to attain "unity of temper" in sympathy with society or art and "unity of expression" in an individual. Those charges recall *The Sacred Wood*'s contention that the romantics lacked adequate form in which to "confine" their impressions. (*SW* 62) To Eliot their careers were parables of the need for control and discipline of the violent forces of poetic composition and affect. Similarly, they showed the necessity of ordered morality in both art and life. "The Lesson of Baudelaire" (1921) condemned romantic morality in the accents of Babbitt. The French seventeenth century offered a coherent classical account of good and evil. "Romanticism endeavored to form another Morals —Rousseau, Byron, Goethe, Poe were moralists," intoned Eliot with immediately to be abandoned temperance. "But they have not sufficient coherence; not only was the foundation of Rousseau rotten, his structure was chaotic and inconsistent."[43] For his 1923 review of Joyce's *Ulysses* he posed the antithesis with equal extremity: " 'Classicism' is not an alternative to 'romanticism'. . . . It is a goal toward which all good literature strives."[44] In *The Sacred Wood* Eliot lamented that Babbitt had not "preached of discipline in a more disciplined style." (*SW* 42) So, too, with his disciple. Eliot protests against the romantics too much in his middle period; they came too close to his own concerns and fears, and had already demonically possessed him in his youth. That made them terrifying.

Religious conversion shaped the new stresses in Eliot's second phase of anti-romanticism. While he continued his technical and thematic critiques, developing more precisely his objections to Coleridge's doctrines of imagination and to Shelley in general, he grew increasingly prone to attack romantic philosophy or theology in themselves, without reference to poetry. That happened in his neglected because unreprinted review of six Blake books in "The Mysticism of Blake," written in the year of his conversion, 1927. He raged against Blake's ignorance and heresy with all the fury of a learned convert:

> Blake was not even a first-rate visionary: his visions have a certain illiteracy about them. . . . Was he, then, a great philosopher? No, he did not know enough. . . . [through his] Isolation . . . and Pride . . . Blake is philosophically an autodidact amateur; theologically, a heretic. . . . The [Prophetic] Books are full of poetry, and fine poetry, too. But they show very sadly that genius and inspiration are not enough for a poet. He must have education, by which I do not mean erudition but a kind of mental and moral discipline.[45]

Again, Eliot has his eye on himself. Blake was certainly an autodidact and possibly a heretic, but even autodidacts and heretics may have "mental and moral discipline." Blake quite possibly possessed more of either than Eliot, enough for him to risk living as the "naked man" who so terrified Eliot. Instead, Eliot reached out to professional education and religious orthodoxy to restrain his innate "genius and inspiration."[46]

Eliot forged the principles of his second Blake essay in a debate with John Middleton Murry that ignited in the *Adelphi* and *Criterion* in 1923 and flared up again in 1927. In "On Fear; and on Romanticism"[47] Murry had argued for romanticism (intuition, inner voice, concern with inner reality) as the native British tradition, opposed to foreign classicism (reason, external authority, restraint); romanticism was British and Protestant, classicism Latin and Catholic. Eliot answered in "The Function of Criticism" (1923). Partly, he reiterated the cachets by which he had freed himself earlier from nineteenth-century British poetry. Romanticism was fragmentary, immature, and chaotic, while classicism was complete, adult, and orderly. Similarly, romantics lacked the "sense of fact" of classicists.[48] So far Eliot repeats the battle cries of his own psychic war. But he also sounds a new call, ghost-written by Babbitt and Arnold, against the "inner voice":

> My belief is that those who possess this inner voice are ready enough to hearken to it, and will hear no other. The inner voice, in fact, sounds remarkably like an old principle which has been formulated by an elder critic in the now familiar phrase of "doing as one likes." The possessors of the inner voice ride ten in a compartment to a football match at Swansea, listening to the inner voice, which breathes the eternal message of vanity, fear, and lust. (*SE* 16)

Besides the snobbery of this, we notice the near-hysteria in Eliot's denunciation. His rhetoric distorts its object; it is as though Murry were to hold that obeyers of external authority ban books (a position Eliot later accepted in theory) and burn people at the stake.[49] In a familiar forensic maneuver Eliot attacks a debased caricature of his adversary's position. Significantly, he couples his fear of unrestrained action with "lust," which he had associated with romanticism from adolescence. Murry issued a restrained reply, urging Eliot to distinguish naive from sophisticated romanticism and making the Socratic argument that "to know what you really like means to know what you really are; and that is a matter of painful experience and slow exploration."[50] His plea failed, for in attacking romanticism Eliot combated not a historical force but a projection of his own problems.

The religious element of Eliot's anti-romantic compound, present in solution during his 1923 exchange with Murry, crystallized during the 1927 sequel. Although they had traded minor sallies in 1924 and 1926, Murry's suggestion of a synthesis of romanticism and classicism called forth another of Eliot's philippics. Following immediately after Yeats' "The Tower" in an issue of the *Criterion* showing Eliot's tolerance as editor, Murry's "Towards a Synthesis" argued for a fusion of romantic stress on immediate perception and classical insistence on patterned cognition. In a splendid missing of Murry's point, Eliot denounced Murry's world as one of shifting truths that tried to make poetry a substitute for religion. He invoked a passage from Jacques Rivière that he admired enough to quote again six years later: "It is only with Romanticism that the literary act began to be conceived as a sort of approach towards the absolute, and its result as a revelation; at that moment literature gathered the inheritance of religion and organized itself on the model of that which it replaced; the writer became the priest; the purpose of all his gestures was solely to induce the descent of the 'Real Presence' into this consecrated Host."[51] To Eliot, the romantics began the substitution of poetry for religion that culminated in Arnold's concept of culture. Characteristically, he chose a passage that treats this alleged romantic trespass in terms of control of superhuman forces. As priest, the poet uses the "gesture" of the "poetic act"—in short, his form of ritual—to induce "revelation," or the descent of a Holy Ghost. This partly describes one form of romanticism but fits even better Eliot's own early strategy as Humanist poet influenced by Babbitt. Only for Eliot poetic and mental discipline apparently failed to contain the violent forces within his psyche, which emerged with special energy during poetic creation. His own Furies drove him to a further stage of development, and romanticism—as before —served as projection for the stage he had left behind.

In condemning romantic poetry for challenging religion, Eliot mistakes its use of polysemous language, which his early verse shared to some degree. His true enemy, properly identified in "Arnold and Pater" (1930), was fin de siècle aestheticism with its religion of art. In contrast, romantic displacement of religious language onto secular experience had aimed at adapting traditional terminology to describe all forms of psychic activity and so to display their unity. The diction of Blake's *Marriage of Heaven and Hell* generates multiple political, sexual, and religious applications. Eliot's preconversion poetry follows a similar tactic. The famous "After such knowledge, what forgiveness?" passage of "Gerontion," for example, applies to historical, sexual, and religious experience, while *The Waste Land* secretes a web of polysemous reference. By the late 1920s Eliot rejected this mode of expression and in poems like *Ash Wednesday* or *Four Quartets* would restore religious terminology to its original significance.

Religion both offered a surer bulwark against chaotic forces and subsumed Eliot's earlier literary demonology. In the preface to *For Lancelot Andrewes* (1928), pertinently subtitled "Essays on Style and Order," came the famous triple declaration Eliot eventually regretted: "The general point of view may be described as classicist in literature, royalist in politics, and anglo-catholic in religion."[52] What these three terms share, of course, is restraint by external authority. Eliot had forged a new connection between his religion, his politics, and his literature that, in its interconnectedness if not in its content, recalls the unity for which he had maligned George Wyndham a decade before. The religious component increasingly dominated the others. Six years later, in *After Strange Gods: A Primer of Modern Heresy* (1934), he lamented the *Lancelot Andrewes* avowal for suggesting that "the three subjects are of equal importance to me." (*ASG* 29) Religion was primary. It both incorporated his earlier distinctions and reduced their importance: "My contrast of heresy and orthodoxy has some analogy to the more usual one of romanticism and classicism; and I wish to emphasize this analogy myself, as a safeguard against carrying it too far." There was even "something wrong when a critic divides all works of art neatly into one group or the other and then plumps for the romantic or the classical as a whole," and in any case practicing poets could not bother to adhere to one camp or the other during actual composition. (*ASG* 26-29) The chief value of the terms was "temporary and political," and by 1934 Eliot's political need of them had waned with his personal need, although he still put himself in the classical lists. He had stronger forms of defense against chaos and could be tolerant of his old literary nemeses, although not, characteristically, of rival religions. He had an incorrigible need of demons.

In turning to Christianity as a defense against inner forces Eliot followed the pattern of his admired Coleridge in "The Eolian Harp." There the speaker renounced "shapings of the unregenerate mind" in the name of Christian orthodoxy. In terms of mental states, he renounced imaginative vision for self-abnegation. But, to the extent that the speaker is Coleridge, not enough to stop being a poet. A similar contradiction troubled Eliot, one that he discussed in *After Strange Gods*. There he came to the remarkable conclusion that his poems might contradict his religious opinions because "in one's prose reflexions one may be legitimately occupied with ideals, whereas in the writing of verse one can only deal with actuality." (*ASG* 30) The remainder of his poetic career may be fairly described as a struggle between his orthodox mind and his unregenerate imagination, between his ideal conceptions and actual perceptions. His critiques of specific poets—principally Baudelaire, Coleridge, and Shelley—during his second anti-

romantic phase develop that paradox and prepare us for understanding both his late reconciliation with romanticism and his
own poetic career.

By the self-revealing essay "Baudelaire" (1930) Eliot had begun
to doubt how far even the most militantly modern poet could
escape his post-romantic heritage. He saw even Baudelaire ("the
greatest exemplar in *modern* poetry in any language," SE 377,
italics Eliot's) as at once "the offspring of romanticism, and by his
nature the first counter-romantic in poetry." (SE 376) Though a
"classical" poet, Baudelaire could not shuck off the "romantic detritus" of satanism, romantic love, and poet *maudit*. Victor Brombert has properly questioned Eliot's accuracy in contending for
Baudelaire's classical tendencies and Christian orthodoxy,[53] for
Eliot again projects his own situation onto a precursor. "A poet in
a romantic age cannot be a 'classical' poet except in tendency," he
admitted in a major revision of his earlier catechisms. He himself
could be only classical in tendency. Particularly, he suffered from
two problems he attacked in romanticism. First was the relation
between poetic form and psychic disorder: he conjectured "that
the care for perfection of form, among some of the romantic poets
of the nineteenth century, was an effort to support, or to conceal
from view, an inner disorder." (SE 375) This describes Eliot's own
preconversion poetry, when the severe discipline culminating in
The Waste Land coexisted with increasing psychic breakdown.
Likewise, when he imputes the sadness of romantic poetry to the
inadequacy of human relationships in satisfying human desires,
and to lack of any further object for desire, we remember the
pervasive tone of much of his own early poetry. He attributed to
Baudelaire the same escape he himself had found—recognition
"that what really matters is Sin and Redemption," especially Sin.
(SE 378-79) Even damnation dispelled the ennui of modern life
and, in contrast to "the modern Protestantism of Byron and Shelley," gave significance to life. Eliot's own conception of Christianity rested on original sin and through that stress tended, ironically, toward heresy, as several commentators have suggested. His
approach to Christianity was relentlessly Pauline, and when he
wanted a Biblical citation for his essay he turned to Romans 6:16.
Toward the end of "Baudelaire" Eliot completed his romantic associations by working around to sexuality. Although Baudelaire
had "an imperfect, vague romantic conception of Good," he at
least understood "that what distinguishes the relations of man
and woman from the copulation of beasts is the knowledge of
Good and Evil." (SE 380) By the time he concluded with a quota-

tion from T. E. Hulme on the virtues of discipline, Eliot had created a remarkable self-portrait under the guise of an essay on a French forerunner.

When in 1950 he looked back on his poetic career, Eliot decided that his chief debt to Baudelaire had been use of "sordid aspects of the modern metropolis" as subject matter. (*TCC* 126) This deflection of poetic interest from adolescent preoccupation with nature to his mature engagement with urban subjects helped Eliot to escape his early romanticism. For although the romantics wrote of modern cities, they were above all nature poets, whereas although Eliot wrote of, say, the rose garden, he was principally a city poet, who once confessed that he could no more live in the country than he could give up cigarettes.[54] The statement recalls Blake's dislike of country life, but whereas Blake feared that nature would overwhelm imagination, Eliot worried that it would vanquish reason. He inveighed tirelessly against romantic nature, only recognizing at the end of his life that " 'Nature' to Wordsworth and to Goethe . . . meant something which they had experienced—and which I had not." (*OPP* 254) When the romantics looked at nature, they in fact wrote poems of mental action, usually hymning imagination's prowess. When Eliot looked at the city he also wrote poems of mental action, but they either expressed merely associationist processes or sought to project a disembodied consciousness. For him, metropolitan subjects helped to restrain the violence from within, or else to siphon it off into tolerable channels.

Eliot both revered Coleridge's criticism and identified with Coleridge the man. "As for Coleridge, he was rather a man of my own type,"[55] he wrote in a late essay. What type that was he had indicated by contrast with Wordsworth in 1932: "[Wordsworth's] inspiration never having been of that sudden, fitful and terrifying kind that visited Coleridge, he was never, apparently, troubled by the consciousness of having lost it." (*UPUC* 69) To establish his contrast, Eliot ignores the Intimations ode and other poems. Wordsworth wasn't troubled, but Coleridge was; both the congruence of "sudden, fitful and terrifying" inspiration with Eliot's own literary experience and his later conflation of himself with Coleridge suggest that Eliot was, too.[56] In more controlled moments he could respect Coleridge as perhaps the greatest of poet-critics, at least the peer of Dryden and Johnson, and hence a model for the kind of critic Eliot thought himself to be. Through his myriad studies Coleridge had injected philosophy, psychology, and aesthetics into literary criticism once and for all. "The criticism of to-day, indeed, may be said to be in direct descent from Coleridge," he wrote.[57] Eliot followed Coleridge in completing literary with extraliterary criticism, even when discussing poetry. Not content simply to dine at Coleridge's table, he made off with as many of Coleridge's spoons as possible, like the notions of suspension of disbelief, balance of opposites, and even clerisy, which he later melted down and recast in his own design.

Yet Eliot managed to admire and utilize Coleridge's criticism even while rejecting its chief tenet, the doctrine of imagination. Weakening the distinction between Fancy and Imagination obsessed him, for that discrimination seemed to Coleridge and to Eliot to restrict the value of the Metaphysical poets whose technique he was adapting in his own verse. He wanted wit to replace imagination as criterion. "The difference between imagination and fancy, in view of this poetry of wit, is a very narrow one," he declared in his early essay "Andrew Marvell" (1921). (*SE* 256) Of Coleridge's many elucidations of imagination, Eliot quoted the celebrated passage from *Biographia Literaria* which he would cite again in his Norton lectures:

> This power . . . reveals itself in the balance or reconcilement of opposite or discordant qualities: of sameness, with difference; of the general, with the concrete; the idea, with the image; the individual, with the representative; the sense of novelty and freshness, with old and familiar objects; a more than usual state of emotion, with more than usual order; judgment ever awake and steady self-possession, with enthusiasm and feeling profound or vehement. . . .[58]

Although those terms shift among the reader's response, work itself, and writer, Eliot apparently took them all as applying to the work and argued that they described Marvell's verse. He cited six passages, one of which ("Annihilating all that's made/ To a green thought in a green shade") corresponded in fact to Coleridge's notions as developed here and elsewhere. The others did not; for example,

> And now the meadows fresher dyed,
> Whose grass, with moister colour dashed,
> Seems as green silks but newly washed.

Those two passages from Marvell's poetry mirror two from Shakespeare's *Venus and Adonis* that Coleridge himself used to distinguish between faculties. Fancy united mainly dissimilar images by one or more points of distinguished likeness:

> Full gently now she takes him by the hand,
> A lily prison'd in a gaol of snow,
> Or ivory in an alabaster band;
> So white a friend engirts so white a foe.

Imagination brought together many images and feelings without discord:

> Look! how a bright star shooteth from the sky,
> So glides he in the night from Venus' eye.[59]

Eliot takes a description of imagination manifesting itself in work, reader, and author as a description of qualities in a work, and then ignores Coleridge's other analyses of imagination in arguing for its presence in Marvell. He thus makes a double claim: the difference between imagination and fancy is slight, and in any case Metaphysical poets show imagination. He wants to shift literary analysis from imagination to wit, which was "absent from the work of Wordsworth, Shelley, and Keats, on whose poetry nineteenth-century criticism has unconsciously been based."[60] (*SE* 262) This change in criticism would rewrite literary history to boost the Metaphysicals, sink the romantics, and provide a favorable background for what Eliot thought he was doing in his own poetry.

His personal motivation becomes even clearer in the several treatments of imagination in the Norton lectures, *The Use of Poetry and the Use of Criticism* (1933). He twice cited Coleridge's remark that "Milton had a highly imaginative, Cowley a very fanciful mind." (*UPUC* 29, 58) It is amusing to watch Eliot—who himself bombarded the romantics with even more heavily loaded rhetoric—complain that Coleridge's choice of Milton and Cowley biases the reader's evaluation of the opposed qualities, and it is instructive to note that his proposed substitution of Spenser and Donne accurately identifies the chief antecedent of Milton and the romantics. As he himself remarked of Coleridge, "When the critics are themselves poets, it may be suspected that they have formed their critical statements with a view to justifying their poetic practice." (*UPUC* 29) But like Hamlet in act 1, Eliot kept being disturbed by the ghost of imagination when trying to swear on the handle of wit. Was he, after all, missing something? In the Norton lectures he thought of following Dryden in using "imagination" to describe the whole process of composition, of which invention formed only a moment. His description invoked the violent metaphors he associated with both composition and romantic poetry: "Dryden's 'invention' includes the sudden irruption of the germ of a new poem, possibly merely as a state of feeling."(*UPUC* 56) To Dryden, invention, fancy, and elocution all belonged to imagination, which thus to Eliot becomes mainly a process for controlling the eruption of feeling that he recognized as the "germ" of his own poetic act.

In his last combat with the Antaeus of fancy and imagination Eliot tilted at the famous distinctions concluding chapter 13 of *Biographia Literaria*.[61] In a masterful smoke screen that makes the reader blush who remembers Eliot's objection to Coleridge's rhetoric, Eliot made four challenges to Coleridge's position:

1. "My mind is too heavy and concrete for any flight of abstruse reasoning."
2. "The difference between imagination and fancy amounts in practice to no more than the difference between good and bad poetry."
3. "It is only if fancy can be an ingredient in good poetry, and if you can show some good poetry which is the better for it; it is only if the distinction illuminates our immediate preference of one poet over another, that it can be of use to a practical mind like mine."
4. "But it seems unwise to talk of memory in connexion with fancy and omit it altogether from the account of imagination." (*UPUC* 77-78)

Eliot's beguiling claim, "It may be that I wholly fail to appreciate this passage," applies to only three of his reasons. The first is irrelevant rhetoric. The second is wrong, for Coleridge uses the distinction to distinguish, at most, good from better poetry, not good from bad. Hence, the third misses the mark, for its precepts are just those which Coleridge had followed. The fourth point usefully advances critical theory by pointing to a need for elucidation. But Eliot dislikes Coleridge's implicit distinction between imaginative memory which "dissolves, diffuses and dissipates" and fanciful memory which plays with "fixities and definites," which at least gives the start of a distinction. For Eliot's own memory seems to have supplied him chiefly with fixities and definites, like the name "Prufrock," or the literary memory of Lancelot Andrewes at the beginning of "Journey of the Magi," or the personal one of the adapted tavern scene in the middle of that poem. Only *Four Quartets* presented imaginative memory extensively.[62]

Despite his respect for Coleridge, Eliot challenged the distinction between fancy and imagination time and again. Need to defend his own critical principles, version of literary history, creative processes, and personal strategies goaded him on. Elevation of Metaphysical wit meant pulling romantic imagination down from its pinnacle. More important, he conceived of his own art as selection and arrangement,[63] which could embody wit; but his art could show imagination only if he could redefine that term virtually to identify it with wit. Eliot revealingly cites Richards on Coleridge with approval, for Richards by his own admission was there a Benthamite trying to understand a Platonist; to some degree, so was Eliot. Finally, his redefinitions and oppositions added to the pattern of restraint that he imposed on his own violent eruptions of feeling—like classicism and Christianity, these literary doctrines made for clothed order rather than naked energy. But Eliot was only partly right about himself, for his mind was orthodox and his imagination heretical, and his poetry a struggle between the two powers. So were his life and criticism, and their uneasy synthesis of Prolific and Devourer regularly went to pieces over Shelley.

Shelley drove Eliot to frenzy. His reactions show a kind of schizophrenia, alternately belittling and praising Shelley for the same trait, not just at different periods but even within the same anti-romantic phase. Thus, in 1917 he commended Pound for making it "impossible to write like Shelley, leaving blanks for the adjectives" as in "what is called the 'music' of Shelley," while in 1920 he praised Shelley's "Music, When Soft Voices Die" for its "beauty of music."[64] In 1921 Shelley's "Art Thou Pale from Weariness" suffered from lack of wit (*SE* 263), while by 1956 Eliot judged the same lines as the highest type of enjoyable poetry not needing any explanation and found they gave him "as keen a thrill when I repeat them to-day as they did fifty years ago." (*OPP* 129) These alterations suggest a mind divided against itself, at once enormously susceptible to Shelley and distrustful of that very susceptibility.

That division causes the Norton lectures to disintegrate when they reach Shelley. By fits and starts Eliot tries to explain how he can condemn Shelley without violating his own principles and practices. Part of his problem was personal. He had never forgotten his adolescent experience of "being enraptured, invaded, carried away by one writer after another," prominent among them Shelley. (*OPP* 244) Hence, he told his Harvard audience that "the ideas of Shelley seem to me always to be ideas of adolescence . . .

and an enthusiasm for Shelley seems to me also to be an affair of adolescence; for most of us, Shelley has marked an intense period before maturity." (*UPUC* 89) But the problem lay not just in Eliot's youth but also in his manhood. "I find his ideas repellent," he declared with growing shrillness, "and the man was humorless, pedantic, self-centred, and sometimes almost a blackguard." Since by abundant testimony Shelley had a fine sense of humor, hated pedantry, and was less self-centered than most, one wonders what drove Eliot to those absurdities. Perhaps the sexuality he always ascribed to romanticism, for the contrast between Shelley the advocate of free (though not licentious) love and Eliot the resolute husband of an increasingly deranged wife could explain the improbable description of Shelley as a blackguard. Four pages later, Eliot singled out the disavowal of exclusively restricted affection in *Epipsychidion* for special abuse.[65]

Eliot's rant circles around the role of belief in poetry. He finds Shelley a combiner of eighteenth-century rationalism and cloudy Platonism who "never quite escaped from the tutelage of Godwin." (*UPUC* 90) In trying to derive his distaste for Shelley from "a peculiarity in the poetry and not in the reader" (*UPUC* 96), Eliot finally reached a modification of Coleridge's notion of suspension of disbelief as filtered through I. A. Richards: a poet's "view of life" need not trouble the reader if it is mature and coherent, but Shelley's was "childish or feeble." (*UPUC* 96) This is nonsense about Shelley, but why did Eliot avow it? First, he typically projected onto Shelley his own adolescence. Second, that projection freed him from seeing Shelley as another naked man terrifying the clothed Eliot. For Shelley in his poetry shows a heroic skepticism in confronting experience without comforting beliefs, even that in his own powers; he is in many ways the most honest of poets. When Eliot attacks Shelley's use of creeds outworn or tyrants and priests as catchwords, he fights for the principles on which his own precarious mental balance depended—religion, classicism, and monarchy. For Eliot to have imitated Shelley's nakedness would have been disastrous, and in denouncing Shelley he sought to keep down his own *hysterica passio*.

These personal fears coincided with Eliot's rejection of prophetic stance, with its implied suspension of rational control, from his poetry. He thought that romantic claims for poetry "reach their highest point of exaggeration in Shelley's famous phrase, 'poets are the unacknowledged legislators of mankind,' " a step on the way to substitution of poet for priest and Arnoldian elevation of culture. In a misunderstanding of Shelley spectacular even for

125

Eliot, he tagged him as "the first . . . of Nature's M.P.'s" (*UPUC* 26), a phrase from Shaw, as though nature did not threaten imagination in much of Shelley's work from "Mount Blanc" or earlier through *The Triumph of Life*. Earlier, in 1921, he had compared a great chorus of *Hellas* ("The world's great age begins anew ... .") unfavorably with Dryden's "The Secular Masque" (*SE* 265), but made no mention of its debt to Virgil's fourth eclogue. Yet in 1951 Eliot delivered one of his few pronouncements on prophetic poetry apropos of that eclogue. Significantly, his remarks stress the prophet's lack of understanding of his own utterance. (*OPP* 137) For Eliot, genuine prophetic poetry meant abandoning rational power for the entire poetic experience, whereas his own practice was to place immediately the undisciplined moment within a framework of restraint.

In the Norton lectures Eliot used Keats' kind of impersonality as an attractive foil to Shelley's. He quoted letters on Wordsworth's poetry as "sketchy intellectual landscape, not a search for truth" and on men of genius being "great as certain ethereal chemicals operating on the Mass of neutral intellect—but they have not any individuality, any determined character." (*UPUC* 101) Keats' impersonality apparently offered a gentle escape from selfhood without the attendant violence of Shelley's prophetic suspension of self. Eliot himself would seem to have suppressed his Shelleyan side in trying to behave like a good Keatsian.

Yet even in serving chiefly as a negative projection of personal fears, Shelley affected Eliot's poetry positively through his relation to Dante. In 1929 Eliot included grudging praise of Shelley for knowing Dante well (and being the only nineteenth-century poet capable of following Dante's example) in using Shelley to argue that the age had a prejudice against beatitude as material for poetry. (*SE* 225) Characteristically, Eliot there plucked a line—"Our sweetest songs are those that tell of saddest thought"—from its context in "To a Skylark" to treat it as though it were a statement by Shelley the man. By 1950 he could be more generous about his debt to Shelley, particularly to *The Triumph of Life*, the one poem of Shelley's he had consistently admired. In "What Dante Means to Me," he quoted at length "one passage which made an indelible impression upon me over forty-five years ago." This was the same description of Rousseau from which he had also quoted in *The Use of Poetry and the Use of Criticism* and which inspired several lines of "Sweeney Erect." With the grace that often marked his late reconciliation with romanticism, he added, in implicit comparison to his own Dantesque passage in *Little Gidding*, "Well, this is better than I could do."[66]

Rapprochement with Shelley signals a general truce with romanticism in Eliot's later years. Already begun by the mid-thirties, the change was complete by the end of the decade. He had reached a phase of development beyond his earlier divisions of childhood, adolescence, and maturity. Characteristically generalizing his own progress, he described his new schema in a late essay on Goethe. Childhood dropped out, and the first two stages became adolescence ("swept with enthusiasm for one author after another") and a sort of early maturity ("Though we may at this stage enjoy, understand, and appreciate an indefinite variety of artistic and philosophic genius, there will remain obstinate cases of authors of high rank whom we continue to find antipathetic"). Eliot's chief obstinacies had been romantic poets. But now he had purged rancor:

> The third stage of development—of maturation so far as that process can be represented by the history of our reading and study—is that at which we begin to enquire into the reasons for our failure to enjoy what has been found delightful by men, perhaps many generations of men, as well qualified or better qualified for appreciation than ourselves. In trying to understand why one has failed to appreciate rightly a particular author, one is seeking for light, not only about that author, but about oneself. (*OPP* 242)

Eliot properly stressed his late criticism as a kind of self-discovery, for his criticism had always shown as much about himself as about its nominal subjects. After the thirties, that streak intensified, particularly in the passages of autobiographic recollection, many of which we have already inspected. They show less about Dante or Virgil, say, than about what those writers had meant to Eliot. When he does focus mainly on his subject, as in the surprisingly weak essay on Byron (1937), he often slips into banality. After some personal reminiscence there, he suggests considering Byron as a Scottish poet—as though he still had trouble fitting romanticism into English tradition. Touching the familiar bases of Byron's diabolism, posturing, and skill as a tale-teller, he makes his most provocative comment when he comes to the latter part of *Don Juan*: Byron "was right in making the hero of his house-party a Spaniard, for what Byron understands and dislikes about English society is very much what an intelligent foreigner in the same position would understand and dislike." (*OPP* 238) Again, an obvious analogy to Eliot the intelligent foreigner, who himself brilliantly satirized English society, drives this statement. The Byron essay came early enough in Eliot's final stage to display survivals of his earlier anti-romantic militancy, chiefly conflation of poet and man, and an ugly trick of fixing on physical disabilities. As he had earlier ascribed what he disliked in Milton to his blindness, so does he compare Byron's use of ottava rima to conceal metrical defects to his use of a horse to conceal his clubfoot. This nasty lapse soon passes: what is striking about the essay is Eliot's inability to infuse the vigor or stimulation of his earlier onslaughts into his more balanced critique.[67]

If Eliot's late comments on romantic poets interest us chiefly as personal revelation, they at least show a firm desire to repudiate his earlier hostility. By 1944 he undercut his once crucial catchwords "classic" and "romantic" as "a pair of terms belonging to literary politics, and therefore arousing winds of passion" that he now asked Aeolus to keep in the bag. (*OPP* 53) Later he could even allow that under the romantics England had held the lead in European poetry,[68] although he still thought that they would have been "greater poets if they had held a different view of life." (*OPP* 243) His literary wars over, he could appear as statesman of letters, capable of appreciating conflicting claims. When in 1961 he recalled his triple avowal of *Lancelot Andrewes,* he could concede that "as for Classicism and Romanticism, I find that the terms have no longer the importance to me that they once had." (*TCC* 15)

Why did the terms lose importance? Partly because Eliot had ceased being a creative poet. He no longer needed to berate the romantics to repudiate his own past, and he no longer needed to sink their reputations to clear the way for public acceptance of his own school. Now, he could admit that Coleridge had been more industrious than himself, Shelley a better Danteist, or Wordsworth more sensitive to natural experience. Nor did he any longer need them as projections of personal demons. Although suppression of biographical information hinders full understanding, he had apparently succeeded in his lifelong effort to restrain eruptions of inner violence in an outer framework of order. No longer need he rage at romantic lives or psyches for their disorder and chaos. With the end of poetic creation and personal instability, his anti-romanticism petered out. Yet even at his most virulent, Eliot had been in crucial ways a romantic against the grain. Many of his allegedly anti-romantic attitudes toward composition, tradition, and literary analysis presented romantic positions under the guise of a hostile modernism. We have explored his complicated personal and critical relation to romanticism; it is time to look to his poetic links.

II

Like his mind, Eliot's poetry divides against itself. Violence fights with restraint, imaginative eruption with patterned control, detritus of the past with pressure of the present. Viewed historically, these tensions make his poetry post-romantic in some ways and anti-romantic in others. Contrary to his partisans' claims, Eliot's anti-romanticism does not lie primarily in his technique, except for use of abrupt juxtapositions and even those find analogues in Blake. His revolutions in diction and meter parallel those of Wordsworth in modern guise, purifying the dialect of the tribe for current taste. His exaltation of metaphor and image belongs to central romantic tradition, which in this respect he carries to an extreme. Eliot's technical accomplishment finds its true enemy in the debased romanticism of contemporary British letters that surrounded him. His more genuine anti-romanticism derives from his rejection of imagination both as theme and, often, as process. Although his poems contain moments imaginative in the romantic sense, they more often display the selection and arrangement of fancy's fixities; likewise, they do not seize on imaginative processes as subjects and structures in the varied manner of "Ode to a Nightingale," "Ode to the West Wind," or Blake's Prophetic Books. Partly because of this break, as a group they reverse romantic displacement of religious terminology to secular experience. Although Eliot starts from romantic displacement, by *Four Quartets* he has restored religious diction to its original subject.

Yet just as Eliot ruefully concluded that Baudelaire could be anti-romantic only in tendency because he lived in a romantic (or post-romantic) epoch, so does his own poetry develop as much as break with the work of his predecessors. Above all, he like them makes mind his principal subject and acts of mind his determining structure. And he does this in a direct post-romantic mode rather than in an earlier indirect fashion. To that end he marshals familiar forms like the Greater Romantic Lyric and psychodrama, internal quest, and a particular kind of polysemous language and systematic imagery. He does not so much imitate romantics as adopt similar strategies to resolve similar poetic dilemmas. The early nineteenth century had set ground rules that survived changing the shape of the bat or the weight of the ball. Even his social satires project states of mind, and his greatest poems do so more immediately. Their peculiar relation to imagination generates both their originality and their weakness and makes Eliot a modern, though anguished, Andrea del Sarto.

"The Love Song of J. Alfred Prufrock" reverses Eliot's earlier imitations of romanticism point for point. As the greatest poem in his first great lyrical outburst (1910-12), it may be taken as emblematic of his reaction. Formally, irregular rhymes and meters replace regular ones. These support a dictional shift from derivative poeticisms to an idiom blending everyday raciness, Latinate aloofness, and calculated allusion. Ironic doubt supplants orthodox confidence in tone, and the irony suggests a disciplined restraint and self-control. In theme, varieties of mental triumph yield to a mental defeat, or at best a standoff. Finally, city replaces country as setting, and nature shrinks to a fringe source of metaphors for psychic states. Only Byronic rhymes like "ices" and "crisis" survive the sea change, and the context transforms even them into something rich and strange. Originality has banished convention, although not tradition.

The poem is a dramatic monologue, that species of Greater Romantic Lyric manqué deriving from what Langbaum calls the romantic dramatic lyric. The speaker's mind determines its structure, and his progressive self-revelation its purpose. Eliot takes the form to its extreme by causing the auditor virtually to vanish. While at the beginning of the poem we may think that Prufrock is addressing a companion, or perhaps playing a soul in hell to Eliot's Dante, by the end we suspect that the mysterious "you" is not wholly separate from "I," that both belong to the same psyche. This division of the self into constituent elements occurs regularly in romantic psychodramas, like *The Four Zoas* or *Prometheus Unbound*, but less often in lyrics. Like Blake and Shelley, Eliot may have derived the technique partly from Dante, but he stands closer to the romantics in abandoning traditional Christian divisions of faculties for less programmatically symbolic ones. But while the romantics usually identify the psychic fragments precisely, Eliot leaves them vague; we know only that one suffers and reveals, and tries to instruct the other. Like its larger forebears, the poem builds to a crisis of possible reintegration but then veers away from them by aborting that synthesis. The two selves fail to fuse, and both drown in the chambers of the sea. Such extreme bifurcation in the speaker verges on madness. Its poetic management requires strict control by the poet to avoid the fallacy of imitative form.

The forces for order in the poem are basically associational. However confusing the lyric may have appeared to early, uninitiated readers, after more than half a century it shows an almost mechanical regularity. The apparent leaps in subject signaled by spacing between sections correspond to associations of Prufrock's mind. The sequence repays examination. His introductory "Let us go" leads to the introduction of "visit" at the end of the first section;[69] the next two lines on women coming and going describe the goal of the visit. He then shifts to the fog en route, which returns him to thoughts of time to prepare for the visit and then again to the chatting women he will meet there. This leads to constructing a scenario of what will happen in the room and thus to a sequence of associations first with voices, then with eyes, and finally with arms. He next fancies telling the women of men in shirt-sleeves and arrives at the startling lines "I should have been a pair of ragged claws/ Scuttling across the floors of silent seas." Even these have a close associative link, for they provide an alternate image of how he would look to the men gazing down on him. Associations of silence and animals lead him back to the evening as cat and to death. Thought of death prompts him to frame a hypothetical question about value in life and, after two more paragraphs, he breaks off his monologue and recalls that other great questioner, Hamlet. After rejecting the prince's role he selects that of Polonius and, in the next section, pictures his own advancing old age. With the shift to Prufrock as *senex* strolling the beach, the poem approaches its most imaginative moment, the lyrical climax of mermaids riding the waves, and concludes with figurative drowning in the chambers of the sea.

Such an account of the sequence oversimplifies in quantity but not in quality: there are more links, but they are still discrete connections rather than imaginative fusions. For example, the self-portrait as a crab connects to recurrent sea imagery (begun as early as the oyster-shells of line 7), animal motifs, contrast between voices and silence, various kinds of movement, and —through "floors"—with the room of the salon itself; ironically, Prufrock is already a "pair." But these all constitute separate connections, multiplying variety in a wilderness of mirrors, and depending on laws of association rather than of imagination. It is no accident that Eliot's early poetry found a champion in I. A. Richards, for its construction perfectly suited Richards' earlier theories reducing imagination from fusion to interaction between independent entities. Richards meant essentially what Eliot did in his prose attempts to conflate fancy and imagination in accord with his own methods and needs. Except for its conclusion, "Prufrock" acts out Eliot's critical theories. Even in defending St.-John Perse's *Anabasis* against charges of disorder, Eliot attributed "any obscurity of the poem, on first readings . . . to the suppression of 'links in the chain,' of explanatory and connecting matter."[70] His metaphor of a linked chain underscores his constant contention that poetry depends on placement and arrangement of discrete entities, and thus implies why he had to revise Coleridge. When he goes on to paraphrase his great predecessor in declaring that "There is a logic of imagination as well as a logic of concepts,"[71] he means imagination in his own sense, virtually as fancy, which we have already examined in his criticism. He immediately adds that this "arrangement of imagery" requires the sort of "fundamental brainwork of the reader" that a barrister expends on a complicated case. His remarks apply equally well to the juxtapositions of fancy in his own works.

What is shocking in Eliot's poetic world is the violent metaphoric content of his poetic "links," which the restrained tone and tight logic lull many readers into missing. In "Prufrock" alone we find an etherized body, insidious intent, time to murder and create, a body pinned and wriggling on a wall, ragged claws, a head on a platter, a corpse returned from the dead, a slide show of nerve patterns, and the final drowning. When analyzing the creative process in his accounts of Dryden and Coleridge's poetics, Eliot glossed Dryden's term "invention" as "a finding, a trouvaille," in which the germ of a new poem (possibly as a state of feeling) suddenly erupts. "Fancy" then consciously elaborated the original donnée. To the extent that the root metaphors of sections of "Prufrock" represent the original germ of those passages, they both represent a violent eruption and are themselves violent in content. All the formal and technical discipline of the poem arrays itself against this root violence and catches it in an ambush of order. In terms of speaker rather than poet, Prufrock confines the vitality that drives his mental actions, and that centers in metaphor, within a dictional and tonal framework of restraint built of polite aloofness, irony, and social formula. These complement the governing associational logic to support conscious control. In this way the language of the poem reenacts the predicament in the life of its speaker, which is also the predicament in the poetic life of its creator.

The strategy of entrapment creates the haunting independence of the conclusion. Like Pound's "Cino," Eliot's poems often end on a lyrical high:

> I have seen them riding seaward on the waves
> Combing the white hair of the waves blown back
> When the wind blows the water white and black.
>
> We have lingered in the chambers of the sea
> By sea-girls wreathed with seaweed red and brown
> Till human voices wake us, and we drown.

The poem everywhere prepares for but nowhere demands this conclusion. Women, hair, chambers, lingering, desire to escape—all link these lines to the body of the poem. The lines slough off restraints present elsewhere in an isolated lyrical outburst. But unlike the Greater Romantic Lyrics of Keats or Yeats, the mental action of the poem does not demand such an apex or prepare us for its achievement. The poem arrives there by the same processes of association that motivate it throughout. The eruption could have come earlier, or later, or not at all. It simply flares up in front of us, and Eliot wisely chooses to end on it. Not, however, before the brutal canceling of vision in the last line. At the end of Keats' Nightingale ode, as in many romantic poems, the speaker questions the validity of his vision. It is a genuine questioning. In contrast, Eliot has Prufrock end with total repudiation. He makes the poem's most genuinely imaginative passage into a flash of futile escapism, creation of an artificial dreamworld to satisfy Prufrock's frustrated erotic desires. That was, of course, a principal charge Eliot leveled against romantic poetry, but "Prufrock" shows in practice what Eliot's prose shows in theory—that the real impetus of the charge was need to domesticate his own imagination. The last line contradicts the lyrical thrust of the passage itself in accord with its creator's own drives.

Location of vitality under the sea reflects the tendency of romantic imagery to locate sources of power downward and within, rather than upward and outward. To an extent the whole poem takes place in the landscape of Prufrock's mind; from the opening image of evening as an etherized patient, nature becomes an objective correlative to his own psychic topography. The mermaids in the chambers of the sea, which are down, contrast with the fashionable women at the tea party, which is up. That is, energy lurks below and vitiation reigns above. Although the strategy of the poem is to reduce the downward energy to escapism, the restraints do not wholly succeed, and we are left with a sense of contrast between the sea and tea worlds. This spatial projection follows the change initiated by the romantics, which the breathing earth and volcanic eruptions of *Prometheus Unbound* exemplify, particularly in the overthrow of Jupiter's court by subterranean forces. It is another example of Eliot's imagination opposing the anti-romantic thrust of his intellect.

A similar spatial contrast governs "Mr. Apollinax," one of the poems written at Oxford in 1915, which describes Bertrand Russell's descent on Harvard several years earlier. Again, the situation contrasts submarine vitality with an enervated tea party, and the diction plays off vibrant imagery against discursive precision. Besides invoking centaurs' hooves and sexuality in the shrubbery, the speaker describes Apollinax as a libidinous Proteus:

> He laughed like an irresponsible foetus.
> His laughter was submarine and profound
> Like the old man of the sea's
> Hidden under coral islands
> Where worried bodies of drowned men drift down in the
>   green silence,
> Dropping from fingers of surf.
>
>   (23)

The lines contain Eliot's familiar cluster of vitality from below, eroticism, and irresponsibility or immaturity. The subtheme of death by water which is not wholly death will reappear in *The Waste Land,* and that of a silence at the center in *Coriolan;* both began in "Prufrock." The war between Mr. Apollinax and Professor and Mrs. Cheetah takes place not directly but only in the mind of the speaker. His bathetic naturalism ("I remember a slice of lemon, and a bitten macaroon") neatly skewers his academic hosts, while his more fanciful mental action (first "thought" and then metaphors) seems to exalt the Priapean visitor. But Eliot has carefully defended against undue admiration for Apollinax and the forces he triggers. Comic exaggeration tinges the metaphors of vitality, and the polite background intensifies the discrepancy. This ambivalence culminates in nearly oxymoronic description of Apollinax's talk as at once "dry and passionate." Apollinax's head does not after all grin over a screen with seaweed in its hair; it smiles politely over taking of toast and tea. The true conflict exists in the mind of the speaker, who is the most interesting—perhaps the only—character in the poem. As in "Prufrock," both language and situation act out a psychological division in the narrator on which the poem itself imposes a framework of order. Only toward the end of the underwater rhapsody, with sudden intrusion of the drifting corpses of the drowned, does the language seem to break loose from its controlling frame in a sudden burst of autonomous power.

Eliot ended his first book, *Prufrock and Other Observations,* with his only poem to mention imagination directly, "La Figlia che Piange." Written about the same time as "Prufrock" and sharing its failed eroticism, the poem begins with the speaker constructing a farewell scene.[72] He speaks as stage director to actress, coaching the girl to stand, lean, weave, clasp, and fling. With the second stanza's shift into subjunctives, we realize that he has not been addressing her directly but has been arranging her in his mind. By switching from "I" to "we" he sets up the ambiguity in his role that marks the poem: we wonder whether he was onlooker or participant in the physical action. The disturbing final stanza explicitly presents the mental action that has been implicit all along:

> She turned away, but with the autumn weather
> Compelled my imagination many days,
> Many days and many hours:
> Her hair over her arms and her arms full of flowers.
> And I wonder how they should have been together!
> I should have lost a gesture and a pose.
> Sometimes these cogitations still amaze
> The troubled midnight and the noon's repose.
>
> (26)

The calculated tension of these lines cuts imagination down to little more than the size of fancy but utters an undersong of protest at the shearing. The opening statement seems to reduce the girl by putting her on a par with autumn weather as a compeller of imagination. Yet autumn suggests not merely dilettantish seasonal sensation but also death and loss, and this is a poem of loss in several ways. As his poetic cache of corpses shows, death compelled Eliot as strongly as it did the romantics. Ensuing realization that union of the lovers would have lost the speaker "a gesture and a pose" deflates the incident to insignificant titillation. Again, though, it plays against traditional romantic insistence on necessity of continued loss, which Yeats proclaimed in modern times. Finally comes implied identification of "imagination" with "cogitations," in accord with Eliot's critical tenets, which the last eight words obliquely question. For "amaze" reverses the Latinate abstraction of "cogitations" (not simply "thoughts"), while the last line transfers Eliot's spatial projection of downward energy and upward calm into temporal terms, troubled midnight and noon's repose. As with the drifting corpses of "Mr. Apollinax," the poem here seems to struggle against its ironic frame.

Comparison with Stevens and Yeats supports glossing imagination with the same meaning it carries in Eliot's criticism. Stevens' "Of Modern Poetry" exploits similar dramatic metaphors but both prescribes and offers at the end completed figures, like a woman dancing or combing, who reappear more fully elsewhere in his poetry. Yeats' "Among School Children" ends with twin images of dancer and great-rooted blossomer. Both poems discuss and project imaginative processes. In contrast, "La Figlia che Piange" dramatizes fanciful ones. Its quintuple directions to the girl in stanza 1 deal in fixities and definites; they select and arrange discrete actions, but lack that unity which animates Stevens' or Yeats' figures. Correspondingly, the verb sequence stand-lean-weave-clasp-fling moves from rest to action but cannot be read as a parable of imaginative activity in the manner of Stevens' rest-think-collect-are-forget-feel-say-make progression of "Final Soliloquy of the Interior Paramour," another analogue for Eliot's poem. Finally, the directions are deliberately sentimental, for Eliot regularly mocks creation of a dreamworld as a romantic corruption. Then, too, the poem trivializes rather than heightens creation of the action, reducing the girl at the end to "a gesture and a pose." The speaker remains in the situation of the poet of Stevens' *The Man with the Blue Guitar*, section II:

> I cannot bring a world quite round,
> Although I patch it as I can.
>
> I sing a hero's head, large eye
> And bearded bronze, but not a man.

So, too, does Eliot, not from sentimentality, but from fear of the forces that troubled his own midnights.

Mental conflict between imagination and association, like the linguistic war between imagery and discourse, continues in "Gerontion," the masterpiece of Eliot's second volume in the *Collected Poems* ordering. Depending on one's point of view, the poem either marks Eliot's closest approach to a Greater Romantic Lyric or *is* a Greater Romantic Lyric written by a man afraid of his own imagination. Like its romantic ancestors and modern cousins, "Gerontion" both begins and ends with the speaker placing himself in a specific setting, here an old house in a dry season. After initial description Gerontion neither engages imaginatively with an object in his surroundings like Keats' nightingale nor, until the end, creates an imaginative vision like Coleridge's animated harps. Instead, he develops a series of linked meditations on themes of renewal, perverted devotion, and history, continually circling back to his associational nexus, the house. He leaps in turn from his own "dull head among windy spaces" to ambiguous signs of religious renewal, perversions of devotion by internationalized enthusiasts of china, art, and clairvoyance, history, decay, and the final vision of destruction, all described in language at once erotic, religious, and historical. Only toward the end does his imagination erupt:

> What will the spider do,
> Suspend its operations, will the weevil
> Delay? De Bailhache, Fresca, Mrs. Cammel, whirled
> Beyond the circuit of the shuddering Bear
> In fractured atoms. Gull against the wind, in the
>   windy straits,
> Of Belle Isle, or running on the Horn,
> White feathers in the snow, the Gulf claims. . . .
>
>   (31)

These lines, which carry the customary violent content of many of Eliot's most imaginative passages, do not depend on the finite, disparate links of the other sections, for which their polysemous meanings are a linguistic analogue, but rather on direct assertion of imaginative power. But the poem does not demand this sudden transformation of its creeping corruption into the nearly apocalyptic image of the fractured atoms of De Bailhache, Fresca, and Mrs. Cammel whirled beyond the ambiguously shuddering bear. Nor does it demand the lovely image of the gull against the wind, which recalls Yeats' sea-borne bird balanced on the air at the end of "On a Political Prisoner." The poem does not demand these achievements because Gerontion's mental processes do not: he has progressed by chance associational links, rather than by ordered preparation for vision. Although the passage culminates the poem by relation to theme and diction, it does not do so by organic role in developing mental action. It is discontinuous with its psychological context. Partly because of that, it has no effect on Gerontion except to exhaust him. As with "Prufrock," the very end ("Tenants of the house,/ Thoughts of a dry brain in a dry season") undercuts the imaginative vision, whose dangerous content signals its dangerous origin. Unlike the speakers of early and late Greater Romantic Lyrics, Gerontion ends where he began. The vision makes no difference to him.

Hugh Kenner has written the best account of this poem and its ending. I co-opt it here partly in admiration, partly to show a congruity in observation if not in conclusion between my arguments and the best of orthodox Eliot scholarship, and partly to disagree with one aspect of Kenner's provocative interpretation. His terminology here particularly suits the present argument:

> The poem ends with a plausible bridge into the world where images have a Lockean patness and applicability:
>
> > Tenants of the house,
> > Thoughts of a dry brain in a dry season.
>
> This has a look of exegetic universality, clearing up everything, resolving all, and restoring us to daylight. Actually it is an index of the speaker's failed imagination, at the furthest extreme from his earlier polysemous intensity. He begins to talk what we are accustomed to regard as sense only at the instant when he is too fatigued to hang onto the rich vision any longer.[73]

This is right: the lines do have a Lockean quality signaling failed imagination. They do not, however, contrast with the polysemous passages of the body of the poem, but with the imaginative section immediately preceding them. For the polysemous passages display highly charged fancy rather than imagination. Consider the fine "After such knowledge, what forgiveness" sequence. It applies to historical, religious, and sexual experience, not just in series but simultaneously. "Knowledge," for example, carries Biblical, sexual, and historical applications, in addition to referring directly to Gerontion's obsession with self-knowledge. But multiple associations do not constitute imaginative fusion. Nor are signs symbols, and whatever else "the wrath-bearing tree" is in the poem, we do not believe it is also a tree. The many-leveled associative passages represent brilliant tours de force, but they remain semantic Rosetta stones.

The manipulation of polysemous meaning both follows romantic convention and marks an important stage toward Eliot's attempted correction of it. As we have seen, the romantics sought a common language for all forms of experience. Eliot's combination in "Gerontion" of religious, sexual, and historical significance recalls similar multiplicities in *The Marriage of Heaven and Hell* or *Prometheus Unbound*. Romantic strategy often displaced religious terminology to secular experience. That application Eliot increasingly sought to reverse after his conversion, in accord with his conviction that romanticism tried to substitute poetry for religion.

"Gerontion" forms a halfway house in Eliot's progress: although religious meanings do not dominate the others, they have become increasingly important in their own right, and they grow steadily more so in his poetry, first in the ecumenical constructions of *The Waste Land* and then in his specifically Christian verse.

Failure to integrate the imaginative outburst into a developing pattern of mental action provides a clue to the peculiar quality of both Prufrock and Gerontion as speakers. Hugh Kenner again has suggestively labeled both personae "a zone of consciousness."[74] Although I think he takes Eliotic impersonality at face value and relies too heavily on Bradley's metaphysics, the notion can be expanded differently. Prufrock and Gerontion fit the spatial metaphor of a zone because the chronological progression of their mental actions does not matter. While the poems progress and develop, the speakers' mental actions do not: they simply change, and form a sequence but not a consequence. In "Frost at Midnight" or "Among School Children" the order of the actions matters: first description, next memory, and then either future projection or present vision. This is not the case with Eliot's two speakers. They progress by associative links arranged serially but not causally, until imagination arbitrarily and briefly erupts; but the sequence of links does not cause the eruption, which need not have occurred at just that place. Further, the eruption has no effect on the speakers, who remain as they were before. They are failed visionaries.

The isolated imaginative eruptions rework Browning and Pater's cult of the privileged moment.[75] For an instant the speaker breaks through into intensity; to invoke a third analogue Eliot would have hated, the persona's buried life surfaces. These moments come gratuitously, but as interruptions of associative sequences rather than as consequences of negative capability. In regard to the speaker, they come as chance epiphanies, having nothing to do with his ordinary self. For a moment his imagination autonomously asserts itself against a web of Lockean restraints. But what are they for Eliot? Both his prose and the poems themselves suggest that they are something quite similar, a revolt of imagination at the constraints of intellect, which to Eliot appeared as an upheaval of violent and irrational forces. He inserts them into a restraining framework, and even embodies them in disciplined form, but he does not integrate them into a developing mental process. Eliot's radical contribution to the tradition of the ecstatic moment is fear, resulting in defense.

"Gerontion" invites comparison with Yeats' "An Acre of Grass," in which another old man ruminates in an old house at life's end. Besides sharing similar speakers and settings, both poems begin with books, juxtapose bodily decrepitude to need for renewal, move from the mill of the mind to imaginative exertion, pern on the problem of knowledge, invoke Renaissance foils, and end on images of upward flight contrasting with the original, stationary position of the speaker; furthermore, both evince a close relation between poet and persona. Yet they offer contrasting patterns of mental action, for "An Acre of Grass" portrays imagination's triumph and "Gerontion" its failure. Yeats accepts imagination as a violence from within and can pray for "frenzy." As his old man's prayer progresses, it acts out its own request, moving the poem from initial quiet through growing excitation to the final, successful image of the old man's eagle mind overcoming both nature ("pierce the clouds") and mortality ("shake the dead in their shrouds"). In contrast, Eliot fears imagination's interior violence, and the last thing he prayed for was to be reborn as Blake; during his whole career he struggles to be reborn as an anti-Blake. His poem therefore ends with defeat: Gerontion's mental actions lack the teleological progression of Yeats' old man's, and after a final flare of imagination he sinks back into his Lockean associationism, into what Yeats calls "the mill of the mind." Eliot's commentators often liken his early poetry to a journey through Hell, but for all Eliot's overt intentions, his nether regions belong as much to Ulro as to Christian cartography.

Most of the poems accompanying "Gerontion" in the 1920 volume display an increase in overt technical order. Their rhymed quatrains extend the subtle discipline of "Prufrock" and "Gerontion" to more obvious formal arrangement. Their impetus came partly from a joint decision by Eliot and Pound to combat growing "floppiness" engendered in English verse by lesser imitators of their own early success. As Pound in 1932 recalled their resolve:

> That is to say, at a particular date in a particular room, two authors, neither engaged in picking the other's pocket, decided that the dilutation of *vers libre*, Amygism, Lee Masterism, general floppiness had gone too far and that some counter-current must be set going. Parallel situation centuries ago in China. Remedy prescribed 'Emaux et Camées' (or the Bay State Hymn Book). Rhyme and regular strophes.
>
> Results: Poems in Mr. Eliot's *second* volume, not contained in his first [(]'Prufrock' Egoist, 1917), also 'H. S. Mauberley.'
> Divergence later.[76]

Of the seven resultant poems in quatrains, "Sweeney Erect" (1919) relates most closely to romanticism, for its description of the epileptic woman draws on Shelley's rendering of Rousseau in his last major work, *The Triumph of Life*.[77] Eliot quoted the Shelleyan passage twice in his prose, once the seven pertinent lines alone and once at greater length.[78] He introduced the longer citation in 1950 by confirming that it "made an indelible impression upon me over forty-five years ago." With the passage anticipating "Sweeney Erect" italicized, the section that impressed Eliot so indelibly reads:

Struck to the heart by this sad pageantry,
Half to myself I said—"And what is this?
Whose shape is that within the car? and why—"

I would have added—"is all here amiss?"
But a voice answered—"Life!" I turned, and knew
(O Heaven, have mercy on such wretchedness!)

That what I thought was an old root which grew
To strange distortion out of the hill side,
Was indeed one of those deluded crew,

And that the grass, which methought hung so wide
And white, was but his thin discoloured hair,
And that the holes he vainly sought to hide,

Were or had been eyes:—"If thou canst, forbear
To join the dance, which I had well forborne!",
Said the grim Feature (of my thought aware).

"I will unfold that which to this deep scorn
Led me and my companions, and relate
The progress of the pageant since the morn;

If thirst of knowledge shall not then abate,
Follow it thou even to the night, but I
Am weary."—Then like one who with the weight

Of his own words is staggered, wearily
He paused; and ere he could resume, I cried:
"First, who art thou?"—"Before thy memory,

I feared, loved, hated, suffered, did and died,
And if the spark with which Heaven lit my spirit
Had been with purer nutriment supplied,

Corruption would not now thus much inherit
Of what was once Rousseau,—nor this disguise
Stain that which ought to have disdained to wear it. . . ."[79]

141

Eliot condenses the grisly images of distorted root, withered hair, and holes for eyes into the fourth stanza of his own poem on a deluded crew:

> This withered root of knots of hair
> Slitted below and gashed with eyes,
> This oval O cropped out with teeth:
> The sickle motion from the thighs

and continues:

> Jackknifes upward at the knees
> Then straightens out from heel to hip
> Pushing the framework of the bed
> And clawing at the pillow slip.
>
> (34)

These passages sound contrasting tones in their critiques of natural man. In Shelley's poem Rousseau functions as expounder and guide, a sort of Virgil to Shelley's Dante, explaining the meaning of Life's triumphal progress and her thronging captives. Himself the prophet of nature, he is reduced here to the condition of natural man, fit companion for Blake's Nebuchadnezzar and a dehumanized part of the nature he once celebrated. Yet for all the horror of Rousseau's degeneration, Shelley's poem at least implies compassion for his fallen state. No such sympathy permeates the description in "Sweeney Erect," or, for that matter, analogous ones throughout Eliot's poetry. The speaking voice combines anger and loathing in a savage intensity of barely contained violence. Reductions to both vegetable ("root") and animal ("clawing") nature combine with emphasis on isolated actions and features to encourage us to view the epileptic woman as an object rather than a human being. Only Doris' late entrance with smelling salts and neat brandy injects a response in any way humane. That is, the speaker's attitude actually complements in its inhumanity the attitudes of Sweeney, the ladies of the corridor, and Mrs. Turner, although his outright disgust contrasts with their more detached and self-serving reactions. This radical hatred of the natural human condition, often mingled with social disdain, intrudes often in Eliot's poetry, whether he sneers at "the damp souls of housemaids" (19), the human "crawling bugs" of a draft of *The Waste Land*,[80] or "men and bits of paper" in *Burnt Norton* (179). It plays ironically against the passage's humanistic source, and the discrepancy constitutes one of the true differences between the two poets.

Undoubtedly, Shelley's critique of Rousseau delighted Eliot and helped him to conclude that this late work showed signs of growing maturity in the previously adolescent sensibility of its author. Eliot had always seen Rousseau as the great original of romantic failings and criticized him for betraying reason, discipline, and religion to emotion, impulse, and nature. "Sweeney Erect" coincides with those charges. Yet, typically, Shelley analyzes the problem of Rousseau's failure more complexly than Eliot. For Eliot's commendation of his Shelleyan source's "very interesting comment on Rousseau" suggests that he took Rousseau's explanation at face value. Rousseau traces his corruption to lack of a "purer nutriment" (presumably purer than nature and his own natural desires) for "the spark with which Heaven lit my spirit." This would accord both with Eliot's early New Humanism and his later religious outlook. But it does not accord with the remainder of *The Triumph of Life*. Rousseau later remarks of his fall, "Why this should be, my mind can compass not,"[81] for one of the poem's subtlest ironies is Rousseau's continuing incomprehension of his error and false attempt at explanation. His personal narrative suggests that his mistake lay in seeking absolute vision directly rather than indirectly through created things. Shelley's fine elaboration of that distinction reveals his skeptical honesty at its strongest and makes an attractive contrast to the credulous Eliot. One of the deepest perversions in modern critical adoption of Eliot's own contrast between Eliotic maturity and Shelleyan adolescence is its neat reversal of the truth.

Mental action in the poem shows Eliot's characteristic tension when confronting the twin themes of sexuality and creative power. The first two quatrains may have a different speaker from the main text, perhaps a figure like Aspatia in *The Maid's Tragedy*. At any rate, their elevated rhetoric contrasts with later diction, while the theatrical metaphors of "La Figlia che Piange" here find analogues in the fine arts ("Paint me . . ." and "Display me . . ."). The scene called for also suggests the posed artificiality of the earlier poem, in contrast to the sordid realism that follows. In the lines deriving from Shelley, the speaker erupts in one of Eliot's powerful unions of violent content and imaginative expression. It is as though a geyser forced its way up, impelled by irresistible subterranean forces, and the speaker's tone nearly escapes his control. The moment passes, however, and the remaining six stanzas consist of tight, understated observation, without the figurative language inspired by the epileptic. Eliot fields his familiar array of restraints against a moment of violent imagination and a subject that prompted it.

Progressive mythologizing of speakers and suggestions of their multiplicity culminate in *The Waste Land* (1922). Prufrock seems a zone of consciousness of a single character, albeit one split into two parts. Gerontion appears a more ambiguous persona—he may be just an old man, but like his house he disconcertingly shades off into the mind of Europe. "Sweeney Erect" changes tone so abruptly that it suggests two speakers. *The Waste Land* exponentializes these complexities. Its principal speaker, Tiresias, comes directly from mythology and unites in his bisexuality both masculine and feminine voices in the poem, as well as male and female characters. He opens up possibilities in prophetic stance that Eliot had previously avoided, but Eliot carefully restricts his persona's powers to observation rather than revelation, just as he restricts the Cumaean sybil to passive suffering. Although Eliot cobbled up the anthropological notes partly to meet a publisher's need for more pages, unwittingly misdirecting future scholarly energy, he included one prolonged comment on his own technique:

> Tiresias, although a mere spectator and not indeed a "character", is yet the most important personage in the poem, uniting all the rest. Just as the one-eyed merchant, seller of currants, melts into the Phoenician Sailor, and the latter is not wholly distinct from Ferdinand Prince of Naples, so all the women are one woman, and the two sexes meet in Tiresias. What Tiresias *sees*, in fact, is the substance of the poem. (72)

Partly a desperate attempt to mitigate the confusion of speakers left after Pound's editorial efforts, Eliot's statement hints at a fundamental way of encountering his poem. If the individual speakers melt into separate male and female groups that unite in the one mind of Tiresias, and if what Tiresias sees is the substance of the poem, then how he reacts *is* the poem. Seen in this way, *The Waste Land* becomes the mental actions of a presiding, perceiving mind of whom the individual speakers form parts. C. K. Stead has written in a different context: " 'The Waste Land' is composed of a series of projections of 'states of feeling', having no fixed centre but their common origin in the depths of one man's mind. . . . The poem is a representation, not of the visible world, but of a state of mind."[82] As Stead makes clear, this approach preserves us from thinking of the poem as a discourse from which we should abstract a system of ideas, which Eliot's critics often take to be asserted qualifications. Stead's understandable eagerness to focus on projection rather than material, however, leads him here to reject Eliot's notion of links in a chain. This we need not abandon, for the associational links of the speakers' mental actions complement the semantic links of the material.

This kind of modern poetry derives from romantic psychodramas, like Blake's *Four Zoas* or Shelley's *Prometheus Unbound*. The romantic poems, too, consist of actions in a single mind, whether Albion's or Prometheus', of which the separate personages form parts. Such division drives the structure into myth, both to develop a vocabulary for presenting intricate psychological phenomena and as defense against vision dropping into allegory. Further, like *The Waste Land* such poems do not advance chronologically. Much of the action takes place simultaneously —nearly all of *Prometheus Unbound*, for example, occurs in the moment that Prometheus retracts his own curse on Jupiter. Simultaneity makes all three poems amenable to notions of spatial form—ideally, we apprehend all their parts at the same time. Finally, these psychodramas incorporate both past and present historical material. Just as Blake and Shelley can include both Biblical events and the French Revolution, so can Eliot coordinate both Augustine's life and World War I. Like Prometheus, Tiresias is tortured by his vision of human suffering.

Psychodramas tend to be quest poems. By taking consciousness as subject, they inevitably run into the inadequacy of current human sensibility. Hence, they turn on notions of rebirth or apocalypse, replacement of the old, fallen consciousness with a new risen one. Just here Eliot's poem diverges from quest analogues. These present successful apocalypse in which new consciousness succeeds the old. *The Waste Land* does not, although it allows for hope. Consequently, the poem becomes an exploration of current consciousness, whether of society as a whole if we think of Marie, Madame Sosostris, and the other speakers, or of a collective representation of maximal awareness if we think of Tiresias. Although references to quests of the grail knights, fisher king, and others riddle the poem, they nowhere reach conclusion. Moreover, they do not even reach execution. This lack separates *The Waste Land* from romantic poems even of failed quests, like *Alastor*. In *Alastor* the hero actively pursues his quest. Even Blake's cyclic *Mental Traveller* shows progression. Not so *The Waste Land*, which is a static poem in that the material progresses but the mental action does not. Hence, the emotion of the mental actors, the perceivers, rather than the physical ones, the perceived, is passive suffering, which Yeats once tried to read from the ranks of acceptable poetic subjects.[83] He did so because purely passive suffering contradicts the living romanticism within which he stood. Contrary to hostile interpreters, his objection centered on passivity, not suffering, which blocked the decisive mental action of romantic tradition. By *The Waste Land* Eliot had not yet found the active conception of suffering that Christianity later opened to him,[84] and absence of such dynamism constitutes the true anti-romanticism of the poem.

The Waste Land develops its twin themes of personal and cultural disorder, in which need for rebirth unites dominant sexual and religious motifs, without corresponding mental progress in the speakers (or speaker, to the extent that they all merge in Tiresias). "The Burial of the Dead" moves from Marie in the mountains to a prophetic voice under the red desert rock back to *Tristan and Isolde* and the hyacinth girl, on to Madame Sosostris' Tarot and horoscopes, and concludes with the crowd in the unreal city. The splendid links between these sections, and intricate connections within each, advance theme but not mental action: the limited consciousness of individual speakers (this section alone uses Marie, her cousin, the desert prophet, a sailor from *Tristan*, the hyacinth girl, Madame Sosostris, and Stetson's friend) or the presiding consciousness of Tiresias do not develop but simply succeed each other in accord with thematic links in the material and associative ones in its treatment, and the more they change the more they remain the same. The same process governs "A Game of Chess" and "The Fire Sermon," while the brief "Death by Water" has only one speaker but bears a similar relation to the rest of the poem. Only the final "What the Thunder Said" allows a meaningful progression, but it follows the abortive pattern of "Prufrock" and "Gerontion." The poem's nearest approach to triumph, the impressive give-sympathize-control section, provokes a final collapse back into dissociation. While the unity created in its materials makes the poem a whole, the continued fragmentation of its speakers and passivity of Tiresias make it an abortive psychodrama: it presents an anatomy rather than transformation of fallen consciousness.

The poem locates its scanty regenerative forces downward and within, in accord with post-romantic spatialization of imagery and its own pervasive invocation of vegetation mythology. But we do not need Asian arcana to read the first seven lines:

April is the cruellest month, breeding
Lilacs out of the dead land, mixing
Memory and desire, stirring
Dull roots with spring rain.
Winter kept us warm, covering
Earth in forgetful snow, feeding
A little life with dried tubers.

(53)

Impelled by vigorous participles enacting theme by engendering new syntactic structures at the death of each line, the passage follows Eliot's normal conception of energy as subterranean, a force from below.[85] He characteristically underlines the painfulness of its power by making April the cruelest month, with its agonies of rebirth. Even more important, however, the imagery reduces the vitality below ("feeding/ A little life with dried tubers") in contrast to the rhapsodic though doomed undersea world of Prufrock. The insistence on rain from above initiates one crux of the poem: the wasteland cannot regenerate itself but depends on external forces from above for salvation. The implications of this condition for the wasteland taken as a state of mind point to need for regeneration from outside the psyche. The whole poem pleads for rain, for rejuvenation of wasted powers within by a quickening force from without. The opening lines begin a major train of imagery in the poem, including the balancing of their Christian connotations by the Neoplatonic nuances of those describing Phlebas the Phoenician. Just as Asia in *Prometheus Unbound* "passed Age's icy caves,/ And Manhood's dark and tossing waves,/ And Youth's smooth ocean,"[86] so has Phlebas "passed the stages of his age and youth/ Entering the whirlpool." (65) But Shelley accepted the subterranean forces that Eliot both spurned and craved.

His fear of downward energy flickers through his prose. R. P. Blackmur has identified the abyss as one of Eliot's obsessive images.[87] Energy lay below, but it was dangerous; it could erupt at any moment and shatter the structures of order. We have already noticed this in his critiques of romanticism and in his poetry. Likewise, in an essay written just before most of *The Waste Land*, Eliot spoke of Jacobean playwrights whose "words have often a network of tentacular roots reaching down to the deepest terrors and desires." (*SE*135) So, too, do those of Eliot's poem. He used a line that also appears in *The Waste Land* to gloss Coleridge's alleged failure in "Kubla Khan": "The imagery of that fragment, certainly, whatever its origins in Coleridge's reading, sank to the

147

depths of Coleridge's feeling, was saturated, transformed there—'those are pearls that were his eyes'—and brought up into daylight again." (*UPUC* 146) Bringing to daylight was also the function of the successful objective correlative—to "drag to light, contemplate, or manipulate into art." (*SW* 100) For Eliot, subterranean forces most often consist of emotions and feelings.

Fear of forces downward and within in both Eliot's poetry and prose suggests why *The Waste Land* shuns the regeneration of romantic psychodrama and implicitly looks toward an external cure. In romantic poems imagination creates interior apocalypse, which transforms the perceived world as well as the perceiving psyche. But imagination is just what Eliot feared. He identified it with autochthonous energies and emotions from within, which demanded structures of restraint; he could conceive imagination as rage, but not as rage for order. Consequently, his speakers lack means of self-transformation. Their mental passivity denies the very power that would revitalize and reintegrate them. Likewise, the poem itself excludes that power. Yet its themes obsessively return to the sexual drives Eliot associated with romanticism and the forces of his own psyche. There are no powers of interior regeneration in the poem, although there are innumerable defenses against the pain of obsessive consciousness. The spring rain reawakening the dried tubers with their little life can come only from without. This external salvation fits the situation of Eliot himself as well as of his creations, and he would shortly find an external redemptive power in Christianity.

Recent publication of both the *Waste Land* manuscripts and pertinent letters allows a rare biographical glimpse into Eliot's development and infuses considerable poignancy into the persona who sets fragments against his ruin at the end of the poem. Eliot both drafted his great work in emotional derangement and himself could not make order out of it. In one of the apparently milder letters, written to Richard Aldington from Margate in 1921 ("On Margate Sands./ I can connect/ Nothing with nothing" [64]) he attributed his " 'nerves' . . . not to overwork but to an aboulie and emotional derangement which has been a lifelong affliction."[88] Intolerable strains in his personal circumstances combined with that lifelong nemesis to drive his mind to the end of its tether, although characteristically Eliot sought to assign the disease to his emotions. "Nothing wrong with my mind," he continued to Aldington. As he had before, Eliot turned to poetry as defense and drafted most of *The Waste Land* during the period at Margate and then Lausanne ("this decayed hole among the mountains" [68]).

These biographical revelations put the references to madness throughout the poem in new perspective, and charge with new intensity the pervasive impression of a sensibility fighting to keep its balance. They also prompt second thoughts about Eliot's vaunted impersonality. Like his admired Samuel Johnson, he constantly strove to hold forces of mental darkness at arm's length, and the precarious struggle gives his overtly ordered style its underlying dynamism.

But the manuscripts reveal that this time Eliot's resources for order failed. Before Pound's efforts, the poem was a chaotic, sprawling mass, by turns brilliant and pathetic, and with nothing like its eventual coherence. The drafts show Eliot's pervasive attempt to transvalue in modern guise eighteenth-century strategies for city poems on London played off against Latin ones on Rome,[89] and they also show its failure. Mostly by excision, Pound extracted from the inchoate draft an ordered poem. Lack of developing mental action in Eliot's scheme eased Pound's practice of his own ideogrammic method on his friend's work. He could omit and juxtapose at will, following organizational principles dependent on the material rather than dynamically developing consciousness, for the natural, wakeful life of a Poundian or Eliotic ego is a perceiving. The same strategy enabled Eliot to build his poems by accretion of separate elements over long periods of time. Just as *The Waste Land* incorporated material composed at diverse intervals, so had "Prufrock." Pound had earlier tried to remove the Hamlet passage from that poem but had told Harriet Monroe regretfully that "it is an early and cherished bit and T. E. won't give it up."[90] Sporadic composition of discrete passages favored lack of progressively developing mental action and promoted thematic links between sections as a chief system of organization. Only in forming *The Waste Land* Eliot could no longer complete his own structures of order, but relied on Pound to salvage them from fragments shored against his ruin. To adapt Yeats' phrase for the "new naturalism" of Pound's *Cantos* and Joyce's *Anna Livia Plurabella*, Eliot was a man helpless before the contents of his own mind.

Eliot's response to feared forces within himself by denial, restraint, and projection onto others led to his many anti-Semitic passages, among them some in the *Waste Land* manuscripts. Contrary to his more ardent supporters' attempt to explain his hostility away or more honest students' tendency to dismiss its manifestations as regrettable and even mild lapses, they formed an organic part of his sensibility, which incorrigibly needed external de-

149

mons. Besides nasty manuscript material ("Graves' Disease in a dead jew's eyes"[91]), we have the Jewish slumlord in "Gerontion" (just barely justifiable to determined exegetes because partly identifiable with Christ), the systematic disgust of "Burbank with a Baedeker: Bleistein with a Cigar," and a host of references to Rabinovitz, Klipstein, Krumpacker, and the rest. For Eliot, Jews aroused persistently negative responses. Additionally, he thought that introduction of Jewish names was somehow funny and could be used to show Western degeneration ("She entertains Sir Ferdinand/ Klein" [33]). After his conversion, these slurs reach their nadir in his famous remark at a public lecture shortly after Hitler's rise to power that because of need for cultural homogeneity "reasons of race and religion combine to make any large number of free-thinking Jews undesirable." (ASG 20) Just as the romantics symbolized deviation from Latin tradition, so did Jews represent refusal of Christian orthodoxy.[92] A man anxious to deny forces within himself has an insatiable need of scapegoats, and Eliot maintained one of the most plentifully stocked demonologies of modern times. Given Eliot's occasional denials of anti-Semitism, partly on grounds that such prejudice constituted a sin in the eyes of the Church,[93] one wonders what he thought anti-Semitism was.

Themes and tensions of the decade culminating in *The Waste Land* dominate the poems published between 1925 and 1930, the years surrounding Eliot's confirmation in the Church of England in 1927. Far from a discontinuity, his Christian poetry finds what will suffice the growing needs of his poetic career. The notion of two states of being, implicit since "Prufrock," finds full expression in "The Hollow Men," while *The Waste Land*'s themes of death and rebirth appear everywhere, as in *Ash Wednesday* or "Journey of the Magi." Christianity answered the need for a force without to combat chaos within, providing both social orthodoxy and individual grace. It also transformed many of Eliot's continuing poetic obsessions. His vision of a woman at the top of stairs signified an upward but enervated order in "Prufrock" or "The *Boston Evening Transcript*" and a creation of artificial fancy in "La Figlia che Piange." By *Ash Wednesday* the image becomes a climb by renunciation to a Beatrice-like figure of grace, and the order she represents vitalizes rather than vitiates. Ascent remains a mental quest, however, in which the persona mounts by "steps of the mind." (89)

Eliot's Christianity provided a new frame for his repudiation of nature. Although the rejection parallels those of Blake and Yeats, its motivation does not. The crucial (and beautiful) passage occurs near the end of *Ash Wednesday:*

> And the lost heart stiffens and rejoices
> In the lost lilac and the lost sea voices
> And the weak spirit quickens to rebel
> For the bent golden-rod and the lost sea smell
> Quickens to recover
> The cry of quail and the whirling plover
> And the blind eye creates
> The empty forms between the ivory gates
> And smell renews the salt savour of the sandy earth.
>
> (94)

Having extinguished his own will to find peace in God's, the poet discovers that nature threatens to revive it by double appeal to his emotions ("heart") and spirit. The flowers, and sound and smell of the sea, try to reattach him to the world. But love of created things does not lead the soul to God in Eliot's theology. He does "not wish to wish these things" because they disrupt the spiritual discipline that seeks to resolve his old problem of unmanageable inner drives by turning his volcanic core into a vacuum to be filled by God. Should he succumb instead, he will return artistically to the spiritual state of a "blind eye" creating the delusive forms of the ivory gates, whose association with false dreams in the sixth book of *The Aeneid* makes them fit symbol of poetic vision. These claims reverse those of Blake or Yeats. To Eliot, both those poets create empty forms of delusion. To Blake, Eliot would hypostatize human mental creations and deny imagination in the name of mystery. To Yeats, Eliot would forsake the necessary skepticism and attachment to the world of the visionary poet at his strongest. Eliot rejects nature because he fears it will reawaken his interior powers, Blake and Yeats because it might overcome them. Both would wish Eliot gone, although Yeats might bestow blessings on his head.

Eliot's first poem after his official conversion, "The Journey of the Magi" (1927), suggests that Christianity continued as much as it inaugurated in his poetic career. Written from within Christian tradition, the poem depends on our knowing more than the speaker—for example, he finds "no information" (100) in a landscape crying out for symbolic interpretation.[94] Perhaps under the pressure of mass appeal (the poem was Eliot's first contribution to the most distinguished series of Christmas cards in British literary history), Eliot makes more concessions to narrative plot than ever before. Yet in theme and form the poem belongs to his characteristic concerns. Like "Prufrock" and "Gerontion," "The Journey of the Magi" is a dramatic monologue presenting another of Eliot's failed questers. Its themes of death, rebirth, and contrasting spiritual worlds all develop earlier tendencies. Most important of all, the poem still avoids imaginative mental action: it relies almost wholly on the speaker's memory, although it partly substitutes narrative for associational order. Its tripartite structure, marked by breaks in spacing, could easily have become a Greater Romantic Lyric in which the speaker leads up to a moment of vision, followed by evaluation of it. Instead, Eliot presents another consciousness inadequate to such demands. Before he attempted direct, devotional poetry, continued adherence to failed vision as theme allowed him to keep his defenses in order.

Although the poem falls within romantic parameters, its distance from imaginative mental action may be gauged by comparing it to Yeats' development of the same subject in his more brief "The Magi" (1913). Of course, some differences derive from Yeats' historic stance outside the Christian tradition and his view of the birth as inaugural only of a new cycle rather than of absolute change. But, more important, Yeats sees the Magi as images of continuing, passionate (in his sense) questing rather than of abortive consciousness. This difference manifests itself in the mental action. Eliot's speaker, himself a Magus, relies on memory, narrative association, and discourse. In contrast, Yeats' speaker conjures up the Magi in "the mind's eye" and thus proves himself their equal in imaginative quest. If Eliot's poem is not a Greater Romantic Lyric because it lacks a moment of vision, Yeats' is not solely because it lacks opening description and final evaluation; it is wholly vision.

The true innovation of Eliot's poem lies in its syntactic structure, which opened a new line of poetic organization for him. The initial quotation from Lancelot Andrewes has made citation of a passage from Eliot's essay on that bishop, published the previous year, de rigueur in commentaries on the poem. My argument causes me here to revalue the importance of this famous description of Andrewes' style, which Eliot lifted from F. E. Brightman:

'But the structure is not merely an external scheme or framework: the internal structure is as close as the external. Andrewes develops an idea he has in his mind: every line tells and adds something. He does not expatiate, but moves forward: if he repeats, it is because the repetition has a real force of expression; if he accumulates, each new word or phrase represents a new development, a substantive addition to what he is saying. He assimilates his material and advances by means of it. His quotation is not decoration or irrelevance, but the matter in which he expresses what he wants to say. His single thoughts are no doubt often suggested by the words he borrows, but the thoughts are made his own, and the constructive force, the fire that fuses them, is his own. And this internal, progressive, often poetic structure is marked outwardly.' (*SE* 303)

Although Eliot had always fitted syntax and style to mental contours, the technique described here allows for more continuous development, both in place of abrupt juxtapositions of earlier poems and even within individual sections. It functions only imperfectly in "Journey of the Magi" and "A Song for Simeon," which, as Bergonzi has observed, tend to "read like summaries of experience rather than enactments of it."[95] From that pair onward, Eliot's major poems increasingly advance in the cumulative manner prescribed in the Andrewes essay, in which ordered, progressive development replaces associational concatenation. Commentators have not stressed, however, that the passage applies to expression of an idea already present in the writer's mind and to only a limited range of mental actions—those concerned with thoughts. It thus forms a new bulwark against eruption of violent forces in the creative process itself and ensures expression only of what was known already to the ego. Further, the same restrictions affect persona as well as poet—the poem will project only mental actions belonging to ordered control. Of course, if Eliot adhered exclusively to this program, he would kill himself as poet. Just at this point the remarks gain interest: they sketch a perfect compositional theory for a poet anxious to snare imaginative eruption in structures of order but unable or unwilling to integrate it in developing mental action of the whole psyche's powers. Resultant poems thus move forward in progressive systole and diastole of discursive structures, waiting for imagination to interrupt. When it does, its brief upheaval is automatically caught in a context of restraint. This describes what happens in the great poem that principally occupied Eliot for the last decade of his career as poet.

Four Quartets demonstrates the suitability of both stylistic and theological Anglican tradition to give Eliot's perennial war between internal drives and external restraints its final formulation. At the same time, it both stands in one line of romantic tradition and perches on the abyss that separated Eliot from his predecessors. Its subject, systematic imagery, polysemous meanings, and spatialization of reality follow romantic norms, while its phrasing and forms often recall specific romantic works. Yet reversal of earlier displacements of religious terminology to secular terms heralds a swerve from romantic tradition, in which grace replaces imagination. This substitution transvalues many of the post-romantic terms Eliot brought to his predicament and drives the poem into a series of conflicts, which reveal themselves as much in what the poem does as in what it overtly says. The principles of the essay on Andrewes inspire the poem's forces for stylistic order, as Christian mythology does its thematic unity and the five-part scheme of *The Waste Land* its formal coherence, but many of the best moments come when Eliot's renegade poetic imagination opposes or transfigures those powers. *Four Quartets* is romantic against the grain.

In projecting mental development as overt subject of a long, first-person poem, *Four Quartets* inevitably recalls *The Prelude*. Both depend heavily on memory and significant moments, assert that ordinary experience can offer revelation if approached in proper receptivity but that "the dreary intercourse of daily life" can block it, insist on duty or observance and discipline as restraining forces, exploit similar techniques (like temporal dislocation), and combine aesthetic, political, psychological, and religious preoccupations.[96] Yet Eliot's "moments" differ from Wordsworth's "spots of time," although both urge a "lifetime burning in every moment." (189) Wordsworth's spots of time "renovate," "nourish," and "repair"[97] our minds by showing mental domination over sense and reminding us to look through the eye rather than with it. They strengthen us for our existence in time. In contrast, Eliot's moments catapult us out of time; our remembering them for any purpose but conquest of chronos shows that we defeatedly remain in time (178) and, likely, "had the experience but missed the meaning." (194) His religious frame takes him as much beyond Wordsworth's 1850 text as that version did beyond its 1805 predecessor; for Eliot, Wordsworth's spots of time still bind us to life in chronos rather than liberate us into kairos, and still allow too much scope for independent human imagination. In this respect *Four Quartets* reads like a third version of *The Prelude*, in which imaginative power is further transferred back to God. It also reads like a coda rather than a prelude to the growth of a poet's mind.

That mind unfolds itself in the multiple meanings and systematic patterns of imagery familiar in romantic poetry but differing from their other near-analogues in medieval practice by allowing the poem greater scope to fix the meaning of its own symbols, even when they come from traditional sources. Except for pervasive echoes of Eden and obvious Christian significance in rose and dove, the poem itself creates the importance of its patterned birds and flowers, while it makes its own use of conventions like the four elements and even a Dantesque pervasiveness of light. Polysemous passages support the organized imagery. One of the poem's most successful figures, the dance, begins by exploiting its traditional applications to marriage (in diction derived from Sir Thomas Eliot's *The Governour* [183]), turns into an image of religious purification (205), and metamorphoses finally into an emblem of successful poetic composition:

> (where every word is at home,
> Taking its place to support the others,
> The word neither diffident nor ostentatious,
> An easy commerce of the old and the new,
> The common word exact without vulgarity,
> The formal word precise but not pedantic,
> The complete consort dancing together). . . .
> (207-8)

These kinds of patterns and multiplicities do not prove the poem "romantic"; rather, they simply suggest that it is a post-romantic poem many of whose devices follow directions prescribed by romantic modification of traditional poetic strategies.

Four Quartets spatializes reality in terms of movements and forces downward and within. Even the dove—at once spirit and warplane—appears as "descending." (207) Most important among inner places is "the still point of the turning world" (177), which we are not to call fixity but which negates all movement. The still point lies within the world, within time, and within ourselves, and is a repository of light. Upon it depends successful dance. But forces of darkness and chaos also lie within, and they can disrupt the dance. Eliot finds a symbol for them in the brown river of *The Dry Salvages*, which is both "destroyer, reminder/ Of what men choose to forget" and "within us." (191) One problem of the poem is to preclude dominance by these darker powers by preparing for fusion of "spheres of existence" into imagination. Otherwise, their triumph turns action into mere movement, "driven by daemonic, chthonic/ Powers." (199) To a degree Christian mythology can incorporate this scheme into traditional notions like the way down being the way up, but Eliot does not wholly unite his post-romantic poetic heritage with Christian norms. To the extent that the poem's spatializations clash with its overt allegiances, Eliot's poetic drives subvert his own orthodoxy.

A poem this imbued with romantic organizations of imagery, meaning, and typography continually suggests romantic analogues in diction and symbol as well. The "Chinese jar" (180) which "still/ Moves perpetually in its stillness" inevitably recalls its more famous Grecian ancestor, as does the jar that Stevens puts in Tennessee. The sun "Reflecting in a watery mirror/ A glare that is blindness in the early afternoon./ And glow more intense than blaze of branch, or brazier" (200) recalls the "cold glare, intenser than the noon,/ But icy cold, obscured with blinding light/ The sun, as he the stars" in *The Triumph of Life*, a poem that affected the superb Dantesque vision later in *Little Gidding*.[98] Like Shelley's West Wind, Time emerges as both "destroyer" and "preserver" (195), while the voice in the rigging descants like the pipes on Keats' urn, "not to the ear . . . and not in any language."[99] (196) *Four Quartets* does not invoke these romantic analogues as direct allusions, but sees similar dilemmas in the relation between life and art, and between physical and mental processes.

The poem's drive into romantic patterns despite itself appears nowhere more clearly than in the first poem of *East Coker*, whose last three sections comprise a Greater Romantic Lyric. Marked by breaks in spacing, they move from description of a landscape to creation of a vision in it (here, the summer dancers) and then to partial evaluation. Spatially, the movements form a here-there-here pattern, while temporally they become overtly afternoon-midnight-dawn and implicitly present-future-present. The speaker ends where he began:

> In my beginning is my end. Now the light falls
> Across the open field, leaving the deep lane
> Shuttered with branches, dark in the afternoon,
> Where you lean against a bank while a van passes,
> And the deep lane insists on the direction
> Into the village, in the electric heat
> Hypnotised. In a warm haze the sultry light
> Is absorbed, not refracted, by grey stone.
> The dahlias sleep in the empty silence.
> Wait for the early owl.
>   In that open field
> If you do not come too close, if you do not come too close,
> On a summer midnight, you can hear the music

Of the weak pipe and the little drum
And see them dancing around the bonfire
The association of man and woman
In daunsinge, signifying matrimonie—
A dignified and commodious sacrament.
Two and two, necessarye coniunction,
Holding eche other by the hand or the arm
Whiche betokeneth concorde. Round and round the fire
Leaping through the flames, or joined in circles,
Rustically solemn or in rustic laughter
Lifting heavy feet in clumsy shoes,
Earth feet, loam feet, lifted in country mirth
Mirth of those long since under earth
Nourishing the corn. Keeping time,
Keeping the rhythm in their dancing
As in their living in the living seasons
The time of the seasons and the constellations
The time of milking and the time of harvest
The time of the coupling of man and woman
And that of beasts. Feet rising and falling.
Eating and drinking. Dung and death.

Dawn points, and another day
Prepares for heat and silence. Out at sea the dawn wind
Wrinkles and slides. I am here
Or there, or elsewhere. In my beginning.

(182–83)

Like many of the best passages in *Four Quartets*, this imaginative eruption seems to counter the thrust of the poem and, in some
ways, to divide against itself.[100] The concrete power of the opening description shocks us after the derivative *ubi sunt* meditation
preceding it, whose closing reminiscences of Ecclesiastes sound
more like empty echoes than genuine prophetic power. The
natural description contradicts in practice Eliot's rejection of nature in *Ash Wednesday* and his denial of the world elsewhere in
Four Quartets. Lingering in the natural world provokes an outburst of poetic power. In the vision section, the dancers may be
actual rustics or, given the witching hour of midnight, ghosts of
past ones; at any rate, the speaker imagines them. Eliot takes two
structural precautions against direct personal vision: first, like
Wordsworth at the end of "Tintern Abbey" or Coleridge in "Frost
at Midnight," he imagines a future visitor experiencing the landscape; and second, he renders the entire episode conditional ("If
. . ."), although by its end we have forgotten the condition. In a
brilliant thematic defense against his own fears, Eliot makes the

vision embody order—a dance around a fire betokening concord—although the lines on leaping through the flames nearly escape this restraint. But shortly the poem begins to go to pieces, as Eliot's work often does under pressure of sex as subject. Return to the meters of Ecclesiastes signals a coming failure in vision, which after paralleling human and bestial copulation arrives at a natural nadir, "Dung and death." That final phrase accords with the intellectual needs informing the general structure of the entire poem but betrays the extraordinary appeal of the rich vision in an often desiccated work. The recovery of the last four lines is swift and a little pointless, for the speaker returns too exactly to his former state. *Four Quartets* wants us to deny the validity of the imaginative experience of this passage, either by seeing it in natural terms as dung and death or in spiritual ones as a moment hinting at Incarnation. Both ways contradict the obvious direction of emotional and imaginative energy.

Such dualities belong to an overall scheme informing the poem and culminating Eliot's lifelong personal and poetic struggles. We may arrange them in the following pairs, in which the left-hand column descends from Eliot's earlier conception of classicism and the right-hand column from romanticism:

discourse	Image
images of fancy	images of imagination
intellect and will	emotion
restraint	eruption
chronos	kairos
Pauline	apocalyptic
orthodoxy	heresy
agape	eros
pattern	movement

The first four pairs and the last one pervade Eliot's poetry generally, as we have seen. I have distinguished between Image in Kermode's sense of Romantic Image and images, which can be produced by either fancy or imagination. In *Four Quartets* the image of the dancers in the first section of *East Coker* derives from imagination, those of the hospital in the fourth section from fancy. The four religious pairs belong to Eliot's postconversion poetry. Eliot the man might have wanted to reverse the placement of chronos and kairos; the arrangement here follows the imagination of the poet in him.

The religious terms restore the primary referent of nineteenth-century displacements, returning metaphors for secular activity and experience to their original meanings, although still carrying signs of their secular excursion. The poem pivots on the relation between chronos (passing or clock time, time as duration) and kairos (the season, a point in time charged with meaning, time as fulfillment), two Greek words whose systematic distinction belongs to Christian thought. "History is a pattern/ Of timeless moments" (208) means that chronos becomes a pattern made up of kairoi, of which the most important to the Christian scheme are the Fall, Nativity, Passion, and Last Judgment, four events that reappear throughout *Four Quartets*. History may be servitude or freedom (205), depending on which kind of time we see in it. The same distinction holds for the individual life as well, where kairos returns Pater's concept of the moment to its original, divine reference. As man Eliot follows the discipline appropriate for a believer caught in chronos, while as poet his imagination continually veers toward kairos; the resultant conflict makes *Four Quartets* a final formulation of Eliot's recurrent dilemmas.

The dogma of the poem crosses its imagery withershins. Eliot's intellect adheres to Pauline tradition, emphasizing restraint, denial, and asceticism. His imagination, in contrast, fastens on apocalyptic imagery appropriate to kairoi—fire, dove, and the moment. The Jesuit scholar William F. Lynch has suggested provocatively that Eliot had an orthodox mind and heretical imagination. He writes,

> For it is hard to say no to the impression, if I may use a mixture of my own symbols and his, that the Christian imagination is finally limited to the element of fire, to the day of Pentecost, to the descent of the Holy Ghost upon the disciples. . . . Eliot's imagination (and is not this a theology?) is alive with points of *intersection* and of *descent*. He seems to place our faith, our hope, and our love, not in the flux of time but in the *points* of time. I am sure his mind is interested in the line and time of Christ, whose Spirit is his total flux. But I am not so sure about his imagination. Is it or is it not an imagination which is saved from time's nausea or terror by points of intersection? . . . Everything that is good [in the poem] is annunciation and epiphany.[101] (Italics Lynch's.)

Father Lynch notes in particular Eliot's insistence on love as immobility, which St. Thomas sustains but also confutes, in accord with the linguistic inadequacy for the ineffable that Eliot elsewhere exploits. Likewise, Augustine had defined love as a motion of the soul toward God. So, too, with Eliot's description of

> Desiccation of the world of sense,
> Evacuation of the world of fancy,

Inoperancy of the world of spirit;
. . . abstention from movement.
(179)

In an ironic confirmation of romantic dialectic, that inner wasteland corresponds to the outer one created by Eliot's version of
agape replacing eros' love of created things.

Eliot's formulation of Christian tradition matches his earlier interpretation of classicism and romanticism in deriving from his
own urgent needs. He transferred his earlier urge for control and
management of daemonic inner forces from a literary to a religious
frame and sought above all to replace the terror at the center with
stillness, abstention from movement, a void in which divine presence could replace daemonic drives. *Four Quartets* expresses his
desperate strategy most fully and leaves little room for further
development. His poetry had always lacked a certain kind of mental action, but now he had an external goal beyond mere contain-
ment of internal forces. Eliot now wanted "Incarnation," "the impossible union/ Of spheres of existence," mentioned at the end of
The Dry Salvages. (199) But poetry depends on the contrary apprehension:

> For most of us, there is only the unattended
> Moment, the moment in and out of time,
> The distraction fit, lost in a shaft of sunlight,
> The wild thyme unseen, or the winter lightning
> Or the waterfall, or music heard so deeply
> That it is not heard at all, but you are the music
> While the music lasts. These are only hints and guesses,
> Hints followed by guesses; and the rest
> Is prayer, observance, discipline, thought and action.
> (198–99)

Trapped in the conflict between "unattended moment" and
"prayer, obedience, discipline, thought and action," Eliot finally
would settle only for an impossible rendering of Incarnation. This
the poem does not and cannot give us, although *Little Gidding* ends
with a moving statement of hope. "I am not sure that there is any
such thing as 'mystical poetry,' " he wrote in a discussion of Blake
published late in the year of his conversion. "Mysticism . . . is a
whole-time job; and so is poetry."[102] It is difficult to tell whether
Eliot's impetus toward mysticism triumphed, or whether it failed
and he reverted instead to prayer, obedience, and discipline.
Either course would have suppressed his long-beleaguered poetic
imagination, and either way his poetic career had ended.

Four Quartets germinated from rejected fragments of Eliot's first play, *Murder in the Cathedral*.[103] While the dramatic career to which he devoted his subsequent creative energies lies outside the scope of our discussion, one passage from *The Cocktail Party* (1950) claims attention as epilogue to Eliot's tempestuous relation to romanticism. Toward the end of that play Sir Henry Harcourt-Reilly asks "Do you mind if I quote poetry?" and then recites these lines from Shelley's *Prometheus Unbound:*

> Ere Babylon was dust
> The magus Zoroaster, my dead child,
> Met his own image walking in the garden.
> That apparition, sole of men, he saw.
> For know there are two worlds of life and death:
> One that which thou beholdest; but the other
> Is underneath the grave, where do inhabit
> The shadows of all forms that think and live
> Till death unite them and they part no more.[104]

Although Reilly's introductory question alerts us to the difference in cadence and diction between romantic and modern verse drama, Eliot clearly means his allusion to be positive, a kind of tribute to the poet whom he had most vilified earlier in his career. It reminds us how much the two poets had in common. Yet it also suggests Eliot's unromantic solution to romantic problems. For Earth's speech in *Prometheus Unbound* immediately continues:

> Dreams and the light imaginings of men,
> And all that faith creates or love desires,
> Terrible, strange, sublime and beauteous shapes.[105]

Shelley makes the phantom world a human creation, and its union with the ordinary world also becomes a human creation in his visionary play. Just here Eliot recoils not only from Shelley, Blake, and Keats but even from Wordsworth or Coleridge. For Eliot unmistakably adopted a world view not just dependent on unhuman powers but requiring repudiation of both nature and imagination, as *The Cocktail Party* elsewhere makes clear. Blake repudiated all hypostatizations, Shelley adhered to a visionary skepticism, Keats was certain of nothing but the holiness of the heart's affections and the truths of imagination, and even the more orthodoxly religious Wordsworth and Coleridge saw both nature and imagination as positive. Eliot did not, and his refusal generated the conflict between the overt and covert mental action of his poems. Unlike Shelley, who equally recognized the dangers of imagination, Eliot could never see "all that faith creates, or love desires" as ultimately human, although he, too, perceived "Terrible, strange, sublime and beauteous shapes." He was romantic against the grain, illustrating in his own career the contention of his essay on Baudelaire that in a romantic age a poet could not be anti-romantic except in tendency. The saint repudiated the swordsman, although not without subterranean vacillation.

4

The
New Romanticism
of Wallace Stevens

"After all, Eliot and I are dead opposites," wrote Wallace Stevens in 1950.[1] Nowhere were they more opposite than in their responses to romanticism. Where Eliot thundered against romanticism in theory even while often developing it in practice, Stevens openly called for a new romanticism that in practice sometimes subverted the old. For Stevens, the romantic meant the new, the vital, and above all the imaginative, and he looked to the British romantics for both illustration and sanction of his own values, even while jealously distancing himself from them to guard his own independence. He confronted romantic problems like the dualism between subject and object or the contradiction between life and art, and accepted key aspects of their aesthetic like the importance of imagination and the kind of defense of poetry to which imagination led. Yet in his drive to develop his own art and personality Stevens saw the necessity of renewing romanticism and adapting it to modern times. He forswore mere repetition. Joyously welcoming the creative violence which Eliot feared, he redefined imagination to emphasize its ferocity while reformulating the cyclic quality of romantic experience. His poetry incorporated new strategies of image, syntax, and presentation of consciousness designed to create provisional rather than final fictions. In the process, he both extended romantic literary theory and reshaped romantic mental action into the poems of our climate. His profound relation to romanticism has been mentioned so much and systematically explored so little that its extensive investiga-

163

tion can open central approaches to both his aesthetic and his poetry.[2]

Stevens' changing attitudes toward romanticism follow the same tripartite pattern whose presence in our other two writers suggests that it may be normative for strong poets of the modernist generation. The breaks coincide with the natural divisions of his writing career. He began with enthusiasm for the debased romanticism of the turn of the century, with strong roots in Keats. This period extends from adolescence until a dozen years beyond Stevens' first abandonment of poetry for publication in 1900. From the recommencement of his career as publishing poet near the outbreak of World War I until the appearance of the *Harmonium* volume in 1923, Stevens entered a mildly anti-romantic phase. During those years allusions to romanticism disappeared from his letters, and two poems, *The Comedian as the Letter C* and a manuscript version of "Anecdote of the Prince of Peacocks," suggested a negative judgment. Yet Stevens remained so centrally in romantic tradition that his reaction involved overt omission more than outright hostility, and *Harmonium* poems like "Earthy Anecdote," "The Snow Man," or "Anecdote of the Jar" imply a modernist reworking of romantic norms. This latent romanticism surfaced after Stevens again resumed publication with "The Sun This March" in 1930. Soon he was advocating a "new romanticism"—which he exalted over false imitations—and for the remaining quarter century of his career worked out its precepts. His startling appearance as a romantic in midst of the warring schools of Marxism or New Criticism in the thirties identifies the mature Stevens as his own man, able on occasion sharply to dissociate himself from his romantic forebears even while fighting through to a modernist art that continued and transformed their own.

Stevens' early letters and journals display the conventional and unremarkable attraction to romanticism of a young man of his day with a literary bent. Stereotypes of romantic solitude coexisted easily with a sense of poetic centrality. In a mood of discontent he would imagine himself with spirits "wandering by 'caverns measureless to man,/ Down to a sunless sea' " but felt "too languid" to name many of his fellow roamers in the Coleridgean landscape.[3] He contrasted Shelley's interest in "humanity" with modern individualism, admired his "poetic thought," and resented an inept mention of Shelley in the funeral service for Stephen Crane. On a walking tour he turned back his shirt and dickey to resemble "that corsair of hearts, le grand Byron." He could also share romantic devotion to nature and even conscripted the arch nature-hater, Blake, for his sentimentalization. Watching the sun light up surrounding hills in the Palisades on a brilliant spring day made him think that "if it had been a bit nearer sunset . . . Blake's angels would have been there with their 'Holy, Holy, Holy.' "

These stock derivations paled beside a passion for Keats, the most important poet for early Stevens personally and the one whom he most grew to resemble poetically. Keats pervades the early prose as poet figure, subject of youthful high jinks, source of quotation, and above all as composer of *Endymion*. The earliest published reference, in Stevens' journal for 1899, praises Keats as a virile rather than effeminate poet, along with Homer, Dante, Shakespeare, Milton, and Browning.[4] The next year he invoked Keats while ragging bartenders during an afternoon walk from Reading. "We asked one fellow whether he had heard that John Keats had been run over, by a trolley car at Stony Creek in the morning," recorded Stevens in snobbishness soon to be outgrown. "He said that he had not—he did not know Keats—but that he had heard of the family. Spirit of Adonais!" In a speculative mood, he could wonder whether the difference between Keats and a longshoreman derived from purely physiological causes. Phrases from Keats popped up in midst of other discussions. An account of a walking trip out of New York sketched a scene with hundreds of robins, some of whom, with other birds, "made 'sweet moan' " for the loitering young knight. A revery on the relation of music and memory mentioned harp chords which "vibrate on more than the 'sensual ear,' " the same gross faculty surpassed by the pipes on the Grecian Urn.

Young Stevens' favorite poem was the quest romance *Endymion*, which he reread periodically with deepening comprehension. Countering the abortive search of Shelley's *Alastor* with Endymion's successful discovery that the Indian maiden, the dream vision, and Cynthia were all one, Keats' insistence on grounding high imaginative experience in our terrestrial world may have shaped Stevens' developing world view decisively. According to his journal, he began with conventional rapture: "The moon was very fine. . . . When home I began the third canto of 'Endymion' which opens with O moon! and Cynthia! and that sort of thing. It was intoxicating."[5] His appreciation presumably grew the following academic year, when he received a grade of A in the course on English romanticism at Harvard.[6] In 1908 he took the trouble to see J. P. Morgan's manuscript of *Endymion* on exhibition at Columbia. "You know the beginning," he wrote to Elsie, " 'A thing of beauty is a joy forever.' " That beginning, with its dedication to "wreathing/ A flowery band to bind us to the earth" fitted Stevens' future desire to write a poem of earth as surely as it presaged Keats' own later development. The next year Stevens reread the poem with new insight: "I've started 'Endymion' and find a good many beautiful things in it that I had forgotten, or else not noticed." He wondered whether a modern poet could still easily write poetry dedicated to Beauty or whether "the growth of criticism" had made it more "difficult." The lessons of *Endymion* reappear in another poem of Keats in the couplets, "Epistle to John Hamilton Reynolds," and Stevens unerringly singled out its famous epitome for citation to his wife:

> It is a flaw
> In happiness, to see beyond our bourn,—
> It forces us in summer skies to mourn,
> It spoils the singing of the nightingale.

Something almost always spoils the singing of Stevens' own nightingales; they tend to niggle or to torture the ear.[7] But Keats' lines signified more than avian aversion to Stevens—they sound the ground note of his own poetry, with its passionate commitment to the human and its heroic refusal of transcendent or suprahuman values.

When identifying "Keats in college" to a later interviewer curious about his important literary experiences, Stevens said he avoided wide reading in contemporary poetry for fear he would " 'pick up something' and unconsciously incorporate it into his own poetry."[8] To judge by the pervasive romanticism in his early verse, the fear had solid grounds, for Stevens did absorb and use what he read. Without degenerating into the kind of critic he disliked, "who spends his time dissecting what he reads for echoes, imitations, influences, as if no one was ever simply himself but is always compounded of a lot of other people" (*LWS* 813), I mean to note briefly the derivation of his juvenilia before proceeding to the greater subject of his mature transformation of romanticism to a creative poetry in which he could be himself. For early Stevens was as imitative as later Stevens was original; his undergraduate verse was still compounded largely of others.

Chief among past Iffucans were the romantics. Like Eliot a decade later, Stevens at Harvard entered a poetic cul-de-sac of outworn convention chiefly derived from English Renaissance and nineteenth-century models, with a dash of recent French verse for the more daring. Inchling poets in this milieu piped predictable themes of love, nature, and mortality in elevated poetic diction; they could also share the world-weariness of English decadents or jaunty posturing of French dandies. The closest student of Stevens' college poems, Robert Buttel, finds them mostly "typical of the undergraduate and magazine verse of the era, verse in the ebbing Romantic and Victorian traditions."[9] The large proportion of sonnets itself indicates attraction to an Elizabethan form rehabilitated by the romantics after a century of relative disuse. Buttel suggests that Stevens' sonnet "There shines the morning star" echoes Keats' famous "Bright Star."[10] Romantic diction pervades other poems as well: the speaker of another sonnet finds "the deep wind brought the scent/ Of flowers I could not see," just as the protagonist of the Nightingale ode "cannot see what flowers are at my feet" but guesses at them from incense borne on breezes.[11] Likewise, the phrase "and like fresh clouds they roam" echoes Wordsworth's "I wandered lonely as a cloud."[12] More important, the poet cranks out the stage apparatus of derivative romanticism—images of wind, star, moon, and domes of light; speakers contemplating pastoral landscapes; and poeticisms like " 'tween" mingled with invocations of faith, hope, joy, or glory.

This fustian continues in Stevens' next poetic productions, the manuscript June Books he made for Elsie in 1908 and 1909. "Ancient Rendezvous" ("Winter Melody" in the 1908 version) combines the old devices with a new spareness:

> I went into the dim wood
> And walked alone.
> I heard the icy forest move
> With icy tone.
>
> My heart leaped in the dim wood
> So cold, so bare;
> And seemed to echo suddenly
> Old music there.
>
> I halted in the dim wood
> And watched; and soon
> There rose for me, a second time,
> The pageant moon.[13]

The central stanza combines memories of Wordsworth's "My heart leaps up" with the recurrent music so prominent in his "The Solitary Reaper," Coleridge's "Kubla Khan," and Keats' Nightingale ode as well as early Stevens generally. The entire poem recapitulates romantic experience; in the first quatrain a lone wan-

derer enters a cold and alien wood; in the last he finds an imaginative response through forsaking activity (his walking) for a wise
passiveness in which he halts and watches. The rising of that
standard prop, the moon, signals his conventional victory.

Immersion in romantic and especially Keatsian verse-craft continued to color even the romantic reversals of Stevens' later productions. He sanctioned the phrase "half pales of red" in *Credences of Summer* (*CP* 378) by citing Keats as precedent. "When
using the word pales I validated the use by thinking of the use that
had been made of gules," he told Renato Poggioli. "Keats used
words something like this: 'and cast warm gules of red.' " (*LWS*
781) Keats had in fact written that the wintry moon "threw warm
gules on Madeleine's fair breast" in stanza xxv of *The Eve of St.
Agnes*. There the "rose-bloom" on her hand adumbrates the
"roseate characters" of Stevens' poem, even while Stevens' overall
description reverses Keats' not just by turning winter moon to
summer sun but by turning colors into characters instead of
characters into colors. Such metamorphosis culminates in Stevens'
remarkable "The Poem that Took the Place of a Mountain." (*CP*
512) That work transforms Keats' analogy between himself encountering Chapman's Homer and Cortez discovering a new
ocean into an analogy which emphasizes the provisional correspondence between poem and mountain even while developing it
in more detail, and which suggests discovery not of a new world
but of one's home[14]—even if like a good modern refugee from Ox-
idia the speaker "breathed its oxygen" rather than "breathed its
pure serene." But late Stevens' characteristic subjunctives plague
the vision of his lyric and its brave attempt to find a home. He
knew that we live in a place that is not our own, and hard it is in
spite of blazoned days. An immense chasm separates his derivative early romanticism from the stunning transformations of the
later poems. A look at the qualified and transitional anti-romanticism of *Harmonium* will make more understandable the innovative
romantic redemption of his mature art.

In the decade from 1914 to 1923 when he worked on the *Harmonium* poems, Stevens cast off the detritus of his college verse to
produce genuinely modern works that, paradoxically, sometimes
came closer to high romanticism than had his youthful adapta-
tions. Like Yeats and Eliot, Stevens needed to escape fin de siècle
convention. Always sensitive to charges of escapism, he feared
most that his earlier devotion would lead him to a literary dreamworld which he sought to shun by contemporaneity in technique.
He experimented most obviously with diction, sometimes

deflating romanticistic pomp by substituting, say, a "jar" for an "urn," while elsewhere breaking into a linguistic gaudiness that ironically mocked its own pretensions. Continual probings to find his own voice replaced the regular rhythms and forms of his earlier verse. He flirted briefly with Imagism but later decried its indiscriminate subject matter. "When HARMONIUM was in the making there was a time when I liked the idea of images and images alone, or images and the music of verse together," he recalled. (*LWS* 288) Imagism became a halfway house en route to his true subject, which was less images alone than mind's relation to them, less product than process.

"Anecdote of the Prince of Peacocks" (1923) illustrates Stevens' use of modern techniques to evolve a strong romanticism out of attack on a weak variety. An early and imperfect draft makes at least the object of attack clearer:

> In the land of the peacocks, the prince thereof,
> Grown weary of romantics, walked alone,
> In the first of evening, pondering.
>
> "The deuce!" he cried.
>
> And by him, in the bushes, he espied
> A white philosopher.
> The white one sighed—
>
> He seemed to seek replies,
> From nothingness, to all his sighs.
>
> "My sighs are pulses in a dreamer's death!"
> Exclaimed the white one, smothering his lips.
>
> The prince's frisson reached his fingers' tips.[15]

The pejorative "romantics" here ambiguously applies both to personalities, perhaps those of poets, and to the whole gamut of outworn romantic paraphernalia and postures, which the colloquial "The deuce!" tries to counteract. But the prince has grown weary of such poses too late, for as prince of peacocks he embodies them. The remainder of the draft oscillates between mocking romantic conventions and equivocally imitating them. The crudeness of "smothering his lips" and the archness of "frisson" both suggest burlesque, but the overall action repeats romantic quest devices and the last line carries some conviction. The mysterious white philosopher reflects the prince's own condition, and the frisson suggests recognition that the unanswered sighs and dreamer's death apply to both. The error ("He seemed to seek

169

replies,/ From nothingness, to all his sighs") lies in a favorite romantic target, the linked excesses of egotism and humility in which mistaken egotism demands a response from uncaring nature and false humility refuses to recognize that such meaning comes only from the self.

In revising the poem Stevens focused more precisely on dissolution of a dreamworld in a way that adumbrates his later reworking of romanticism. The prince of peacocks has become the speaker, wanderer in a blue and moonlit landscape "in the midst of dreams." (CP 58) The white philosopher has become the red Berserk, setter of traps for the forgetful escapist. By the end of the poem the prince knows not just the beauty of moonlight but now also "the dread of the bushy plain" whose ground lies "full of blocks/ And blocking steel." Stevens later wrote that "The imagination loses vitality as it ceases to adhere to what is real,"[16] and that fate has befallen the prince already. Then Berserk's red vitality threatens to demolish his imaginative blue world, whose "milky" hue suggests its etiolation. Berserk's name signifies the violent rage of both true reality and—Stevens increasingly insisted —true imagination as well. Identification of the quester's error as loss of frenzy marks an innovation in romantic tradition, one the later Yeats would have understood well. It helped Stevens to avoid his own blocking steel, his precursors' works, first as trivialized convention and then as genuine challenge.

Once he had broken with degenerate modes, Stevens could begin the recovery of true romantic themes. Three of the many resultant poems in *Harmonium* serve to plot the thematic recovery, technical innovations, and incipient transformations particularly well; they are "Earthy Anecdote," "Anecdote of the Jar," and "The Snow Man." Stevens signaled the importance of "Earthy Anecdote" (1918) by placing it first in both *Harmonium* and *Collected Poems*. Just as the last poem of the larger volume ends with the word "reality," so does the first present a parable of imagination ordering perception. In "Earthy Anecdote" (CP 3) the leaping and bristling firecat changes the bucks' clattering into "a swift, circular line" to the right or left. As so often in Stevens, the lyric has a strong literal sense; he insisted that he meant "something quite concrete: actual animals." (LWS 209) But a firecat is not an actual animal, and the poem drives us to its implications. The firecat orders the bucks the way the imagination orders perceptions; its ferocity changes their disorganized clatter into an ordered pattern of motion. The firecat thus becomes center to the bucks' moving circle in a dynamic design for which each term needs the other. While the poem's diction and rhythms modernize this romantic theme, the firecat's "bright eyes" belong to orthodox romantic tradition. There such eyes accompany the presence of imaginative power, whether inspiring awe or joy. Coleridge's "bright-eyed Mariner" or the poet's "flashing eyes" in "Kubla Khan," the "shooting lights/ Of thy [Dorothy's] wild eyes" in "Tintern Abbey," and Blake's fiery-eyed tyger "burning bright" stand behind Stevens' firecat. Yet the eyes are not symbols. Stevens claimed that his poem had "no symbolism [but] a good deal of theory." (*LWS* 204) This is true in that the poem's separate parts remain images or concrete details and it implies a larger meaning by its overall pattern rather than its individual components. Stevens called the lyric an "anecdote," as he did several other parables on imagination and the relation between art and life. By choosing that term he denied an authoritative status to the lyric and instead labeled it something minor, illustrative, or incidental. In so doing he anticipated his crucial later notion of the poem as provisional rather than final artifact.

The related "Anecdote of the Jar" (1919) shifts from the attractions of process to the problems of product. Like Keats' "Ode on a Grecian Urn," the poem develops the tension between art and nature, mind and mutability, through meditation on a crafted object. Stevens shares Keats' conclusion that the urn remains ultimately a cold pastoral but already introduces those deflections which lead to his mature art. By replacing a grand "urn" with a more pedestrian "jar" he deviates into an acceptable modern diction and implicitly begins a contrast that continues beyond *Harmonium* in the green "jar of the shoots of the infant country" and ashy "venerable urn" of "Someone Puts a Pineapple Together" (*NA* 83) or the "gigantic, solitary urn,/ A trash can at the end of the world" in "Mr. Burnshaw and the Statue."[17] More important, Stevens changes the relation of the urn to nature from mimetic to antithetic opposition. Where Keats' ornate urn represents a flowery tale, Stevens' jar stands "gray and bare" (*CP* 76) against the bird and bush of Tennessee; the contrast lies between wilderness and its ordering nemesis rather than its heightened mimesis. As with the firecat and bucks, the jar and wilderness need each other to compose a circular pattern, but the first pair relate to ongoing perception and the second to completed result of imaginative activity. Hence comes the contrast between the attractive firecat and the nearly repellent jar. A supreme fiction must change, but the jar, like the urn, cannot; unlike the urn, it also cannot give pleasure. In separating art from nature in his anecdote, Stevens

171

deepens the Keatsian duality. He would later advance a few provisional solutions in a duet with the undertaker.

The nadir of imagination following its metamorphosis from process to product lasts but briefly, as "The Snow Man" (1921) suggests. This poem belongs with Shelley's "Mont Blanc" and Yeats' "Meru" as one of the great expressions of romantic winter vision. A technical tour de force (its fifteen lines comprise a single sentence), it both attacks a sentimental pathetic fallacy and incarnates a tough-minded one in which an internal mind of winter matches an alien landscape. This is the point reached in "Meru," where thought ravens its way through illusion into the desolation of reality, or in Stevens' own "Man and Bottle" (1940), in which "The mind is the great poem of winter, the man,/ Who, to find what will suffice,/ Destroys romantic tenements/ Of rose and ice." (CP 238) Yet as in "Mont Blanc," the destructive power issuing from mind will eventually transform itself into a beneficent force for life and reinitiate the entire cycle. Winter implies eventual summer in a seasonal rotation, and upon finally beholding "nothing that is not there and the nothing that is" (CP 10), the mind will immediately begin to generate new fictions. "The Snow Man" anticipates the double consciousness informing some of Stevens' own later constructions, which present one mind's apprehension of another. Here, the speaker does not have a mind of winter himself; rather, he imagines such a mind, appropriate to a snow man. Like "The Idea of Order at Key West" or "Connoisseur of Chaos," the poem refracts one consciousness through a second.

Just as he began to redefine romantic themes even in the act of their recovery, so did Stevens mutate romantic tone and setting even while following it most closely. That happens in the famous conclusion of "Sunday Morning" (1915), derived from Keats' "To Autumn":

> Deer walk upon our mountains, and the quail
> Whistle about us their spontaneous cries;
> Sweet berries ripen in the wilderness;
> And, in the isolation of the sky,
> At evening, casual flocks of pigeons make
> Ambiguous undulations as they sink,
> Downward to darkness, on extended wings.[18]
>
> (CP 70)

The most acute commentator on these lines' relation to Keats, Helen Vendler, rightly says that they show "Stevens' divergence from his Romantic forebears, even when he is echoing them."[19]

172

Vendler's subtle analysis demonstrates the passage's surprisingly programmatic exemplification of preceding general statements in the poem and concludes that the scene "is being used largely as an instance of a thesis, not surrendered to in and for itself," in contrast to Keats. The argument succeeds, for Stevens was in some ways a Shelleyan poet who aspired to be a good Keatsian, and the ending to "Sunday Morning" moves us most by depicting a beautiful, sufficient vision that Stevens' temperament could never quite accept. Yet the passage carries more conviction than Vendler allows. What Stevens could accept—indeed, could not avoid—was romantic cyclicity, which he later developed in new ways. Following the great summer chant of paradise, Stevens' undulating and sinking pigeons (another figure of patterned movement) with their extended wings suggest assent to a cycle leading from the summer chant through the auroras of autumn to the snow man's winter mind and perhaps again to the sun each March.

How to keep an ongoing cycle from turning into either a bleak endgame or meaningless repetition temporarily baffled Stevens in *The Comedian as the Letter C,* the last major poem completed for *Harmonium.* An ongoing scholarly tradition relates the poem helpfully to Wordsworth's *Prelude* as tracing the growth of a poet's mind, but *Comedian* derives even more directly from Shelley's *Alastor* and Keats' *Endymion,* to which it constitutes an ironic riposte.[20] Like them, it narrates a quest romance in which the hero becomes an "introspective voyager" (*CP* 29) through exotic landscape. Stevens' first long poem and the only one with a strong narrative plot, *Comedian* further shares the chief themes of its forerunners, concern with imagination's relation to reality and the poet's relation to society. *Comedian* crosses its prototypes not only in its self-mocking language but also in what Stevens later called its "anti-mythological" mode. The epithet meant more than the jettison of Keats' revivified Greek mythology or Shelley's more improvised apparatus; it meant selection as hero of "an every-day man who lives a life without the slightest adventure except that he lives it in a poetic atmosphere as we all do." (*LWS* 778) That later claim clashes with Crispin's adventures in Yucatan and elsewhere but does suggest that Stevens wanted to substitute a quotidian for an exceptional hero and to scant the literal level of events.

As everyone recognizes, the poem itself works as both individual development and literary history. In an early article lavishly praised by Stevens himself as "not only correct but keen" (*LWS* 350), Hi Simons argued that *Comedian* "tells both how a representative modern poet tried to change from a romanticist to a realist and how he adapted himself to his social environment. The hero's development may be summarized as a passage from (1) juvenile romantic subjectivism . . . to (7) an 'indulgent fatalis[m]' and skepticism."[21] Crispin's journey thus loosely recapitulates both Stevens' own career and one view of the progress of poetry over the preceding century and a quarter. He begins by valuing not "that century of wind in a single puff" but "mythology of self." (CP 28) Stevens identifies romanticism as the exaggerated egotism he had escaped after his youth: "the last distortion of romance/ Forsook the insatiable egotist." (CP 30) Crispin must learn not that "man is the intelligence of his soil" (CP 27) but that "his soil is man's intelligence" (CP 36), not to dominate but to express his native grounds. He does this by passing beyond the Maya sonneteers who, like the derivative ones of Stevens' early literary milieu, shunned the savagery of reality and "still to the night-bird made their plea" in countless Keatsian imitations. (CP 30) By Carolina the moonlight fiction disappears. Crispin throws off the past to make the present, and throws over his precursors to make himself:

> Exit the mental moonlight, exit lex,
> Rex and principium, exit the whole
> Shebang. Exeunt omnes. . . .
> What was the purpose of his pilgrimage,
> Whatever shape it took in Crispin's mind,
> If not, when all is said, to drive away
> The shadow of his fellows from the skies,
> And, from their stale intelligence released,
> To make a new intelligence prevail?
>
> (CP 36-37)

But making a new intelligence prevail proved more difficult than either Crispin or Stevens had thought. Projection of a colony including the Georgian pine-spokesman, Floridian banjo-plucker, and other intelligences of their soil leads to perception that "return to social nature" (CP 43) can swamp the solitary poet as well as buoy him up. Stevens ends the poem as he ended his *Harmonium* phase, with uncertainty. Its cyclical ("sown again") and startling final image of eating the world-as-turnip is glossed by the poem as leaving Crispin in either "deluging onwardness" or else a "concluding fadedly." (CP 45, 46)

The same dilemma confronted Stevens himself after *Harmonium* and resulted in his again abandoning the publication of poetry, this time for six years until 1930. He generalized both his own problem and that of Crispin in his letter responding to Simons'

article on *Comedian:* "The way of all mind is from romanticism to
realism, to fatalism and then to indifferentism, unless the cycle
re-commences and the thing goes from indifferentism back to
romanticism all over again." (*LWS* 350) But Stevens did not want
merely to inaugurate a new personal cycle by returning to the
watered down old romanticism of his youth. The world needed "a
new romanticism, a new belief," and so did he. "About the time
[after *Harmonium*] when I, personally, began to feel round for a
new romanticism, I might naturally have been expected to start on
a new cycle," he told Simons. "Instead of doing so, I began to feel
that I was on the edge: that I wanted to get to the center: that I was
isolated, and that I wanted to share the common life." (*LWS* 352)
Stevens saw the choice between periphery and center as the major
decision of his later career. He liked the figure well enough to
reuse it eight years later in the lecture "Effects of Analogy," where
he contrasted two theories of modern poetry. One valued individual imagination as part of a larger power, tried to utilize reality
for its own ends, caused the poet (like Valéry) to live "on the verge
of consciousness" and often resulted in a marginal poetry. The
other theory valued imagination as a purely internal power,
sought simply to understand reality, enabled the poet to live "in
the very center of consciousness," and resulted—"or should
result"—in a central poetry. (*NA* 115) Stevens clearly favored the
second theory. Desire to write a central poetry sharing in some
way in the common life returned him from the art-for-art's-sake
aestheticism of the romantic aftermath to the dedicated humanism
of the original romantics. He sought to avoid degeneration into
indifference partly by incorporating cyclicity itself into his basic
theory and practice.

Creating that new but central romanticism involved at least partial preservation of the old, just as we should expect from a man
who kept an Eolian harp in his garden and positioned his bed to
catch the sound most directly.[22] Stevens distinguished two types
of romanticism, rejecting the pejorative and derivative for the
positive and vital. He nearly identified romanticism with imagination and used that faculty both to defend poetry in the manner of
Shelley and to grapple with reality itself in a new variation of a
recurrent romantic struggle. He carried to their ultimate conclusion earlier displacements of religious patterns onto secular experience, and continued romantic organization of imagery and
spatial projection of reality. Yet Stevens rightly insisted that his
doctrines were his own. He introduced a radical provisionality
into his work while reformulating and elevating notions of the

175

violence and cyclicity of imagination. These deflections in aesthetic theory hint at the radical innovations in mental action that pervade his later poetry.

Just as resuming periodical publication in 1930 with "The Sun This March" suggested renewed commitment to cyclicity, so did introducing his next book, *Ideas of Order* (1935), with "Sailing after Lunch" identify new romanticism as the crux of Stevens' recent exfoliation:[23]

> It is the word *pejorative* that hurts.
> My old boat goes round on a crutch
> And doesn't get under way.
> It's the time of the year
> And the time of the day.
>
> Perhaps it's the lunch that we had
> Or the lunch that we should have had.
> But I am, in any case,
> A most inappropriate man
> In a most unpropitious place.
>
> Mon Dieu, hear the poet's prayer.
> The romantic should be here.
> The romantic should be there.
> It ought to be everywhere.
> But the romantic must never remain,
>
> Mon Dieu, and must never again return.
> This heavy historical sail
> Through the mustiest blue of the lake
> In a really vertiginous boat
> Is wholly the vapidest fake. . . .
>
> It is least what one ever sees.
> It is only the way one feels, to say
> Where my spirit is I am,
> To say the light wind worries the sail,
> To say the water is swift today,
>
> To expunge all people and be a pupil
> Of the gorgeous wheel and so to give
> That slight transcendence to the dirty sail,
> By light, the way one feels, sharp white,
> And then rush brightly through the summer air.
> (*CP* 120-21)

The word *pejorative* hurt Stevens often, for it often applied to other words that he valued besides *romantic*. Later prose discussions of *escapism, personal,* and *temperament* all distinguished a favorable from a "pejorative" sense.[24] His gloss on *escapism* fits his usage in "Sailing after Lunch" as well: "The pejorative sense applies where the poet is not attached to reality, where the imagination does not adhere to reality, which, for my part, I regard as fundamental." (*NA* 31) But we do not have to depend only on *The Necessary Angel,* for Stevens glossed his own line in a letter to his mysterious publisher Ronald Lane Latimer acknowledging the personal importance of the poem to him:

> This particular poem is one that I have had in mind for the first poem in the book. Perhaps it means more to me than it should.
> . . . the thing is an abridgment of at least a temporary theory of poetry. When people speak of the romantic, they do so in what the French commonly call a *pejorative* sense. But poetry is essentially romantic, only the romantic of poetry must be something constantly new and, therefore, just the opposite of what is spoken of as the romantic. Without this new romantic, one gets nowhere; with it, the most casual things take on transcendence, and the poet rushes brightly, and so on. What one is always doing is keeping the romantic pure: eliminating from it what people speak of as the romantic. (*LWS* 277)

"A temporary theory of poetry" was the only kind Stevens would henceforth formulate, for a permanent one would by its permanency contradict the new romanticism's insistence on continual renewal.

The poem itself protests just such fixing, which belongs to the pejorative sense of *romantic.* In its primary meaning the second line, "My old boat goes round on a crutch," both exemplifies a worn-out metaphor and, by its inappropriateness (a boat does not go round on a crutch), establishes the boat as figurative rather than literal. But a possible secondary meaning—*crutch* in its nautical sense of a support to relieve strain on the boom while at rest on the mooring—plays against that overt stock sense in prelude to the more general rehabilitations that follow. In that enterprise our would-be romantic at first seems out of joint with his time, an "inappropriate" man in an "unpropitious" place. Like the draft of "Anecdote of the Prince of Peacocks," the third stanza inserts a French phrase, "Mon Dieu," into consideration of the romantic. The poet prays for the romantic to arise in different places but never to "remain" or to "return" in the same form. The "historical sail" reminds us that the boat represents the speaker's poetry, propelled by past survivals which the poem has just condemned as falsely romantic. In modifying the blue of imagination, "mustiest"—like "milky" in the peacock anecdote—indicates loss of contact with reality by a decaying or stuffy dreamworld. The poet's modernist situation in his boat is "really vertiginous," but attempt at a free ride on past power (the "historical sail") is "the vapidest fake."

Having condemned pejorative romanticism, the poem offers a program for creating a new and positive kind in its difficult last two stanzas. Success depends least on mere observation and most on projection of imagination from within. "It is only the way one feels" means not random impulses of feeling but the way it feels to do the actions described in the following infinitives—the way it feels to say that where my spirit is I am, to say that the wind worries the sail, to say that the water is swift, and to be a pupil of the gorgeous wheel. All these actions are imaginative, and the way it feels to do them is exhilarating. As Daniel Fuchs has suggested, "Metaphors like 'the light wind *worries* the sail' and 'the water is *swift* today' reflect not observation, but imagination."[25] So, too, do the other actions. To say "where my spirit is I am" restores divinity to man in a displacement reaching back through Coleridge's definition of imagination as finite repetition of "the infinite I AM" to Hebrew definitions of God (for example: "I am that I am"). Pursuit of individual imagination means at least temporary independence from society, for which expunging all people makes a nasty image. The final term, "to be a pupil/ Of the gorgeous wheel," connects to the sleight-of-hand man's apprehension of the sun of reality ("It is a wheel, the rays/ Around the sun," *CP* 222). That usage suggests that being a pupil of the gorgeous wheel also means returning to the flow of imaginative perceptions of reality. The process restores the power of the outmoded sail —itself a figure for stale convention—and enables it finally to power the boat.[26] Words like "light," "white," and "brightly" carry their usual Stevensian association with imagination. In some ways crabbed and difficult, this poem ends on a note of triumph that answers the entropic cyclicity of *Comedian* with a parable of romantic renewal, acted out by the dictional progress from the outmoded crutch to rushing brightly through the summer air.

The double sense of *romantic* advanced in "Sailing after Lunch" underlies Stevens' ambivalent use of the term in his prose criticism. He can either praise or condemn, depending on which kind of romantic he has in mind. One of the last Adagia restates the distinction concisely:

It should be said of poetry that it is essentially romantic as if one were recognizing the truth about poetry for the first time. Although the romantic is referred to, most often, in a pejorative sense, this sense attaches, or should attach, not to the romantic in general but to some phase of the romantic that has become stale. Just as there is always a romantic that is potent, so there is always a romantic that is impotent.[27] (*OP* 180)

This romantic duality became a two-handed engine for Stevens to wheel out at the door of poetry during the thirties. His review of Marianne Moore's *Selected Poems* delightedly detected her as a new romantic. The essay, "A Poet that Matters" (1935), makes an instructive contrast to T. S. Eliot's introduction to that volume. Both poets value Moore's precision of language and feeling and see her as technical master of intricately patterned verse. But each makes Moore into something of a self-projection. Eliot praises her "fusion of the ironic-conversational with the high-rhetorical,"[28] a fair enough description of his own verse as well. Stevens lauds rather her rescue of "romantic" relics by either fusing them with the actual ("imaginary gardens with real toads in them") or by "hybridizing" diction with a negative, as in "There are no banyans, frangipani nor/ jack-fruit trees; nor an exotic serpent/ life." (*OP* 251) This, of course, parallels Stevens' own method, as with the angel of reality who has "neither ashen wing nor wear of ore/ And live[s] without a tepid aureole." (*CP* 496) Michel Benamou has termed Stevens' continual negative enumeration of romantic paraphernalia "an anti-rhetoric, the begrudging heir to romantic style."[29] More largely, Eliot contrasts Moore's descriptions with the use of scene to provoke meditation in eighteenth-century or romantic poetry ("from Byron at his worst to Wordsworth at his best") and hence aligns her with Imagism and Poundian precision in expanding "association" from "concentration upon something visual."[30] Stevens instead identifies her as creator of a new and vital romanticism opposed to the obsolescent and embodying the "violent feelings" necessary to a violent time like our own.[31] He corrects Irving Babbitt (whose courses he had attended as an undergraduate) for forgetting the "sense of living intensely" necessary to romanticism, and he impishly conscripts Eliot himself as "the most brilliant instance of the romantic in this sense." (*OP* 252) Each poet sees in Moore the image demanded by his own needs, and the contrast exemplifies one way in which Stevens and Eliot were "dead opposites."

"People think in batches," Stevens told T. C. Wilson in 1935.

"The predominating batch today seems to think that the romantic as we know it is the slightest possible aspect of the thing." (*LWS* 282) That batch included both socially conscious Marxists and aesthetically alert formalists; Stevens wanted to divorce himself from both. His new romanticism tried to combine something from both positions in a *tertium quid*. After 1935 he dropped "new romantic" as slogan from his writing but continued his allegiance to its goals. Like a literary west wind, he both preserved and destroyed romantic theory through the lectures and essays (1942-51) collected as *The Necessary Angel* and through the theoretical hypotheses in his own poetry. During the dark years of the Depression and Second World War he traced the lineaments of a romantic response to the problems of the age. "The spirit of negation has been so active, so confident and so intolerant that the commonplaces about the romantic provoke us to wonder if our salvation, if the way out, is not the romantic," he speculated. (*NA* 17)

Specific citations from Wordsworth's "Composed upon Westminster Bridge," Shelley's *Defence of Poetry*, and Coleridge's *Biographia Literaria* offer ways into the pervasive romanticism of *The Necessary Angel*, particularly since they reverberate in Stevens' own poetry. In "The Noble Rider and the Sound of Words" Stevens adduces these lines from Wordsworth's sonnet to show "how poets help people to live their lives":

> This City now doth, like a garment, wear
> The beauty of the morning, silent bare,
> Ships, towers, domes, theatres, and temples lie
> Open unto the fields, and to the sky;
> All bright and glittering in the smokeless air.
>
> (*NA* 31)

Poets help us to live our lives by restoring our sense of the world. To escapism in the pejorative sense, Stevens contrasts the firm adherence to reality of Wordsworth's imagination; for him, Wordsworth's lines replace a blank, insubstantial, and static world with a full, solid, and dynamic one, an intimation of "the world in which we shall come to live" through the poet's fictions. He must have delighted in Wordsworth's unwitting use of Stevens' own image for such fictions, the metaphor of the garment.

"Of Hartford in a Purple Light," one of six poems published as "Illustrations of the Poetic as a Sense" in 1939, swerves from its Wordsworthian model even in invoking it. Addressing his poem to the sun (which figured so prominently in "Westminster

Bridge"), Stevens creates an alteration of clear masculine and purple feminine light:

> But now as in an amour of women
> Purple sets purple round. Look, Master,
> See the river, the railroad, the cathedral . . .
>
> When male light fell on the naked back
> Of the town, the river, the railroad were clear.
>
> (CP 227)

"Purple" here carries its normal Stevensian association with rite and ceremony, paralleling the religious connotations of Wordsworth's poem. Both lyrics present sudden imaginative perception of an urban panorama, unexpectedly transforming it into an organic body. But where Wordsworth arrests a moment, Stevens presents two lights in a sequence suggesting a cyclical process. The male light arranges the forms of the town like sculptures into "heroic attitudes," and the female light dissolves them back into fluidity in an "ever-freshening" round. Stevens' poem suggests a parable of renewal, which his switch from solemnity to slang ("slops away") reinforces. To him the poet's subject was "his sense of the world" (NA 121) rather than objects themselves.

Not surprisingly, the problem of relating poet and subject to a social context drove Stevens back to Shelley's proud explorations in the *Defence of Poetry*. He invoked Shelley's approximate definitions of poetry:

> Shelley gives us an approximation when he gives us a definition in what he calls "a general sense." He speaks of poetry as created by "that imperial faculty whose throne is *curtained* within the invisible nature of man." He says that a poem is the very *image* of life expressed in its eternal truth. It is "indeed something *divine*. It is at once the *centre and circumference* of knowledge . . . the record of the best and happiest moments of the happiest and best *minds* . . . it arrests the vanishing *apparitions* which *haunt* the interlunations of life." (NA 44, italics mine)

Quoted with evident approval, these sentiments match those of Stevens himself. He, too, saw poetry as a creation of imagination, an image of life and expression of the most fortunate mental states. Equally important, the diction here follows Stevens' own: "curtained" imagination reveals itself only through its coverings (as Nanzia Nunzio discovers); "image" is one of his favorite words and "centre and circumference" a favorite metaphor; and diction like "divine," "apparitions," and "haunt" deliberately displaces religious terms to secular frames in both poets. The *Defence,* in fact, pervades *The Necessary Angel.* When Stevens distinguishes approaching truth through reason from approaching it through imagination (*NA* 41) he follows the opening paragraph of the *Defence,* and when he claims that poetry "leaves its mark on whatever it touches" (*NA* 170) he echoes Shelley's belief that it "transmutes all that it touches." Further, he can argue that the poet has no specific social or moral obligation, just as Shelley warned against the poet embodying local conceptions of right and wrong, because "the imagination and society are inseparable" and the poet affects society by influencing the imagination.[32] (*NA* 28-29) Yet Stevens, like Shelley the man, refused naive belief in the ideal efficacy of art, and as anti-mythological poet he carefully established its limits, which Shelley as artist had conscientiously mentioned but deliberately deemphasized. He invoked Shelley twice in "Mr. Burnshaw and the Statue," his self-defense against young Stanley Burnshaw's Marxist critique of *Ideas of Order.* There he made clear that "Astral and Shelleyan" lights (*OP* 47) might alter our sense of the world but not the structure of nature and that even creation on earth of a Shelleyan "Italy of the mind" (*OP* 48) would not suffice the perpetual subversions of ongoing imagination.

If Stevens evolved his view of the social role of imagination from Shelley, he adapted his formulation of its dynamics in *The Necessary Angel* from Coleridge. Like Eliot, he sometimes used I. A. Richards' redactions, but unlike Eliot he more often departed from their reduction of imaginative power to "links of relevance."[33] Under guise of citing Richards on Coleridge, "The Noble Rider" introduced its own revisions in assigning the statue of Andrew Jackson in Lafayette Square to fancy rather than imagination. "Fancy is an activity of the mind which puts things together of choice, *not* the will, as a principle of the mind's being, striving to realize itself in knowing itself," wrote Stevens. "Fancy, then, is an exercise of selection from among objects already supplied by association . . . for purposes which are not then and therein being shaped but have been already fixed." (*NA* 10-11) This is Coleridge distorted by Stevens' insistent view of mind as a force. Coleridge in *Biographia* saw choice not as opposed to will but as an "empirical phenomenon" of it and defined not the purposes but the objects of fancy as fixed. In contrast, Stevens characteristically shifts all terms to process, with will (and implicitly imagination) becoming the mind striving to know itself in realizing itself and fancy the use of mind for secondary purposes.

Only fear of losing touch with reality could make Stevens falter in distinguishing imagination from fancy. That happened most glaringly in his discussion of imagination's limits in "Three Academic Pieces": "There is a limit to its power to surpass resemblance and that limit is to be found in nature. The imagination is able to manipulate nature as by creating three legs and five arms but it is not able to create a totally new nature as, for instance, a new element with creatures indigenous thereto, their costumes and cuisines." (*NA* 74) This contradicts both traditional Western notions of the poet as creator of an alternate nature or world, which particularly pleased the romantics, and Stevens' own notion of the mundo of imagination.[34] The limit reduces imagination almost to fancy, which creates three-legged or five-armed creatures out of fixities and definites. Stevens the poet knew better. His comic "Oak Leaves Are Hands" used metamorphoses of the formerly twelve-legged Lady Lowzen to explore the degeneration of imagination into fancy. As Helen Vendler has observed, "The aim is to suggest that as the Imagination approaches Fancy, to use Coleridge's terms, it becomes no longer revelatory but nonsensical, embodied in absurd and fabulous creatures like Lady Lowzen."[35] Imagination here ceases to help mind realize itself and instead becomes capricious, trivial, and outlandish, like the vocabulary of the poem itself.

The rest of *The Necessary Angel* continues Stevens' stress on imagination as process and as "power," a word Coleridge had also used. He variously sees imagination as "manifesting itself in its *domination* of words," as "a *process*," and as "the *power* of the mind over the possibilities of things."[36] He identified its function in phrases recalling Coleridge on the balance or reconciliation of opposites: "The imagination is the power that enables us to perceive the normal in the abnormal, the opposite of chaos in chaos." (*NA* 153) As both the sum of our faculties and a class rather than a single thing, imagination created our various ideas of order. Only its loss of contact with reality and withdrawal into a dreamworld could sap its power, as had happened in Stevens' youth. But what was reality?

Reality was also a force. Stevens thought of reality as "not that external scene but the life that is lived in it" and judged such life "spiritually violent" in the modern period. (*NA* 25, 27) Things as they are were not objects but forces, not static but dynamic. These doctrines reach tentative conclusion at the end of *An Ordinary Evening in New Haven:*

> It is not in the premise that reality
> Is a solid. It may be a shade that traverses
> A dust, a force that traverses a shade.
>
> (*CP* 489)

These lines build an ascending conditional scale from solid to shade to force, in which each further step reveals itself only by its effect—which would be a ripple or patterned motion—on a grosser element. The curious verb "traverse" probably carries as a secondary sense its legal meaning of formal denial, here denial that reality is a solid or a dust. The increasingly insubstantial triad contrasts with Shelley's similar tactic at the beginning of "Hymn to Intellectual Beauty," where the shadow of an unseen power floats itself unseen among us, for Stevens' shade and force remain essentially human. Reality remains at least a human product, at best a human process. In his dialectical struggle for vision, which to Stevens meant seeing the world as process rather than product, society often replaces nature as necessary antagonist to human imagination. "A generation ago we should have said that the imagination is an aspect of the conflict between man and nature," he wrote. "Today we are more likely to say that it is an aspect of the conflict between man and organized society." (*NA* 150)

Stevens significantly chose *Essays on Reality and the Imagination* as subtitle for *The Necessary Angel* to remind readers of the interdependence between the two terms. He wanted their relation to be "precise equilibrium." But that was impossible except momentarily. Dominance oscillated between them, and the extremes of their excesses provided the driving power for Stevens' pervasive cyclicity. He described their dynamic relation in the famous concluding remarks on nobility in "The Noble Rider": "The mind has added nothing to human nature. It is a violence from within that protects us from a violence without. It is the imagination pressing back against the pressure of reality." (*NA* 36) This violent psychomachia of opposing forces marks one of Stevens' most original turns in romantic theory. Before exploring it in detail, however, I mean to complete the picture of his development of central romantic strategies by examining his displacement of religious frames onto secular experience and his organization of imagery in a spatial projection emphasizing verticality.

Our argument fits Stevens' often-noticed displacement of reli-

gious to secular into a broader structure as a distinctive completion of romantic tendencies. Unlike his predecessors, Stevens
casts off traditional belief altogether, so that religion becomes
merely a quarry for the stones of his lay temple. In contrast, Blake
bound up his identification of Jesus and imaginative man with
left-wing Protestant radicalism, Wordsworth and Coleridge alternately shrank from or tried to reconcile the clash of secular imagination with orthodox belief, and even anti-Christian Shelley often
posited a suprahuman Power. But for Stevens, Phoebus and all
other gods lie in autumn umber. "In an age in which disbelief is
so profoundly prevalent . . . poetry and painting, and the arts in
general, are, in their measure, a compensation for what has been
lost," he wrote. "Men feel that the imagination is the next greatest
power to faith: the reigning prince." (*NA* 171) Yet he did not want
simply to substitute imagination for faith, or poetry for religion,
but continually held them distinct and hedged his assertions with
conditionals. Haunted heaven belonged to the past; adherents of
the opposing law confronted themselves. Stevens explicitly distinguished Biblical from poetic imagination, making clear that
poetry could not do everything the Bible formerly did. (*NA* 144)
Particularly, poetry made no claims of absolute and final truth,
instead offering us fictions which, if supreme enough, might inspire belief even while known to be false. Hence the poet was not
a *vates.* Only after a series of conditionals remarkable even for
Stevens would he arrive at a moving vision of "the poet himself,
still in the ecstasy of the poem that completely accomplished his
purpose" as seeming "a man who needed what he had created,
uttering the hymns of joy that followed his creation." (*NA* 50-51)

Stevens was in some ways a gnostic without a god and sought in
his own hymns to exalt rather than abase man. "We give our good
qualities to God, or to various gods, but they come from ourselves," he remarked in parallel to Blake's "All deities reside in the
human breast." (*LWS* 295) So Hoon discovered in *Harmonium.*
Descending in the purple of ritual, he learns the true source of the
ointment and hymns:

> Out of my mind the golden ointment rained,
> And my ears made the blowing hymns they heard.
> I was myself the compass of that sea:
>
> I was the world in which I walked, and what I saw
> Or heard or felt came not but from myself;
> And there I found myself more truly and more strange.
> (*CP* 65)

Here mind and ear create their mighty world not half but wholly. The mind's ointment marks Hoon as a human, the ears' hymns as a poet. As creator of his world, he merges with it in an act of self-discovery matching the description of will in "The Noble Rider" as a principle of mind "striving to realize itself in knowing itself." The grandeur of Hoon abated in Stevens' later work, but the function of poetry did not. Only he voiced it with increased sympathy for the pathos of the human condition. *The Man with the Blue Guitar* (1937) continued to insist that "Poetry/ Exceeding music must take the place/ Of empty heaven and its hymns,/ Ourselves in poetry must take their place," and in the very late "Final Soliloquy of the Interior Paramour" (1951) the Blakean axiom that "God and the imagination are one"—qualified by the crucial "we say"—rescues us from poverty to make a sufficient dwelling in the evening air. (*CP* 167, 524)

Displacement from religious to secular involved overall patterns as well as minute particulars. Although she does not say so, Adelaide Kirby Morris' thoughtful précis of Stevens' psychohistoriography falls within romantic bounds: "If God is the imagination, then biblical history becomes personal history: Genesis the moment of awareness which creates the world through the word of the poem; the Fall the moment of self-awareness which separates us from the world; grace, as in 'The Sense of the Sleight-of-Hand Man,' the moment of fortuitous delight."[37] Familiar to readers of Blake and Wordsworth particularly, schemes such as this regularly end in apocalypse, the stripping away of illusive covering to reveal a transformed world. Morris omits apocalypse partly because Stevens himself often turns from it, both in his distrust of transcendentalism and in his uncertainty that we can ever escape from fictive coverings. A desire to restore this world to us inspired his celebrated aphorism, "The great poems of heaven and hell have been written and the great poem of the earth remains to be written." (*NA* 142) Yet the religious analogy to the result of his great poem of earth would be an untranscendental apocalypse revealing this world to us properly. That impulse brings paradise down to the world and, alternately, internalizes it. Wordsworth in *The Prelude* spoke of those who

> in the region of their peaceful selves
> Did now find helpers to their hearts' desire
> . . . in the very world which is the world
> Of all of us,—the place in which, in the end,
> We find our happiness, or not at all!
> (Book X, lines 720-38, 1805 text)

In Stevens this becomes the questions of *Sunday Morning:*

> Shall our blood fail? Or shall it come to be
> The blood of paradise? And shall the earth
> Seem all of paradise that we shall know?[38]
>
> (*CP* 68)

The desire to answer these questions affirmatively informs Stevens' plot against the giant and for the ephebe.

Romantic use of organized imagery and emphasis on movement downward and within reinforced Stevens' displacement of religious to secular. He thought that "a group of images in harmony with each other would constitute a poem within, or above, a poem." (*NA* 78) Full examination of the poem within his own poems would require a book by itself.[39] Here we need note merely that like the romantics he created a pattern of imagery deriving its significance more from his own work than from received tradition and embodying a psychic projection centered on imagination, with the difference that his usages often have some roots in romanticism itself. The chief images he used in a romantic manner were the moon of imagination, sun of reality, star of desire, urns, birds, wind, and marriage. After identifying "the Mind of Man" as his theme in *The Recluse,* for example, Wordsworth adapted Christian marriage between the soul and Christ to his secular song of mind's union with nature, "the spousal verse of this great consummation." Stevens, too, evokes the marriage of man and nature in displaced Christian metaphors of conjugality: from Bonnie and Josie "celebrating the marriage/ Of flesh and air" through the ignorant man's chance "to mate his life with life/ That is the sensual, pearly spouse, the life/ That is fluent in even the wintriest bronze" and the "mystic marriage in Catawba" to the final soliloquy of the interior paramour.[40]

The spatializations of this imagistic world locate power and energy as moving downward and within, in normative romantic fashion. Thus, the triumphant poet descends in "Tea at the Palaz of Hoon," the pigeons sink downward to darkness in "Sunday Morning," the voices of the lions come down at Stevens' resumption of publication with "The Sun This March," and the figure of capable imagination "arrogant of his streaming forces" clatters down the mountain in "Mrs. Alfred Uruguay."[41] Yet Stevens' skeptical cyclicity kept him from absolutism, and he incorporated flashes of upward movement into a pervasive verticality most reminiscent of Shelley's up-and-down motions. Like Crispin, he came to conceive

> his voyaging to be
> An up and down between two elements,
> A fluctuating between sun and moon,
> A sally into gold and crimson forms,
> As on this voyage, out of goblinry,
> And then retirement like a turning back
> And sinking down to the indulgences
> That in the moonlight have their habitude.
>
> (CP 35)

This maneuver enabled Stevens to incorporate his developing sun symbol into his scheme, but even its power descends to earth, like the Great Captain who marries Bawda at noon for love of the marriage place. At the end of *Collected Poems* both the sun and the scrawny cry move "from outside" but *to inside*.

As all this suggests, the mature Stevens worked out his own development of romantic positions, sometimes helped by his predecessors and sometimes arriving at similar strategies on his own. He rightly insisted that he not be classed as a mere repetitor. "While, of course, I come down from the past, the past is my own and not something marked Coleridge, Wordsworth, etc.," he wrote in a letter of 1953. "My reality-imagination complex is entirely my own even though I see it in others." (*LWS* 792) Although that letter's exaggerated claims of originality ("I know of no one who has been particularly important to me") both imply irritation with all too obvious affinities and contradict other avowals, Stevens was in the main correct. We have already seen how he introduced his own variations into romantic theory and diverged from earlier poets even while following them most closely in his poetry. The dark italics of his two principal turns, in the directions of radical provisionality and psychic violence, need to be propounded even more precisely.

Stevens' provisionality derived first from his emphasis on change. He thought of primary imaginative apprehension of reality as fluid. A metaphor could embody such sensuous perception, but subsequent elaboration of it into either codified mythology or abstract statement falsified and deadened by arresting fluidity in a static structure. "The fire eye in the clouds survives the gods" (*CP* 222) means among other things that the imaginative perception generating metaphor (sun as fire eye) outlasts its codification into either theology or theogony and can be returned to when the myths themselves atrophy. The rays as wheel around the sun survive their myths of elaboration into sun chariots. To live with imaginative perception of reality means to live with change. That is why the speaker of the final address to the celestial paramours of "Mr. Burnshaw and the Statue" tells them that "it is only enough/ To live incessantly in change." (*OP* 50) Since there can be lives in which imagination has the same value it does in letters, these changes need not be apocalyptic or poetic. They can inform everyday life. The midday air swarms "with the metaphysical changes that occur,/ Merely in living as and where we live." (*CP* 326) The same drive to change informs Stevens' record of his own imaginative perceptions in his poetry. As Helen Vendler has observed in a different context, "He tries and discards mode after mode, genre after genre, form after form, voice after voice, model after model, topic after topic."[42] At every turn he avoids being fixed. We come to understand one of the tripartite requirements of a supreme fiction: it must change.

Yet such changes were not wholly random but tended to arrange themselves in cycles, which could either liberate or subjugate. They could liberate by turning us from victims to connoisseurs of chaos, aware that a great disorder is an order. (*CP* 215) Stevens' seasonal and diurnal cycles work in that way. But cycles could also ensnare, by either destroying imagination through too rigid a pattern or dooming it to meaningless repetition. Stevens feared the latter in *Comedian*, with its inexorable cycle from romanticism to fatalism. He tried to escape endless repetitions of the grim round by breaking through to the central. This is, of course, a high romantic aim, from Blake's struggle with the Orc cycle to Shelley's with worlds on worlds rolling ever. But Stevens exceeded even Shelley's skepticism about realizing such a goal. He came to doubt that it could be even represented, let alone attained. In place of *Jerusalem* or *Prometheus Unbound* he gives us *notes* toward a supreme fiction. He rings even his closest approach, toward the end of *Notes*, round with conditionals and interrogatives, and by his very fervor of desire makes us doubt its consummation. "It is possible, possible, possible," he writes. "It must/ Be possible." (*CP* 404)

Basic distrust of language completed Stevens' drive toward provisionality. His doubts again surpassed even Shelley's, whose Demogorgon announced that "the deep truth is imageless," or Eliot's, whose new raids on the inarticulate ended with shabby equipment always deteriorating. Stevens preoccupied himself with language as both instrument and symbol more than most poets, making it into a second subject of many poems. Yet in releasing earth from its man-locked set, even the necessary angel offers only liquid lingerings of watery words awash. The gaiety of language, not its adequacy, was Stevens' seigneur. He feared that

189

language inherently falsified, if not by initial distortion then by permanent codification. "I am evading a definition," he declared in "The Noble Rider." "If it is defined, it will be fixed and it must not be fixed." (*NA* 34) Combined with his views on change and cyclicity, Stevens' distrust of language demanded provisionality as the only viable poetic strategy. The true purpose of his endless conditionals, interrogatives, and syntactic legerdemain is to remind us continually that his poetic fictions are only fictions and to prevent them from fixing what must never be fixed. Poetry can only exist "in the intricate evasions of as."[43] (*CP* 486)

The continuous constructions and destructions of provisionality demanded such enormous inputs of energy that Stevens came to exalt the necessary violence of imagination. The romantics had recognized such violence; one thinks of Blake's tyger, Coleridge's sacred river, or Shelley's west wind. But Stevens' insistence on process heightens and extolls the fury of mind's search for what will suffice. He still speaks of mental marriage with the world but shows a modern obsession with the libido it subsumes. For Keats' "diligent indolence" or Wordsworth's "wise passiveness" Stevens substitutes his own oxymoron for imaginative action—"violent idleness." (*CP* 514) He thought such stress obligatory for a new romantic. After stipulating "uncommon intelligence" in the review of Marianne Moore, he added that the romantic "means in a time like our own of violent feelings, equally violent feelings." (*OP* 252) Miss Moore had reciprocated in advance by praising Stevens' "ferocity" in the *Dial* of 1924.[44]

Thinking of imagination and reality as forces fathered such dragon's teeth. The definitions of "The Noble Rider" set up a field theory valuing dynamic drives: imagination was "a violence from within that protects us from a violence without"; it pressed back against the pressure of reality. (*NA* 36) Poetry lived in the interface. Stevens saw progression to psychic violence as the ultimate goal of the ephebe seeking mastery of his own faculties. Like an adept of religious contemplation he advised fledgling poets to begin by studying imagination in exercises and then to "proceed little by little . . . to those violences which are the maturity of his desires." (*NA* 63-64) The imaginative maturity of the master himself appears in the famous apostrophe exalting "rage for order" in "The Idea of Order at Key West," particularly in view of *The Necessary Angel's* later definition of imagination as the power to perceive "the opposite of chaos in chaos." These dynamics reverse Eliot. Fearing violence from within, Eliot sought protection in external ideas of order. Stevens instead feared violence from without and sought to defend himself by a corresponding violence from within. For Eliot order itself was blessed, for Stevens the rage for it.

These ideas permeate not only Stevens' careful considerations but also the more casual pronouncements of his letters. They turn up especially in discussions of literature and fine arts throughout his life. "I expect to read violently all week," he announced (1909).[45] Or, thinking of creation rather than consumption of literature, he could confess "a real fury for indulgence" in writing (1922). Belief in poetry was "a magnificent fury," while Florida had been "violently affective" (1943). Stevens looked at the fine arts with the same eye. He valued Tal Coat over Arp because Tal Coat assimilated the violence of creation. Stevens here and elsewhere used the word "force" not as a dead metaphor but with implicit awareness of its primary meaning. He rapped in staccato: Arp "lacks force. His imagination lacks strength. His feelings are incapable of violence." Hence Arp was "fastidious not forceful" and "his forms will never constitute a 'visionary language' " (1949). In contrast, Tal Coat had painted "a violent still life" (which Stevens admitted sounded "queer") in which the objects had "aggressiveness." His work constituted "a display of imaginative force" (1949).

The painting by Tal Coat, of course, inspired Stevens' corresponding display of imaginative force in "Angel Surrounded by Paysans." But sometimes the violence of that force became itself the subject of poems. His favorite images for it were destructive wind and war, as in "Man and Bottle," and animal ferocity. While the animal imagery appears in *Collected Poems* as early as the firecat of "Earthy Anecdote," Stevens first developed it definitively in *The Man with the Blue Guitar*, whose player seeks to create "a savage blue" with the "claws" and "fangs" of the mind. (*CP* 166, 174) That drive climaxes in the spare vocabulary and complicated syntax of poem XIX:

> That I may reduce the monster to
> Myself, and then may be myself
>
> In face of the monster, be more than part
> Of it, more than the monstrous player of
>
> One of its monstrous lutes, not be
> Alone, but reduce the monster and be,
>
> Two things, the two together as one,
> And play of the monster and of myself,

Or better not of myself at all,
But of that as its intelligence,

Being the lion in the lute
Before the lion locked in stone.
(CP 175)

James Baird has correctly seen but too simply dismissed this as "clear refutation of Stevens' supposed agreement with Wordsworth and Coleridge . . . imagination is not an agent patiently synthesizing: it is a raw faculty."[46] What it more precisely shows us is how much Stevens needed his swerve into imagination's violence to prevent his complete absorption into romantic tradition. For otherwise the poem presents a typical romantic confrontation of the poet with nature. Further, the speaker progresses from a naive egotism ("That I may reduce the monster to/ Myself") to the absence of selfhood characteristic of imaginative activity ("Or better not of myself at all"). The imaginative moment of art temporarily heals the breach between subject and object, and man first becomes "as one" with the monster and then, better, "its intelligence." This quasi union occurs only in the act of playing, when both "I" and "monster" can be described by the specific term "lion," as they are for the first time in the last couplet, still separate but united in the song and in the words of the song. Stevens himself glossed imagination's savagery in the passage in terms obviously parallel to the definitions of *The Necessary Angel:* "I want to face nature the way two lions face one another—the lion in the lute facing the lion locked in stone. I want, as a man of the imagination, to write poetry with all the power of a monster equal in strength to that of the monster about whom I write. I want man's imagination to be completely adequate in the face of reality." (LWS 790)

Mind's violence could destroy as well as create. Specifically, it could demolish imprisoning structures of the past to clear the ground for new imaginative activity in an ongoing cycle. Stevens often used wind to embody this kind of imaginative violence, as in his description of the "turbulent Schlemihl" Ludwig Richter who

Knows desire without an object of desire,
All mind and violence and nothing felt.

He knows he has nothing more to think about,
Like the wind that lashes everything at once.
(CP 358)

In Stevens, the object only suffices in the act of finding it, and then becomes inadequate. The old images have turned to meaningless stage props, and Richter must lash them to pieces before building new ones. Such violence takes its place in the necessary revolutions of imaginative life. Stevens adapted Simone Weil's term "decreation" to distinguish it from mere "destruction": "She says that decreation is making pass from the created to the uncreated, but that destruction is making pass from the created to nothingness. Modern reality is a reality of decreation, in which our revelations are not the revelations of belief, but the precious portents of our own powers. The greatest truth we could hope to discover . . . is that man's truth is the final resolution of everything." (*NA* 174-75) Mind's violence thus becomes the driving force of change in an unending round of creation and decreation; it provides the power for Stevens' provisionality.

"If mind is the most terrible force in the world, it is also the only force that defends us against terror," wrote Stevens in *Adagia*. (*OP* 173) Frank Kermode rightly observes that the first statement about mind here refers to "intellect" and the second to "imagination."[47] As Yeats did in "Meru," Stevens sees intellect as destroying imagination's illusions to deliver man to the desolation of reality, for only there can imagination rightly begin anew. "The Well Dressed Man with a Beard" opens," After the final no there comes a yes/ And on that yes the future world depends," and concludes, "It can never be satisfied, the mind, never." (*CP* 247) Stevens found that formulation crucial enough to be included among his circus animals during the enumeration of old themes in the late "As You Leave the Room"—"that poem . . . about the mind as never satisfied." (*OP* 117) Mind was never satisfied because it found a provisional sufficiency only in the act of finding, not in the objects themselves. Poems sought to render such mental actions rather than to record their objects.

In *The Necessary Angel* Stevens sketched a brief and beautiful image of the poet emerging from the past, using the seventeenth century as example:

> When we look back at the face of the seventeenth century, it is at the rigorous face of the rigorous thinker and, say, the Miltonic image of a poet, severe and determined. In effect, what we are remembering is the rather haggard background of the incredible, the imagination without intelligence, from which a younger figure is emerging, stepping forward in the company of a muse of its own. . . . This younger figure is the intelligence that endures. It is the imagination of the son still bearing the antique

imagination of the father. It is the clear intelligence of the young man still bearing the burden of the obscurities of the intelligence of the old. It is the spirit out of its own self, not out of some surrounding myth, delineating with accurate speech the complications of which it is composed. For this Aeneas, it is the past that is Anchises.[48] (*NA* 52-53)

Stevens found his personal poetic Anchises not in the seventeenth century but in the early nineteenth. We have already investigated his creative transformation of romantic theory and its effect on his poems. It is now time to consider the kind of mental action he evolved in carrying the old, high romanticism on his shoulders into the world he made as twentieth-century new romantic.

II

Stevens' innovations resulted in a mode of mental action distinct from that of both his romantic forerunners and his modernist contemporaries. He shares most with that other towering pro-romantic, Yeats, who also sought to modernize romanticism through attaining his own individuality. But Stevens did not share Yeats' vacillating belief in an external spiritual or transcendent order and developed a correspondingly different attitude toward his art. The speaker of "Sailing to Byzantium" longs to be gathered into "the artifice of eternity," but the pursuer of "A Quiet Normal Life"—a significantly contrasting title—sees no fury in transcendent forms and instead rejoices that "his actual candle blazed with artifice." (*CP* 523) This differing attitude toward artifice resulted in a different status for poetic fictions. Stevens made his fictions more self-canceling than even Yeats' fierce irony allowed; he wanted them not to constitute either a human order analogous to eternity or a maximum human achievement in nature's spite, but rather to collapse on themselves and so return the reader to their human source. Further, Stevens deliberately undermined the status of the image, which for Yeats nearly assumed ontological independence. And finally, Yeats often presented mental actions directly, while Stevens preferred to refract them through a second consciousness. As a result, the passionate originality of each often fits his own self-description, Yeats as a last romantic and Stevens as a new one.

Yeats became at least a tacit ally,[49] but Eliot emerged as implicit enemy to Stevens in his poetic quest (he knew neither personally).

Since Stevens accepted and welcomed the creative violence that
Eliot rejected and feared, his qualifications of vision serve wholly
different ends. Eliot's incessant defenses try to protect the ego
against furious processes of imagination; Stevens' provisionality
aims to preserve the imagination from taking its own products as
final. While Stevens could praise Eliot on one occasion as an "up-
right ascetic" in a "floppy" world,[50] he more often saw him as
antithesis to his own beliefs and more typically described him as
"a negative . . . force." (*LWS* 378) Stevens throughout accepted the
syntax that Eliot (and Pound) often spurned and used it to generate his special brand of provisional vision. He valued process over
product and designed his poems to embody actions rather than
their results. Consequently, Stevens' poems act out what they advocate rather than divide against themselves. But for all their differences, Stevens and Eliot—along with Yeats—have enough in
common to allow a central apprehension of their poetry through
norms derived from romantic mental action. This approach to Stevens can best be made by beginning with an early poem of orthodox mental action, proceeding through the crucial "Idea of
Order at Key West" to his exploitation of double consciousness,
syntax, and image, and concluding with his most ambitious work,
Notes toward a Supreme Fiction.

Stevens comes closest to the direct mental action of his precursors in the early "Domination of Black" (1916). The poem resembles Coleridge's "Frost at Midnight" both in placing its speaker
before a fire in a room at night and in using its collation of inner
and outer (room and nature) as paradigm for relating subjective
and objective. Most important, the tripartite structure approaches
that of the Greater Romantic Lyric:

> At night, by the fire,
> The colors of the bushes
> And of the fallen leaves,
> Repeating themselves,
> Turned in the room,
> Like the leaves themselves
> Turning in the wind.
> Yes: but the color of the heavy hemlocks
> Came striding.
> And I remembered the cry of the peacocks.
>
> The colors of their tails
> Were like the leaves themselves
> Turning in the wind,
> In the twilight wind.

They swept over the room,
Just as they flew from the boughs of the hemlocks
Down to the ground.

I heard them cry—the peacocks.
Was it a cry against the twilight
Or against the leaves themselves
Turning in the wind,
Turning as the flames
Turned in the fire,
Turning as the tails of the peacocks
Turned in the loud fire,
Loud as the hemlocks
Full of the cry of the peacocks?
Or was it a cry against the hemlocks?

Out of the window,
I saw how the planets gathered
Like the leaves themselves
Turning in the wind.
I saw how the night came,
Came striding like the color of the heavy hemlocks
I felt afraid.
And I remembered the cry of the peacocks.

(CP 8-9)

The lines across the page mark the three main divisions in the poem,[51] which progresses from descriptive metaphor to the enigmatic significance of the peacocks and concludes with a new recognition by the persona. Displacements in time and space accompany these shifts. Narrated in past tense, the poem involves two brief spans of time—the opening nocturnal moments in front of the fire and the closing ones looking out of the window, and the intervening recollection of a twilight past including observation of leaves, striding of the hemlocks, and the cry of the peacocks. The speaker begins by comparing the colors of the fire to those of the bushes and fallen leaves. "Yes: but" interrupts the pleasant revery with reminder of the more ominous hemlocks and peacocks' cry. The second verse paragraph compares the peacocks' tails to the turning leaves in color and through the ambiguous reference of "they" connects both to the colors created in the room by the fire. Only then does the speaker enter the second section of the mental action, an interrogative meditation on the peacocks' cry. He emerges with a new perception of his situation. Looking now out the window, he surrenders the implicitly pleasurable reminiscence about the leaves' color to a more ominous sensation. The bleak cyclicity of the planets joins with the turning leaves, black hemlocks, and peacocks' cry to create a fear associated with his own mortality. The poem thus moves from description to meditation to evaluation, with matching tripartite patterns of here-there-here and now-then-now.

One hesitates to label the poem a Greater Romantic Lyric only because of the odd central section. Because his fire simile drags the present back into the past, the persona does not fully enter the time of the peacock apparition. Further, the meditation or vision—if it is a vision—consists wholly of interrogatives. It presents three alternate objects for the peacocks' cry—twilight, leaves, and hemlocks. By providing no means of choice, the series posits as objects all three, with their cumulative connotations of death. The poem's mental powers cannot defend against this fear. They consist of association and memory, with embryonic imagination aborted by the peacocks' cry. For that cry seems to transfix the speaker and to arrest his creative response. He deviates instead into meditation on the cry's significance and can get no further than obstinate questionings. The poem itself constitutes his own cry, less as poet than as peacock, a powerful but not wholly articulate protest at things as they are. The imagination fails to resist fully the pressure of reality, and the poem ends with the domination of black.

Stevens never returned that closely to romantic norms, preferring instead to develop his own imaginative response through the provisionality of double consciousness and distorted syntax already tingeing "Domination of Black." But two poems of the mid-1940s tenuously continue the early approach. "This as Including That" (*OP* 88) frames its intonation by the "priest of nothingness" with a brief opening description of scene and closing return to it in details suggesting sterile discomfort. More complexly, "Recitation after Dinner" (*OP* 86) begins with discussion of the meaning of tradition, progresses to the powerful image of Aeneas bearing Anchises on his back, and returns to an evaluative conclusion. Its passionate central section conjures up an image that the mind reacts to as though it were actually present. Such survivals occur rarely in later Stevens, however, for he had already evolved an alternate artifice.

"The Idea of Order at Key West" (1934) marks the critical transition in Stevens' passage from old to new romanticism. Recognizably—even blatantly—derived from romantic models, it brings together for the first time the still rudimentary innovations that later germinated into his mature work. The poem itself springs from the tradition in which a speaker confronts a landscape made important by his mental action there rather than by its own inherent significance, like Wordsworth's "Tintern Abbey" or Pound's urban "In a Station of the Metro." Were Key West absent from the title, we should not know the place. The comic title also suggests provisionality, as though another idea of order awaited us at, say, Key Largo and still another up at Fort Lauderdale. Yet unlike "Tintern Abbey" the poem is not a Greater Romantic Lyric, although it might have been, and unlike "In a Station of the Metro" it does not simply juxtapose two moments, although it includes them. Stevens has devised his own serenade here, even while ringing changes on familiar romantic tones. The poem sets imagination against nature, displaces religious terms to secular experience (*"blessed* rage for order," *CP* 130), internalizes its quest, and operates within a vertical frame (the sky acutest at its vanishing and the night descending). But it diverges from romantic and modernist paradigms in its manipulation of consciousness, syntax, and image.

The poem displays that "double consciousness" which became a sure signature of Stevens' mature verse. I use the term not in its Wordsworthian sense, where it denotes a second figure introduced into the poem as foil to the first—for example, young Dorothy to mature William in "Tintern Abbey"—but to indicate one mind apprehending the imaginative action of another, as Stevens does the singing girl's in "Key West." The old romanticism presents imaginative action directly: a Wordsworthian speaker encounters the Wye valley, or a Keatsian one interacts with a nightingale or an urn. But the new romanticism presents imaginative action indirectly through the medium of a second mind: a Stevensian speaker often encounters another mind that is itself encountering the world. That is, Stevens refracts mental action of one mind through the apprehension of a second. He builds whole poems of incidental romantic situations where Wordsworth, say, might briefly imagine Dorothy's future encounter with the Wye, or Coleridge end "Frost at Midnight" with Hartley's future relation to nature. He channels the full psychological representation which old romantics poured into conversation poems or Greater Romantic Lyrics into situations that they used only for small parts of longer poems or for slighter lyrics like "The Solitary Reaper."

Most of "Key West" consists of Stevens apprehending the girl's song. For the "I" of direct representation he substitutes the "she" of double consciousness. She is the one undergoing the mental processes that would result in a Greater Romantic Lyric. He but contemplates her creativity, and he does so even in retrospect. He adopts a similar attitude toward his own mental action at the end of the poem. Rather than experiencing the imaginative ordering of night, he again narrates the event in the past tense, replete with the inquisitive probing he had formerly focused on the girl. He filters his past imaginative consciousness through his present meditative one.

What does the speaker do in his meditation? His syntax mimics the mental action he describes, so that while he remains meditative the syntax momentarily fools us into thinking of his act as imaginative. This happens in different ways in each part of the poem. His consideration of the girl begins with negatives and conditionals continually qualifying his assertions but ends with a burst of positive statement. The operative phrases are at first *never formed, yet, was not, although, was not, No more was, were not, Even if, It may be, But . . . not, Whose spirit is this?, If it was only* (twice), *it would have been,* and *But.* But in the last verse paragraph devoted to her they become (with one exception) positive: *It was, She measured, She was, the sea . . . became, she was,* and *we . . . knew.* The syntax thus progresses from qualification to assertion and from weakness to power as the speaker progresses from confusion to knowledge; it acts out at one remove a vicarious participation in her song, causing the reader to respond as if to an ongoing imaginative act rather than to a descant on a past one.

The epilogue accomplishes the same effect by different syntactic means:

> Ramon Fernandez, tell me, if you know,
> Why, when the singing ended and we turned
> Toward the town, tell why the glassy lights,
> The lights in the fishing boats at anchor there,
> As the night descended, tilting in the air,
> Mastered the night and portioned out the sea,
> Fixing emblazoned zones and fiery poles,
> Arranging, deepening, enchanting night.
>
> Oh! Blessed rage for order, pale Ramon,
> The maker's rage to order words of the sea,
> Words of the fragrant portals, dimly-starred,
> And of ourselves and of our origins,
> In ghostlier demarcations, keener sounds.
>
> (CP 130)

The passage begins as a request to Ramon Fernandez for enlightenment. But the interrogative implications of *tell me, Why,* and *tell why* yield to a series of declarative verbs and participles —*descended, tilting, mastered, portioned out, fixing,* and climactically *Arranging, deepening, enchanting.* These are verbs of imagination. More important, as the syntax changes from interrogative to descriptive the scene takes on a life of its own. As the poet sketches the past event, the active verbs and participles assume near syntactic independence so that he seems to be creating a nocturnal seascape which he is in fact recalling. By the line "Arranging, deepening, enchanting night" we have forgotten the opening interrogatives and been caught up in a surrogate act of imagination. The syntax fosters the illusion that he is doing what the girl does: becoming the artificer of his world. He in fact has done that, for the answer to the question "Why?" is "imagination." But the poem acts as if the speaker exercised such imagination now rather than then.

The five final lines provide a third variant of the same strategy. The impassioned rapture at the "rage for order" seems to create a scene under guise of describing the poetic act. We seem to see the sea, portals, and ourselves when the speaker in fact refers only to "words of " those things. The prepositional objects take on quasi-independent status because the passage lacks a main verb. It is static but seems dynamic because enough energy carries over from the previous stanza to make the speaker seem to be creating another scene rather than delivering an apostrophe to the rage for order. "The maker's rage to order words" explicitly refers to the poetry. Both poet and reader order words and so participate in imaginative process. To make them do so is the final purpose of the double consciousness and deceptive syntax, which together prevent direct presentation of mental action and undermine the objective status of the fiction. That act frees us from domination by external products of past mental actions and drives us back to the source of their energy within the self.

The girl at Key West is both a romantic image and a Romantic Image. She derives partly from Wordsworth's "The Solitary Reaper," as a number of critics have noticed.[52] Wordsworth's poem, too, centers on the poet's apprehension of a solitary, singing girl whose distinctively human song (the grand past events or humble present ones of stanza 2) surpasses nature (the Nightingale and Cuckoo-bird of stanza 2) and continues to affect the speaker later. But there are significant differences, ranging from Wordsworth's anchoring of imaginative experience in common labor by the key romantic notion of harvest, through the content of the songs themselves, to their impact on the speaker. In Stevens the speaker acts imaginatively but in Wordsworth he simply bears the music in his heart as implicit future stimulus to imagination. The mental action is, of course, completely different, with Wordsworth's first three stanzas set in the present tense and using simple association and direct syntax. A better and unnoticed parallel lies in Coleridge's response to the maiden with a dulcimer in "Kubla Khan." After the vision of the Abyssinian girl singing of paradise, Coleridge begins with a conditional ("Could I . . .") and then creates the panorama of a human circle around the flashing-eyed poet amid the sunny domes and caves of ice, all of which are syntactically provisional but assume a quasi independence as the constructions progress.

Stevens' singer is also a Romantic Image in the sense propounded by Kermode and embodied in Stevens' own images of a man skating, a woman dancing, and a woman combing at the end of "Of Modern Poetry." Like those, she embodies a Unity of Being and a human ideal fusing opposites into an object of desire. The poem probes her explicit meaning in working out the poet's relation to her. Stevens deliberately separates her song from nature, which it both surpasses ("She sang beyond the genius of the sea") and refuses to merge with ("The song and water were not medleyed sound"). He also repudiates the voice alone ("it was more . . . even than her voice, and ours, among/ The meaningless plunging of water and the wind"). What, then, is left? Although her voice is both beyond and superior to the world, it orders the world ("she was the single *artificer* of the world" [italics mine]). She exemplifies the imagination pressing back against the pressure of reality, a vortex at the intersection of psychic forces. That is why Stevens values her so highly. But she is a particularly transitory Image. "Song" implies both brief duration and change within even that limited span, while the absence of details about the girl makes her presence seem even more ephemeral. The title supports this temporal limitation with a spatial one by reminding us of relativity. She will endure as Image little longer than the moment in which the lights measure the night at the end. These qualities inhere in Romantic Images, but the poem heightens awareness of them. Stevens does not revamp the Image the way he does mental action through double consciousness and deceptive syntax; he rather adds a nuance, and the nuance is in the direction of increasing the Image's transience. The technique becomes more apparent with images rather than Images, as the manipulation of consciousness, syntax, and image already present in "Key West" increasingly informs his later work.

Like Stevens' other chief devices, double consciousness generated not uniformity but diversity among his poems. He exploited its potential in continually shifting ways, for simple repetition would have contradicted the impulse toward provisionality that it supported. By treating imaginative actions at one remove he underscored their impermanence in a world of constant change. Thus, he could employ double consciousness to render the imaginative act itself ("Connoisseur of Chaos"), to explore its relation to image and to self-knowledge ("The Sick Man"), to invert normal perspective ("God Is Good. It Is a Beautiful Night"), or even negatively to present a cautionary example of mind-forged manacles ("Landscape with Boat"). Those four mature poems epitomize the diverse uses to which Stevens put this technique, with which he had experimented as early as "Disillusionment of Ten O'Clock" (1915).

Perhaps the most compact example of double consciousness in Stevens appears in "Connoisseur of Chaos" (1938). The poem concludes its investigation of order with the figure of the pensive man:

> The pensive man . . . He sees that eagle float
> For which the intricate Alps are a single nest.
> (CP 216)

Seeing "the intricate" as "single" involves detection of unity in diversity and, given the lines' context, of order in chaos. Seeing the Alps as nest means viewing a beautiful but foreign and perhaps harsh landscape as a comfortable home, as though we lived in a place that were our own. To make the intricate Alps into a single nest is to perceive them imaginatively. *The pensive man does not do that directly.* He sees the eagle, who sees the Alps as nest. The eagle "floats" in surrender of imposed purpose to the gratuitous discovery on which imagination depends. But an eagle, of course, cannot be imaginative. The eagle, then, must be an image for an imaginative perceiver. The pensive man sees an image of the perceiver who can see the Alps that way. He perceives the image directly and the order only indirectly, and only through the image does he perceive the order at all. The poem's speaker operates from a further remove yet, for he stands in the same relation to the pensive man that the pensive man does to the eagle.

In attenuating the idea of order by multiple removes, the final couplet supports the provisionality that the entire poem seizes as overt theme. The poem begins with two pseudophilosophical statements. "A violent order is disorder" because it both distorts reality to fit its own preconceived premises and excludes what it cannot appropriate. "A great disorder is an order" because it allows for the fortuitous change and inclusiveness on which a true imaginative order depends. The deliberate paradoxes accentuate the provisionality inherent in valid ideas of order. The squirming facts exceed the squamous mind. The paradoxes are "things chalked/ On the sidewalk so that the pensive man may see." That metaphor combines both the improvised play of childlike perception and the provisional status of the statements themselves. Further, the pensive man shares the perceptual verticality that characterizes imagination in Stevens: he looks down (at the sidewalk) and up (at the eagle). The poem itself only chalks its statements and its images.

While double consciousness can occur anywhere in Stevens' poems, it often climaxes them, as our examples already show. In "The Sick Man" (1950) the concluding act of double consciousness reveals what we knew all along—that the ultimate goal of imagination is recognition of our transformed selves. Opening with a contrast between Southern black harmonica players or guitarists and Northern vocal choirs, the poem proceeds to a hypothetical listener:

And in a bed in one room, alone, a listener	7
Waits for the unison of the music of the drifting bands	8
And the dissolving chorals, waits for it and imagines	9
The words of winter in which these two will come together,	10
In the ceiling of the distant room, in which he lies,	11
The listener, listening to the shadows, seeing them,	12
Choosing out of himself, out of everything within him,	13
Speech for the quiet, good hail of himself, good hail, good hail,	14
The peaceful, blissful words, well-tuned, well-sung, well-spoken.	15

(OP 90)

As usual, the complicated syntax obscures relationships in the interest of illusion. "The listener" of line 12 may indicate a new syntactic start returning us to the situation of line 7, but more probably it refers back only to the "he" of line 11, who is an imagined future self of the original listener. That is, the original listener lies in bed and imagines himself at a future time imagining reconciliation of the opposite sounds. He will meet them with words of greeting that become words of self-recognition, "good hail of himself." An external order figures forth an internal order; these two things are one. As in "Connoisseur of Chaos," the speaker stands at an additional remove from the entire process —here, he imagines the listener who imagines—in reinforcement of the provisionality of the fiction.

The speaker finds a different form of self-knowledge in the inverted "God Is Good. It Is a Beautiful Night" (1942). The poem is a sort of ode "To a Skylark" written mostly from the bird's point of view. Stevens keeps the relation between his syntactically equal "brown moon, brown bird" (*CP* 285) ambiguous, so that we wonder whether the moon is a metaphor for the bird or vice versa. Semantics supports syntax, for the image has "light" like the moon but "wings" like a bird. The speaker begins by addressing the bird (or moon) as it prepares for flight. Double consciousness enters when he shifts to imagining what the bird will see as it looks down in its flight. Unlike the eagle of "Connoisseur of Chaos," the bird gazes not at intricate Alps but at the speaker himself, who has become a Stevensian poet. He has turned into a "scholar" because he perceives accurately; he plucks thin music "on the rustiest string" because as poet he reanimates old tradition; and he squeezes red fragrance from the stump of summer because he transforms the intense (red) poetry of life into the poetry of his song. This contrasts with the "venerable song" falling from the bird's "fiery wings" because the bird creates the poetry of life and the poet only the poetry of the poem. The bird merges with the moon because nature is a sleight-of-hand man, whom the speaker imitates even in opposition. Like Yeats in his tower seen by Aherne and Robartes, the speaker appears faintly ridiculous in his quest to capture what the observer already knows, but the poem itself provides an ironic example of his success.

Finally, "Landscape with Boat" (1940) extends at length a negative double consciousness. The speaker contemplates a "floribund ascetic" (*CP* 241) who, like Mrs. Alfred Uruguay, brushes away illusion to get at the real but, again like her, lacks the capable imagination to follow decreation with new geneses. The speaker first imagines the floribund ascetic's razing of romantic tenements and then imagines his inability "to suppose" new worlds. The speaker ends by imagining the floribund ascetic transformed into an imaginative man:

Had he been better able to suppose:
He might sit on a sofa on a balcony
Above the Mediterranean, emerald
Becoming emeralds. He might watch the palms
Flap green ears in the heat. He might observe
A yellow wine and follow a steamer's track
And say, "The thing I hum appears to be
The rhythm of this celestial pantomime."

(CP 243)

The emeralds and ears indicate imaginative perception by metaphor. Could the floribund ascetic do that, he would be able to identify his song with the rhythm of the universe, the poet's final aim. Stevens gives us a vision of that with its pomposity deflated by slangy diction, but the entire vision is conditional—a supposition by the ascetic of which the speaker has pronounced him incapable in advance. Double consciousness here allows a vision of earthly paradise in a fiction that ultimately collapses on itself.

Syntax has intruded into the discussion of double consciousness so prominently because it continually shapes and supports Stevensian mental action. "Domination of Black," "The Idea of Order at Key West," "The Sick Man," and "Landscape with Boat" best exemplify Stevens' manipulation of negatives, subjunctives, interrogatives, and direct statements to mimic mental action while maintaining provisionality. But syntax could work another way, not miming an external act but rather creating one inside the poem itself by generating vision out of the verbal and semantic structure. Such self-begotten shapes triumph over chaos and yet maintain their provisional status through deriving from language itself rather than its referents. We can best understand their appearance in poems like "Of Modern Poetry" or "Prologues to What Is Possible" by first reviewing the elements of Stevens' syntactic provisionality.

Helen Vendler has analyzed brilliantly the creation of tentativeness by syntax in what she terms Stevens' "qualified assertions." She writes:

> Stevens can be chiefly distinguished from the other poets who share his theme, not only by words of uncertainty . . . but by syntactic uncertainty. . . . Stevens resorts repeatedly to may, might, must, could, should, and would to resolve his poems. . . . Stevens never puts his hypotheses into the present tense. . . . Often, where one of Stevens' Romantic predecessors might have made a straightforward claim, Stevens temporizes, either by "might" or by "may," and these forms compose some of his most

characteristic aphorisms. . . . These are programs for action, not descriptions of action; manifestos, not reports; potentialities, not completions. . . . The effect is of something half-glimpsed, half-seen, and that is, finally, what Stevens achieves over and over.[53]

My argument extends hers by shifting attention from statement or aphorism—even statement about action—to mental action itself. Stevens' syntax makes not only his assertions "tentative" (Vendler's word) but his mental actions provisional, even while itself mirroring those actions. Watching actions rather than assertions changes response to the poems. Thus, I do not think that the opening complications of "Key West" "simply serve to implicate the various alternatives ever more deeply with each other,"[54] but rather that they constitute preludes to provisional vision and act out the initial stage of that process.

In Stevens' redaction the central lines of Keats' "Ode to a Nightingale" would become:

> It is as if to be already with thee:
> Tender would be the night . . .

But then he would likely shift into pseudoindicatives giving a provisional autonomy to the vision after all. That happens in Stevens' reworking of romantic lunar voyages in "Extracts from Addresses to the Academy of Fine Ideas" (1941):

> So that if one went to the moon,
> Or anywhere beyond, to a different element,
> One would be drowned in the air of difference,
> Incapable of belief, in the difference.
> And then returning from the moon, if one breathed
> The cold evening, without any scent or the shade
> Of any woman, watched the thinnest light
> And the most distant, single color, about to change,
> And naked of any illusion, in poverty,
> In the exactest poverty, if then
> One breathed the cold evening, the deepest inhalation
> Would come from that return to the subtle centre.
> (CP 258)

As Vendler notes in passing, the past tense following the subjunctive *if*'s creates an illusion of solidity, as though the event itself were somehow taking place. The extended syntax intensifies that effect. The elaborate development of details causes conditionality to fade and ambushes the reader with a sense of actuality; he must suppose so much that he barely notes his supposing. The passage itself purports to indicate that we can only believe in our own element and engage imagination with it, that we must forgo transcendence and return to reality however barren it may at first seem. The lunar parable simultaneously rejects transcendence as an unreal "if" and follows it with substantive rendering of an earthly scene. It operates in terms of the vertical motion that Stevens associated with true imagination and the moon he often used for imagination falsely separated from reality. Like the key Shelleyan phrase "the breathing earth," borrowed from *Prometheus Unbound* II, ii, 52 for the final address to the muses in "Mr. Burnshaw and the Statue" (*OP* 52), the "inhalation" coming from the center locates energy downward and within, and through the process of breathing implies the rhythmic cyclicity of imaginative experience in which we finally return to earth. The lines exemplify their own doctrine, for they fail to render the moon but present precise details of earth.

Interrogatives function analogously to subjunctives in Stevens' poetry. As questions, they automatically make provisional the mental action that accompanies their presentation; further, as the elaborate questions proceed, their interrogative thrust recedes so that again the syntax struggles toward independent status. At the end of "Key West," for example, the interrogative impetus dissipates itself in the increasingly autonomous presentation of the lights mastering night. Similarly, the final lines of "Esthétique du Mal" (1944) start out as a question but suppress the question mark at the end:

> And out of what one sees and hears and out
> Of what one feels, who could have thought to make
> So many selves, so many sensuous worlds,
> As if the air, the mid-day air, was swarming
> With the metaphysical changes that occur,
> Merely in living as and where we live.
>
> (*CP* 326)

Shortly after completing the poem Stevens explained to John Crowe Ransom what had happened: "The last poem ought to end with an interrogation mark, I suppose, but I have punctuated it in such a way as to indicate an abandonment of the question." (*LWS* 469) Abandoning the question makes the construction seem more real as it goes along; so, too, does following "as if " with "was" rather than "were." The last three lines are a conditional illustrating a question but seem to be a conjuring up of an independently existing air swarming with metaphysical changes.

Finally, pseudologic and mock pedanticism both intensify imaginative acts by contrast and yet destroy their full autonomy by pinning them to a tortuous frame. Resultant poems often seem to struggle against their rationalistic restraints. The early and comic "A High-Toned Old Christian Woman" (1922) interrupts its exuberant imaginings with the language of philosophic discourse—"Thus. . . . Thus. . . . Therefore." (CP 59) Along the way the speaker's initial directives—to make the moral law into a nave and build haunted heaven from it, and to make the opposing law a peristyle and project a masque from that—change into hypostatization of the disaffected flagellants and speculation on what they "may" do. The conditionals thus yield to successful imagination with the provisionality restricted to the further actions of the images. Under camouflage of logical terminology and the language of hypothesis, the speaker has smuggled an imaginative action into the poem.

Even Stevens' most referential mental action—in which a mind interacts with the world, albeit often as though through a glass of double consciousness or duplicit syntax darkly—has a reflexive aspect, in which imaginative action grows out of the speaker's involvement with his own words. Sometimes that procedure becomes dominant. Then the syntax takes a simile or metaphor and through intricate elaboration endows it with a life of its own. The resultant images seem self-sown in that they derive from the ongoing language of the poem itself. They at once embody an act of imaginative vision and yet undercut the status of the image. That happens with the image of the guitarist in "Of Modern Poetry" (1940), discussed in chapter 1: he originates in a metaphor for modern poetry but becomes a quasi-independent figure twanging his instrument on stage in the dark. Such images satisfy mind in the act of creating or first perceiving them but lack both referentiality and integrity enough to continue sufficing once their evolution has been completed. In Stevens' hands they become another device for that provisionality which returns mind from the grail to the quest itself.

Linguistically reflexive mental action occurs throughout Stevens' work from *Harmonium* to *The Rock*. The embryonic technique of "Hibiscus on the Sleeping Shores" (1921) reached its full subtlety and intricacy by the late "Prologues to What Is Possible" (1952). The title itself indicates a double provisionality: it promises only "prologues" and what will follow is only "possible." But those complications pale beside the fecund evolution of vision from the language itself in the poem, which begins:

There was an ease of mind that was like being alone in a boat at
  sea,
A boat carried forward by waves resembling the bright backs of
  rowers,
Gripping their oars, as if they were sure of the way to their
  destination,
Bending over and pulling themselves erect on the wooden
  handles,
Wet with water and sparkling in the one-ness of their motion.
                                                    (CP 515)

Each image engenders its successor: likening ease of mind to
being alone in a boat leads to hypostatization of the boat and then
to detailed evocation of the waves propelling the boat as rowers.
The rowers seem freshly and vitally present but syntactically they
are a simile for a term in an earlier simile. Such serial exfoliation
continues in the following stanza, where description of the boat
leads to the man in the boat, then to his being part of the boat,
then to comparison of him to a man searching for a syllable, then
to the syllable, and finally to the effect of the syllable:

A syllable of which he felt, with an appointed sureness,
That it contained the meaning into which he wanted to enter,
A meaning which, as he entered it, would shatter the boat and
  leave the oarsmen quiet
As at a point of central arrival, an instant moment, much or
  little,
Removed from any shore, from any man or woman, and
  needing none.

The speaker has been trying to enter the images that comprise the
syllables of the poem. But he here envisages a central imaginative
action that would break the bitter furies of complexity in the previous similes and provide a meaning like a center. The lure of such
centrality drives the quest of Stevens' poetry, but he expects
neither to win that goal nor even to represent it. He has rendered
it here a multiple conditional, a figure of speech within so many
other figures of speech that its momentary appearance of adequacy
lies encased within a syntactic Chinese box of inadequacy. His
destiny lies in those images that yet fresh images beget and not in
Byzantium. He recoils from his own metaphor in the second half
of the poem, abjuring extended projection of his likeness but then
qualifying even that with an "unless" (unless his "enclosures of
hypotheses" provide points of recognition). Finally, he starts a

209

question that turns into a provisional mental action through engendering a new series of similes, with his snarling self of imagination beautifully modulating into a spring light and human touch. The poem is a triumph of Stevens' mature art.[55]

Referential and reflexive use of language to evolve imaginative mental action out of syntax merge in "Final Soliloquy of the Interior Paramour" (1951). It is one of Stevens' few dramatic monologues spoken not by a character but by a principle of mind. Like Yeats in *The Wind Among the Reeds*, Stevens transplants the device from romantic psychodrama to lyric, as Blake himself occasionally had done. The exact identity of the interior paramour remains uncertain, and Ronald Sukenick may be right in suggesting "the lover of reality within us" who acts through imagination.[56] The word "paramour" in the title invokes the male-female relation of inner and outer, or imaginative and real, which Stevens took over from romantics like Wordsworth, just as "soliloquy" plays on the metaphor of theater he often associated with imaginative acts. The phrase "final soliloquy" reinforces Stevens' sense of provisionality and his bent toward the merely preparatory, for after a final soliloquy comes the climactic action of a play. Here is the poem:

Light the first light of evening, as in a room
In which we *rest* and, for small reason, *think*
The world imagined is the ultimate good.   3

This is, therefore, the intensest rendezvous.
It is in that thought that we *collect* ourselves,
Out of all the indifferences, into one thing: 6

Within a single thing, a single shawl
Wrapped tightly round us, since we *are* poor, a warmth,
A light, a power, the miraculous influence.   9

Here, now, we *forget* each other and ourselves.
We *feel* the obscurity of an order, a whole,
A knowledge, that which arranged the rendezvous.   12

Within its vital boundary, in the mind.
We *say* God and the imagination are one . . .
How high that highest candle lights the dark.   15

Out of this same light, out of the central mind,
We *make* a dwelling in the evening air,
In which being there together is enough.   18
                        (CP 524, italics mine)

210

This recapitulates several of Stevens' favorite syntactic devices: a simile that threatens to become independent ("as in," line 1), pseudologic ("therefore," line 4), mitigation of conditionality by extended appositive (line 9), omission of a verb (line 13), and qualification ("we say," line 14). But Stevens surpasses his usual devices by arranging the verbs governed by "we" into a model of imaginative process: in order, we rest, think, collect ourselves, are, forget, feel, say, and make. The verbs enact a normative sequence of romantic mental action, in which we suspend pointless bustle and irritable reaching after fact, enter a state of negative capability, and then exert our faculties: *rest, think,* and *collect* prepare for vision; *are* and *forget* mark a stage of ready potentiality; and *feel, say,* and *make* form a progressive action based on the paradigm of poetic composition. Syntax supports sense here, for the first half of the soliloquy uses the "we" verbs as subordinates and the second half as main verbs. Despite the devices of provisionality, the poem creates a strong illusion of positive mental action, and its syntax has itself enacted an imaginative process.

Manipulation of images joined with double consciousness and deceptive syntax in a triple alliance against permanence in poetic fictions. Stevens made large claims for the poetic image, valuing it as highly as did Yeats. He wrote in "To the One of Fictive Music" (1922):

> And of all vigils musing the obscure,
> That apprehends the most which sees and names,
> As in your name, an image that is sure. . . .
>
> (CP 88)

But images were rarely sure for Stevens, and they became increasingly problematic as he grew older. Unlike Yeats, he refused to assign them independent or quasi-independent status as emissions of a Great Memory or as elements of a partly magical system. They were not even fragments to be shored against his ruin. Instead, Stevens insisted on the human origin of images as temporary expressions needing continuous revision from ongoing creative perceptions. He designed his poems to present them more as process than as product and thought that once formed they impeded rather than revived imagination. Images became one more weapon in his arsenal of improvisation. He exalted them but qualified his full allegiance by requiring fresh experience, and he reduced them to provisional status even while insisting on their absolute necessity.

Like the romantics before him, Stevens thought that imaginative action demanded a special state of prior readiness. The verbs of "Final Soliloquy" reflect a preliminary process akin to Keats' negative capability. "The Sense of the Sleight-of-Hand Man" (1939) links the same condition to the production of images and metaphors by stressing the verb "occur":

> One's grand flights, one's Sunday baths,
> One's tootings at the weddings of the soul
> Occur as they occur. So bluish clouds
> Occurred. . . .
> To think of a dove with an eye of grenadine
> And pines that are cornets, so it occurs. . . .
>
> (CP 222)

"Occur" indicates an independence from rational control. Imaginative events cannot be predicted or regimented because they require freedom from preconception and preoccupation. This romantic thesis permeated Stevens' poetry, in which fictive things wink as they will and the mind "finds" what will suffice. His prose reinforced the argument: true metaphor was "fortuitous." (NA 73) Stevens called the imaginative perceiver "the ignorant man" to emphasize the freedom from interference by prior knowledge necessary to the creator of images. Ignorance meant not so much lack of knowledge as ability to suspend it in change. This distinction entered a later prose discussion of images which Stevens feared "may suggest that the imagination is the ignorance of the mind." He worriedly added, "Yet the imagination changes as the mind changes." (NA 151) Stevens extended romantic theory by applying such doctrines not just to original creation of images in perception but also to response to their expression in poetry. He wanted the reader as well as the observer to be an ignorant man, and he made his poems provisional to enhance fortuitous discovery.

All images were not created equal. Some encouraged deeper responses and more central poetry than others. The poet needed an "imagination that tries to penetrate to basic images, basic emotions, and so to compose a fundamental poetry." (NA 145) At times Stevens pondered the notion of an absolute image, eventually working out his ideas in Notes toward a Supreme Fiction. That impulse had already sounded in the piping of Harmonium. "Le Monocle de mon Oncle" (1918) proposed that "If men at forty will be painting lakes/ The ephemeral blues must merge for them in one,/ The basic slate, the universal hue." (CP 15) Stevens lacked a year of being forty when he published the poem; he was to learn, however, not a merging of blue into universal slate but rather a cyclical modulation through the entire spectrum. Like the parakeet of parakeets, an ultimate basic image would lack the change necessary to human apprehension. Four years later the man whose pharynx was bad yearned alternately for winter's "final slate" or summer's obverse extreme, for either total lack or total fulfillment of imagination, but that poem already hinted that just such a delusive desire might be the cause of the metrical sore throat.

If the poet could not arrive at an ultimate image, he had to remain with change and cyclicity. Starting from raw perception, he evolved images as basic as possible. These might suffice briefly, but inevitably their freshness faded. The poet then had to choose between returning to ongoing experience and new formulations or surrendering to unreal dream worlds and hackneyed formulas. Stevens knew the importance of that choice as early as "Metaphors of a Magnifico" (1918):

> Twenty men crossing a bridge,
> Into a village,
> Are twenty men crossing twenty bridges,
> Into twenty villages,
> Or one man
> Crossing a single bridge into a village.
>
> This is old song
> That will not declare itself . . . .
>
> Twenty men crossing a bridge,
> Into a village,
> Are
> Twenty men crossing a bridge
> Into a village.
>
> That will not declare itself
> Yet is certain as meaning . . .
>
> The boots of the men clump
> On the boards of the bridge.
> The first white wall of the village
> Rises through fruit-trees.
> Of what was it I was thinking?
> So the meaning escapes.
>
> The first white wall of the village . . .
> The fruit-trees. . . .

> (CP 19)

Improvisational rather than provisional in Stevens' later manner, the poem presents a speaker confronting a landscape and
responding in the present tense. The mental action matches that of
Pound's "Cino" in moving from repeated failure to successful
song. After setting the scene in the first two lines, the Magnifico
first advances conventional metaphors for the twenty men crossing a bridge. He makes them alternately twenty men crossing
twenty bridges to twenty villages or a single man crossing a single
bridge. The point lies not in the metaphysics but the mustiness of
the metaphors: they are "old song." With that recognition the
Magnifico breaks off one botched attempt and starts another. This
time he avoids triteness but ends in tautology: he simply equates
the men, bridge, and village with themselves. He breaks off again,
emphasizing now not the oldness of the song but its failure to
"declare itself." He recaptures his poetic power by returning to its
true source in present perception. His third attempt succeeds
where the others fail by its inclusion of concrete detail. In detect-
ing "the boots" of the men, "the boards" of the bridge, and "the
first white wall" of the village, and adding the new detail of
"fruit-trees," he creates a fresh song convincingly evoking the
scene (and hinting at empathic union with the men by describing
from their point of view the wall rising through fruit-trees). The
lost "meaning" was a false abstraction anyway. He has become a
successful poet by shifting his mode of mental action. Yet the
poem ends not with exultant metaphoric creation but with immersion in concrete perception. It implies that the new images will
come later, now that the Magnifico has become an ignorant man
again. He has entered the state of the poet described in "Effects of
Analogy," who returns to reality "like a man returning from Nowhere to his village" and "sees without images." (NA 129) But his
imageless world turns out to be "full of the obvious analogies"
that eventually will generate new images. As later poems like
"Lions in Sweden" and "The Man on the Dump" attest, Stevens
loved to depict the interlude in which the poet returns to reality
for refreshment from outworn images before creating new ones.

Provisionality of double consciousness, syntax, and even
reflexive rather than referential language came to seem increasingly inadequate by themselves. If the motive for metaphor was
inability to bear the actual, perhaps images and metaphors could
themselves be made provisional in a further push toward process.
Stevens increasingly sought to deny the image its independence
and to remind the reader of its contingency even in the moment of

presentation. That strategy became evident during the forties and manifested itself explicitly in two poems published in 1950. Each took a favorite Stevensian image, a woman or an angel. "The Woman in Sunshine" referred not to an actual woman but to those aspects of sunshine resembling aspects of a woman, in accord with Stevens' notion of the origins of metaphor and image in analogy:

> It is only that this warmth and movement are like
> The warmth and movement of a woman.
>
> It is not that there is any image in the air
> Nor the beginning nor end of a form:
>
> It is empty. But a woman in threadless gold
> Burns us with brushings of her dress
>
> And a dissociated abundance of being,
> More definite for what she is—
>
> Because she is disembodied,
> Bearing the odors of the summer fields,
>
> Confessing the taciturn and yet indifferent,
> Invisibly clear, the only love.
>
> (CP 445)

The first couplet poses the woman as pure analogy, while the second denies her any objective status. The third continues to emphasize her literal basis in sunshine, which is "threadless gold" and "burns us." The fourth and fifth couplets remind us that she lacks a body, and the oxymoron "invisibly clear" in the sixth makes sense only if we think of her as sunshine in air. Both the crucial third stanza and its context refuse the woman independent status; she is an analogy, not a form in air. Yet the reader leaves the poem with a clear sense of her as image, just what the poem denies. How is this possible? First, the poem moves in typical Stevensian fashion from a comparison to a term of the comparison—from warmth and movement being like a woman to the woman that they are like. Second, the change signaled by "But" includes the only strong indicative verb in the poem, "burns," in contrast to surrounding "is" and "are." Then, too, rapid progression obscures the literal basis of "threadless gold" and "burns." Finally, the rest of the poem offers deliberately tangled syntax tending to increase the illusion of the woman's presence. The lyric thus leaves us with a sense of an image directly contrary to its own pronouncements. There is no image in the air, but there is one in the mind, of both speaker and reader. She is a deliberately provisional Romantic Image.

The woman in sunshine finds a counterpart in the angel of reality from "Angel Surrounded by Paysans." (CP 496) That poem recapitulates Stevens' most characteristic reactions to romanticism, including hybridization of elevated diction by a negative ("I have neither ashen wing nor wear of ore"), rejection of a dreamworld ("I am the angel of reality"), sense of change ("Rise liquidly in liquid lingerings"), and, in its derivation from Tal Coat's still life, the violence of imagination. It supports his saving provisionality in mental action through double consciousness, interrogative syntax, and direct undermining of the image. Stevens reverses his customary use of double consciousness by making the mediator rather than the observer into the speaker. The angel says:

> Yet am I the necessary angel of earth,
> Since, in my sight, you see the earth again. . . .

Like the pensive man of "Connoisseur of Chaos," the peasants do not see the earth directly. Just as the pensive man sees the image of the eagle who sees the Alps, so do the peasants perceive the necessary angel and see the earth again in his sight. If they see the earth provisionally, they also do so only momentarily. At the start the countryman sees no one at the door, and at the end the angel describes himself as seen only for a moment:

> Am I not,
> Myself, only half of a figure of a sort,
>
> A figure half seen, or seen for a moment, a man
> Of the mind, an apparition apparelled in
>
> Apparels of such lightest look that a turn
> Of my shoulder and quickly, too quickly, I am gone?

The angel qualifies his speech by casting it as a question, but the syntax works toward quasi assertion by successive apposition and the question comes to seem merely rhetorical. The appositives drastically subvert the status of the image: in a triple qualification they make the angel not just a "figure" but only "half " of a figure "of a sort"; then they make him either "half " or momentarily seen; and finally they assign him, like the woman in sunshine, to the mind as an apparelled apparition. If he is half of a figure of a sort, what would the other half be? As not reality but the angel of reality, he would need not imagination but its interior paramour who searches for him to complete the mystic marriage of imagination and reality in the mind. Stevens continually made notes to arrange that rendezvous, as with the Great Captain and the maiden Bawda, but his radical provisionality prevented its consummation.

Stevens labored to qualify his images and provisionalize their mental production not because they were trivial but because they were so important. They both sustained and created essential humanity. Like the imagination that produced them, they arose powerfully when confronted with bleak winter vision or the absence of humanity. The mind refused to tolerate the vacuity of Newtonian time and space. Polar extremity called forth latent power. "The absence of the imagination had/ Itself to be imagined" (*CP* 503) and Gaston Bachelard was "upside down" in claiming that wintry milieus did not stimulate imagination. (*LWS* 740) Faced with such conditions, imagination generated new images. Stevens even speculated that "the self consists of endless images" (*LWS* 670), which poetry tried to capture in an unending series. The self would also project such images onto the inhuman, or more accurately, mold the inhuman into at least partly human features. That happened in one of Stevens' last poems, "Of Mere Being." He began with a gold-feathered bird singing an inhuman song in the palm at the end of the mind. The bird itself culminates the romantic tradition including Blake's or Wordsworth's lark, Keats' nightingale, Shelley's skylark, and Yeats' golden bird. But it does not herald a revelation, elicit sympathetic imagination, become a model to the poet, or stay altogether changeless metal. Instead, the bird teases creative imagination into action. Recognition that "it is not the reason/ That makes us happy or unhappy" (*OP* 118) implies that it is the imagination that does. In the final tercet, the imagination, like the symbolic wind, blows through the branches and begins to manipulate the image of the bird, endowing it with "fire-fangled feathers" dangling down. The image does not wholly emerge from imagination's forge in the course of the poem, but it begins to, in accord with Stevensian process. Like the englistered woman in "The Sail of Ulysses" a year or two earlier,[57] the bird becomes "A part of the inhuman more,/ The still inhuman more, and yet/ An inhuman of our features." (*OP* 105)

The necessary humanity of a sufficient image informs "A Mythology Reflects Its Region." This late work begins with the relation between soil and intelligence of the early *Comedian as the*

Letter C and aligns itself with Yeats against the conscious cosmopolitanism of Eliot:

> A mythology reflects its region. Here
> In Connecticut, we never lived in a time
> When mythology was possible—But if we had—
> That raises the question of the image's truth.
> The image must be of the nature of its creator.
> It is the nature of its creator increased,
> Heightened. It is he, anew, in a freshened youth
> And it is he in the substance of his region,
> Wood of his forests and stone out of his fields
> Or from under his mountains.
>
> (*OP* 118)

The poem does not present an image but speculates about one and, in the course of speculation, partly evolves one. It begins by affirming the link between region and mythology—which for Stevens meant a systematic structure and elaboration of images—and denying the possibility of successful mythmaking in the modern period. An interrupted conditional ("But if we had—") leads to discussion of the image's truth. Stevens labels his inquiry a "question" to avoid finality and begins with a characteristic "must" expressing—as Vendler notes with other examples—"not a word of faith but a word of doubt, implying as it does an unbearable alternative."[58] Yet again the syntax creates the illusion of an actual image being evolved, first by shifting from "must be" to "is" and then by increasing the specificity of each successive predicate of "is." The provisional figure resembles in its freshened youth the image of the modern poet emerging Aeneas-like from the past. Here he gives life not to tradition but to his surroundings, not to imagination's relics but reality's raw materials, composing himself out of stone from his fields or "under his mountains" in implicit location of energy downward and within. The image remains tentative, for mythology was impossible in Connecticut. Stevens knew, for he had already come as close as he could in his great poem *Notes toward a Supreme Fiction*.

As Stevens' most ambitious work and one he regarded as an imaginative high-water mark,[59] *Notes* (1942) forms a fit conclusion to this consideration of Stevens' poetry. It epitomizes the creative transformation of romanticism so central to his mature career. His favorite devices of double consciousness, distorted syntax, and ambivalent image support favorite themes like cyclical change and mental violence in the lover's quarrel between imagination and world.[60] The resultant provisionality distinguishes his new from

Yeats' last romanticism, even as his acceptance of imagination's violence secures him from the self-division of Eliot's poetry. Stevens neither repeated nor completed his inheritance so much as he revised it. In his lifelong encounter with romanticism, his fecund innovations surpass even his fine congruencies.

The title itself indicates Stevens' ruling provisionality. It offers us neither a supreme fiction nor even a comprehensive plan, but only "notes" toward one. As Stevens wrote a year after composition, "It is a collection of just what I have called it: Notes." (*LWS* 443) Likewise, the poem did not even fully formulate what a supreme fiction might be. "I have not defined a supreme fiction," confessed Stevens with typical horror at "fixing" what he meant. (*LWS* 435) If poetry provides fictions, a supreme fiction would be the highest of them. It might then be an elaboration of a central myth from a central image, perhaps of major man. But it might also be the means of Stevens' breaking out of personal cyclicity into a centrality free from myth and image altogether, a way to "be/ In the difficulty of what it is to be." (*CP* 381) Poetry might incarnate that vision, and Stevens assured alternate correspondents that the supreme fiction was and was not poetry. (*LWS* 407, 438) A supreme fiction might inspire belief even while known to be fictitious. *Notes* itself transvalues romantic psychodrama into a lyric sequence of notes that proceeds less in temporal than in spatial progression toward a climactic provisional formulation of an image for something that never could be named. The three parts—*It Must Be Abstract, It Must Change,* and *It Must Give Pleasure*—delineate chief aspects of the supreme fiction, while a projected fourth section—*It Must Be Human* (*LWS* 863-64)—would have been Stevens' analogue to the fourth act of *Prometheus Unbound.*

It Must Be Abstract begins by adjuring the ephebe to free himself from images and ends with the projected evolution of new ones. The contemporaneously composed essay "The Noble Rider" gives a gloss on what Stevens meant by abstract: the poet "must be able to abstract himself and also to abstract reality, which he does by placing it in his imagination." (*NA* 23) To do that the poet first had to cleanse himself of past incrustations, whether of personal perception or of literary history. The ephebe must "become an ignorant man again" (*CP* 380), seeing the sun of reality with an ignorant eye. He must particularly shun religious images, like those of Phoebus, god of the sun and of poetry, for the supreme fiction involves major man rather than haunted heaven. Yet the result of erasing old images will be the chalking of new ones: the ephebe is only to

219

"begin" by perceiving without them. As Stevens explained, "The first step toward a supreme fiction would be to get rid of all existing fictions." (*LWS* 431) The opening lyric itself enacts that progression. The mature poet starts out in the tones and language of ironic instruction but ends up with a metaphor for the sun, "gold flourisher," even while maintaining that it must bear no name. Further, he in effect tries to place the ephebe in a system of double consciousness: he will perceive the ephebe who will see the sun. The poem advocates the start of a cyclical process, whose goal might be creation of an image so central it will break the cycle. To believe such salvation possible itself constitutes a kind of supreme fiction.

It Must Be Abstract ends with an approach toward major man. Commentators commonly concede the difficulty of interpretation here. In one of the best accounts of the poem Joseph Riddel writes: "The definition of major man continues to perplex. He is, in effect, another version of the abstraction blooded, an image to replace the idea of God. Yet he is not a form so much as sense of human possibility."[61] The problem stems from Stevens' desire to suggest major man but not to confuse him with a limiting image. He accomplishes that through his usual program for provisionality. Poem IX distorts its syntax and undermines its own image. It begins with a convoluted statement of what major man is not. Discrimination of tonal propriety—romantic intoning for apotheosis and reason's click-clack for applications—leads to disavowal of apotheosis as origin and acting out of an alternate source:

He comes,

> Compact in invincible foils, from reason,
> Lighted at midnight by the studious eye,
> Swaddled in revery, the object of
>
> The hum of thoughts evaded in the mind. . . .
>   (*CP* 387-88)

He comes, that is, from all our faculties—"reason," imagination ("Swaddled in revery"), and the unconscious ("thoughts evaded in the mind"). As it progresses, the description of origins seems to act out an evolution, until an injunction to the muse ("My dame, sing for this person accurate songs") breaks the pseudovision. The poet returns to it in the syntax of the next line—"He is and may be but oh! he is, he is." This simultaneously affirms and denies his presence, both explicitly ("is and may be") and implicitly through

220

the patent desperation of the avowal. Stevens lingers on hand and eyes before subverting the imagistic status of major man with the command to "dismiss him from your images." The lyric simultaneously presents major man and denies the adequacy of its own presentation.

Poem X reexamines the origin of major man by generating its pseudovision out of double consciousness. After an opening clarification (at least by Stevens' standards: "The major abstraction is the idea of man/ And major man is its exponent"), the speaker answers his own question about major man's identity:

> What rabbi, grown furious with human wish,
> What chieftain, walking by himself, crying
> Most miserable, most victorious,
>
> Does not see these separate figures one by one,
> And yet see only one, in his old coat,
> His slouching pantaloons, beyond the town,
>
> Looking for what was, where it used to be?
> (CP 389)

The ephebe should concoct major man from the old *fantoche.* But the speaker does not see the man in pantaloons: the rabbi (contemplative man) and chieftain (active man) do that. Further, each is not even a specific rabbi or chieftain, but a rhetorical one encased in a question. The speaker takes his own rhetorical figures and uses them as intervening consciousnesses to apprehend the origin of major man in the pantaloon figure. Likewise, he assigns to the ephebe the transformation of the man in old clothes to major man compact in invincible foils. Both lyrics insist on the origin of major man in man and render their insistence in complementary provisionalities. They speak words of ourselves and of our origins in keener sounds intended "not to console/ Nor sanctify" like Wordsworth but plainly to propound. Stevens' "plainly" is mischievous.

As though recoiling from even its tentative approach to major man, *Notes* immediately moves into its second part, *It Must Change.* Stevens summons a cast including the old seraph, the President, General Du Puy, the planter, and Nanzia Nunzio to dramatize the act of the mind as change. He takes particular care to divorce his vision from that of Shelley, the poet with whom Stevens most resisted his temperamental affinity. Generally, Shelley's terza rima poems stand as intermediary between Stevens' three-part organization and tercets and the patterns of Dante's *Com-*

media. But Shelley gets into two poems of *It Must Change* explicitly, one on change in life and the other on change in art.

The contrapuntal birdsong of poem VI (*CP* 393-94) pits "ké-ké" of the wren, jay, and robin against the sparrow's "Bethou me," in allusion both to French *tutoyez-moi* and the prophetic call of Shelley's "Ode to the West Wind." The sparrow seems to have the poet's sympathy until the difficult last line. Stevens himself wrote contradictory glosses, of which the second and more favorable to the sparrow makes better sense:

> You ask about the relation of this poem to the theme of change. There is a repetition of a sound, ké-ké, all over the place. Its monotony unites the separate sounds into one, as a number of faces become one, as all fates become a common fate, as all the bottles blown by a glass blower become one, and as all bishops grow to look alike, etc. In its monotony the sound ceased to be minstrelsy, all the leaves are alike, all the birds in the leaves are alike; there is just one bird, a stone bird. In this monotony the desire for change creates change. . . . The change is an ingratiating one and intended to be so. When the sparrow begins calling be-thou . . . he expresses one's own liking for the change . . . he mocks the wren, the jay, the robin. . . . In the face of death life asserts itself. Perhaps it makes an image out of the force with which it struggles to survive. Bethou is intended to be heard; it and ké-ké, which is inimical, are opposing sounds. Bethou is the spirit's own seduction. (*LWS* 437-38)

Like the speaker of Shelley's ode, the sparrow (who again belongs to double consciousness, since he and not Stevens' persona says "bethou") longs for a change from the idiot minstrelsy of nature's meaningless round. But he says "Bethou me" not to the west wind of the spirit's power but to the monotonously chanting birds; the source of power is already internalized. In the gloss Stevens qualifies the sparrow's "bethou"s as "the spirit's own seduction." The call of imagination to turn all things into itself would eventually enervate imagination's own power by divorcing it from reality. Hence Stevens undercuts the sparrow at the end; it has made an image of its opposing force but cannot vanquish that enemy without itself capitulating to changelessness, in violation of a controlling axiom of the supreme fiction. Stevens had echoed Shelley's ode before, in "Mozart, 1935." There he had urged the poet to "Be thou the voice" (*CP* 132) of fear and pain as of a great wind howling and had limited his qualification to ironic postponement of Mozart until a future time. In *Notes* he qualifies the call itself, which like hypostasis of major man would obviate the need for change.

Stevens returned to Shelley in demanding change not in life but in art two poems later, when he brought Nanzia Nunzio to confront Ozymandias. He neatly reversed his source. Shelley's sonnet used Ozymandias to demonstrate the change of life and longevity of art, with the ruins of Ozymandias' statue being the only survival of his vanished reign. As though developing the cycle implicit in the decay of the statue, Stevens upholds instead the necessary change of art. Nanzia Nunzio strips off her garments to encounter Ozymandias' "inflexible/ Order" directly. (CP 396) He replies that the bride can never be naked, for "A fictive covering/ Weaves always glistening from the heart and mind."⁶² The metaphor itself brilliantly transforms Shelley's image of the veil separating us from permanence and the One into a fictive garment allowing for saving change and diversity. Nanzia Nunzio herself is a Romantic Image manqué. The mind can never apprehend her nakedly, but only through the continuously changing fictions it continuously creates. The poem has acted out its own doctrine by providing the image of Ozymandias himself with a new fictive covering.

Both Shelleyan sections of *It Must Change* work against romantic norms. The "Bethou me" poem plays against the imaginative violence that Stevens heightened from his predecessors and that pervades *Notes*. The "bloody" wren has already been attacked by sparrow's imaginative violence. This fury erupts most markedly in the roaring lion, blaring elephant, and snarling bear tamed by the poet's "voluble dumb violence" in section V of *It Must Be Abstract* and in the "war between the mind/ And sky" of the military epilogue to the entire poem (where the relation between poet and soldier owes something to Shelley's notion of the power of poetry in the *Defence*). The Ozymandias lyric plays against romantic notions of the sacramental marriage of mind to universe. Nanzia Nunzio wants to be the "contemplated spouse" with her "burning body" but Ozymandias refuses such direct union and insists on the covering of an improvised fiction spun by mind and heart. Here Stevens genuinely reverses Wordsworth, just as the view of art as changing genuinely counters Shelley, in contrast to the "Bethou me" lyric, which reverses only his idea of Shelley.

In *It Must Give Pleasure*,⁶³ the third part of *Notes*, Stevens enters the ultima Thule of his own art. In so doing he extends the province of both romantic and modern poetry. His critique of Canon Aspirin as flawed but imaginative man, a sort of major man manqué, leads to a startling attempt to fuse with an angelic image of his own creation. The fusion would result neither in escape into art nor in metamorphosis into a Yeatsian figure of idealized passion, but rather in achievement of a simple and elusive self-identity without self-consciousness. That transformation would complete one line of post-romantic valuation of images. Stevens follows it with an equally remarkable effort to turn the world itself into an image of the inamorata for the transformed poet, a green and fluent mundo revolving in crystal. For these twin enterprises Stevens enlisted his full array of provisional devices. His accomplishment embodies itself as much in modes of mental action as in overt themes.

The three Canon Aspirin cantos (V-VII) begin with qualified praise and latent criticism, proceed to the magnificent force of his imagination, and end with a shattering critique. His comic name itself suggests both incongruity and inadequacy, as though all we needed were little white tablets. His title implies allegiance to the sort of outworn mythology proscribed in the opening poem of *Notes*, just as the implicit celibacy of his canonical status contrasts unfavorably with the immediately preceding marriage hymn of the Great Captain and Bawda. The canon has only his widowed sister. His praise of her makes us wonder about him, for its terms can be construed both positively and negatively. Her "sensible ecstasy" might imply an anti-transcendent bliss, her "poverty" an adherence to reality fortified by her rejection of dreams, her fighting off "the barest phrase" a desire to catch from the unreasoning moment its unreasoning, and her demand of sleep solely for the children's sake an admirable human feeling. (CP 401-2) But sensible ecstasy might also indicate faintheartedness, poverty an absence of reality, rejecting dreams an uncomfortable affinity with Mrs. Alfred Uruguay, fighting off the barest phrase a refusal of accurate song, and demanding only the unmuddled self of sleep a denial of the imaginative power of dream. As Stevens explained in a letter, "His sister has never explored anything at all and shrinks from doing so." (LWS 445) Palm for palm, poem V leaves the reader where he began, and the following lyrics exploit first the positive and then the negative reverberations of the canon's celebration of his sister.

Poem VI depicts the canon at midnight, the time when, like a Yeatsian figure of passion or mood, major man comes. (CP 388) Stevens characteristically filters the canon's mental action through the speaker's intervening consciousness, presenting one mind's meditation on another's imaginative act. Having reached that romantic limit beyond which "fact could not progress as fact," he reimagines the world, projecting it from "the very material of his mind." At this point he enters his own vision, fusing with the angel ("so that he was the ascending wings he saw") in its vertical movement upward toward the stars and downward to the children's bed. Full of "huge pathetic force" capable of producing what the last poem will call "the fiction that results from feeling" he reaches a second limit, beyond which "thought could not progress as thought." When faced with the limit of fact, he had moved into thought. When faced with the limit of thought, he chooses not to pass beyond but to include it in his vision—"It was not a choice/ Between, but of." Here Stevens breaks off the account. We do not see the canon choose in the same way we saw him become an angel; Stevens simply says that he chose and ends instead with the object of choice, the "amassing harmony."

Yet the repetition of "choose" and its variants four times in three lines suggests a flaw in the canon, which the next poem drastically exposes. The canon exercises his will too consciously. He lacks the negative capability of the ignorant man and foists his conceptions on the world: "He imposes orders as he thinks of them." He has the wrong idea of order, and it issues not in imaginative poetry but in reasonable politics. In contrast, the speaker asserts that "to impose is not/ To discover" and breaks into a chant of desperate yearning:

> To discover an order as of
> A season, to discover summer and know it,
>
> To discover winter and know it well, to find,
> Not to impose, not to have reasoned at all,
> Out of nothing to have come on major weather,
>
> It is possible, possible, possible. It must
> Be possible.
>
> (CP 403-4)

That voices Stevens' great quest and his equal doubt. He hopes to win from cyclical change a knowledge of summery imagination and wintry reality, to perceive them in a climate of major weather appropriate to major man, and to discover rather than impose the objects of his knowledge in a right ignorance. The real will come "like a beast disgorged" to indicate the presence of fortuitous imaginative violence. The concluding apostrophe to the angel—a creation of the speaker's own powers—triggers the daring assertion of poem VIII, the possible fiction that the poet can come upon major weather in his own poetry through identification with his own images of triumphant perception.

Stevens constructs poem VIII to make metamorphosis into the angel both possible and provisional. Last seen in the prologue and a few fleeting apparitions, the "I" now emerges into dominance:

> What am I to believe? If the angel in his cloud,
> Serenely gazing at the violent abyss,
> Plucks on his strings to pluck abysmal glory,   3
>
> Leaps downward through evening's revelations, and
> On his spredden wings, needs nothing but deep space,
> Forgets the gold centre, the golden destiny,   6
>
> Grows warm in the motionless motion of his flight,
> Am I that imagine this angel less satisfied?
> Are the wings his, the lapis-haunted air?   9
>
> Is it he or is it I that experience this?
> Is it I then that keep saying there is an hour,
> Filled with expressible bliss, in which I have   12
>
> No need, am happy, forget need's golden hand,
> Am satisfied without solacing majesty,
> And if there is an hour there is a day,   15
>
> There is a month, a year, there is a time
> In which majesty is a mirror of the self:
> I have not but I am and as I am, I am.   18
>
> These external regions, what do we fill them with
> Except reflections, the escapades of death,
> Cinderella fulfilling herself beneath the roof?   21
>
> (CP 404-5)

The poem heroically collapses double consciousness into single as the speaker identifies with his own created image of the angel. He becomes the angel, as though the pensive man of "Connoisseur of Chaos" were to become the eagle. The angel is both artist playing an instrument and image of existential self-sufficiency, moving, like the pigeons of *Sunday Morning*, downward on extended wings. The speaker chooses the key word "satisfied" in line 8, for like all Stevens' questers he seeks what will suffice. And what suffices is pure being, free from irritable reaching after possession and imposition. The self achieves majesty in dispossession, not just of external encumbrance but of its own self-consciousness and need. It can say: I have not but I am, and as I am I am.

Yet the experience remains conditional. Stevens casts the entire poem into interrogatives, so that it can in nothing lieth since it nothing affirmeth. We do not know what the speaker should believe. Typically, Stevens' interrogatives turn into pseudoassertions pretending to mimic mental action. As his opening description of an angel (lines 1-7) proceeds, the angel surpasses his origin in a conditional ("If . . .") within an interrogative and seems to take on independent existence. The long question of lines 11-18 loses its interrogative status altogether ("Is it I then that . . . ?") as Stevens suppresses the final question mark to intensify the seeming realization of lines 16-18. He expands the moment Satan's watch fiends cannot find into an hour, a day, a month, a year, and an all-embracing "time." The verb pattern of the poem supports the drive to ontological independence, moving from the sequence gazing-plucks-leaps-needs-forgets-grows into a constellation of "am" and "is." The triumphant "as I am, I am" in fact belongs to a complex interrogative conditional. The speaker has become so caught up in the reality of his syntax that he generates vision out of its provisional components. So he has in Stevens before, but this time he identifies with the image of his own creation and becomes the necessary and contented angel of his own devising in a provisional transubstantiation into major man.

The final tercet has sparked diverse interpretations, construing it alternately as dismissal of bondage to space and time now that the speaker has fused with his own image or as disparagement of the vision itself, which has already ceased to suffice. On the one hand Harold Bloom argues: "In that heroic integration, what is outside the self can be dismissed without fear of solipsistic self-absorption, for the self has joined major man."[64] On the other, Helen Vendler contends that the poem "after a heroic expansion, turns despairingly on the mind's ramifying extrapolations and evasions, and ends in disgust. . . . Cinderella's finery returns to rags as the mind turns on its own self-adorning 'escapades.' "[65] Both readings seem to me extreme, for "these" (instead of "those," as Vendler notes) seems to locate the speaker within the regions of death and thus to inhibit Bloom's claims, while Cinderella's escapades did fulfill themselves externally and hence suggest the poet's resignation rather than the disgust posited by Vendler. Further, the speaker himself qualifies the tercet by restoring the interrogative he had repressed at the end of the previous vision. But the tercet's significance lies as much in its contribution to mental action as in its doctrinal formulation. However we interpret it, the tercet embodies a movement back out from identification with the angel and toward a more detached verdict, whether positive or negative. The speaker moves from opening description of the putative angel to union with it and then to an evaluation of the experience. This follows the development of a Greater Romantic Lyric but proceeds wholly by conditionals and interrogatives that create the illusion of actually developing action. Stevens' genius has transformed the structure of a Greater Romantic Lyric into a poem of pure provisionality.

Stevens followed his provisional evolutions of major man, and of union with his own image of the angel, with improvisation of a concluding image of the world in the final poem of *It Must Give Pleasure*. He returned to that enterprise a few years later in a passage of the lecture "Imagination as Value," which illuminates the end of *Notes*:

> The world is no longer an extraneous object, full of other extraneous objects, but an image. In the last analysis, it is with this image of the world that we are vitally concerned. We should not say, however, that the chief object of the imagination is to produce such an image. Among so many objects, it would be the merest improvisation to say of one, even though it is one with which we are vitally concerned, that it is the chief. The next step would be to assert that a particular image was the chief image. Again, it would be the merest improvisation to say of any image of the world, even though it was an image with which a vast accumulation of imaginations had been content, that it was the chief image. The imagination itself would not remain content with it nor allow us to do so. It is the irrepressible revolutionist. (*NA* 151-52)

The prose passage mirrors the techniques of the poetry, in which Stevens discusses the image and evolves it even while denying the validity of his extrapolations. He triply qualifies his statements through subjunctives ("it would be"), adjectives ("merest"), and choice of noun ("improvisation"), which he applies to the notions both that imagination's chief function is to provide an image of the world and that there can be a chief image of the world. In its ceaseless need to change and to return to reality, imagination as revolutionist precludes such status for the image. And yet the whole discussion suggests its opposite, for Stevens dwells almost lovingly on the chief image he is rejecting. The reader wonders whether such an image might not exist after all, and whether it might not itself be a kind of supreme fiction. *Notes* ends with the improvisation of an image of the world in such a way as to suggest its temporary suzerainty and ultimate inadequacy.

Poem X opens with an address to the "fat girl":

Fat girl, terrestrial, my summer, my night,
How is it I find you in difference, see you there
In a moving contour, a change not quite completed?
(*CP* 406)

Stevens calls the fat girl "terrestrial" because she is an image of the earth. Yet he never succeeds in fully tracing her lineaments. He begins by addressing her in an interrogative and calling her "a change not quite completed." Such difficulties in apprehension run throughout the poem, as the speaker finds the fat girl successively "an aberration," an executor of "evasions," a "phantom," and an "irrational/ Distortion." Those epithets clearly keep his formulations provisional, while their context enacts the separate stages of poetic composition. As Frank Doggett was the first to show, "He is expressing in his conclusion, then, the genesis of a poem from the imagination of it pictured in procreant terms ('Fat girl, terrestrial, my summer, my night') through the evasions and transformations of its conception, with the arduous work of composition ('Bent over work, anxious, content, alone'), to the realization of his conception in language (calling it by name), when it is fixed in the crystal of a poem."[66] The poem thus recapitulates the process of its own creation, which, as it has since the romantics, serves as paradigm for imaginative action generally.

The process culminates in the last two tercets:

They will get it straight one day at the Sorbonne.
We shall return at twilight from the lecture
Pleased that the irrational is rational,

Until flicked by feeling, in a gildered street,
I call you by name, my green, my fluent mundo.
You will have stopped revolving except in crystal.
(*CP* 406-7)

The academic abstractions about the irrational at the Sorbonne both amuse and instruct; however, they fail to change. They temporarily suffice the mind, but instead of catching from the irrational moment its unreasoning they reason about it with a later reason, to adopt the language of the first poem in *It Must Give Pleasure*. They only serve until the creative moment itself, when the poet tries to name his paramour. *Green* is Stevens' word for reality and *mundo* for the world transformed by imagination.[67] By bringing the two terms together he indicates a sacramental naming, a marriage of reality and imagination in which he at last possesses the fat girl within the vital boundary, in the mind.

At that point she "will have stopped revolving except in crystal." In that rich line Stevens has cunningly wrought his crystal into provisional process rather than final product. To begin with, the entire line is provisional, occurring after a conditional ("Until") in an imagined future and so twice removed from permanence. "Revolving" doubles the duplicity, for it applies both to the earth (which revolves) and, in Stevens' usage, to the mind. He casually slipped into the latter sense in a letter about the fat girl: "The fat girl is the earth: what the politicians now-a-days are calling the globe, which somehow, as it revolves in their minds . . . ." (*LWS* 426) Such usage was implicit in his idea of imagination, described in the lecture as "the irrepressible revolutionist" both because it overthrows and because it revolves. But Stevens surpasses himself in taking the word "crystal," an image of hardness and permanence, and transforming it into an icon of fluency and change.[68] Most critics rightly identify "crystal" with poetry, but its meanings extend beyond that. The clearness of crystal refracts the light of imagination. Stevens uses "crystal" thus in his poems frequently, and he attaches it particularly to art, to Heaven, to creation out of the self, and, most significantly, to mind. His late poem "The Sail of Ulysses" internalizes the hero's apprehension of the world in a matching of revolutions "In which the world goes round and round/ In the crystal atmospheres of the mind." (*OP* 102) In short, "crystal" denotes mind, which for Stevens is always active. Arresting of the fat girl's motion thus lapses back into provisionality both poetically and personally. For her to stop revolving except in crystal is for her to continue turning. She will do so in the poem because the poem is provisional and in the mind because imagination is an irrepressible revolutionist. She went on revolving in Stevens' own art and life for the many remaining and productive years of his career.

It can never be satisfied, the mind, never.

Notes

NOTES TO CHAPTER 1

1. *The Collected Poems of Wallace Stevens* (New York: Alfred A. Knopf, 1968), pp. 239-40 (hereafter cited as *CP*).

2. *Opus Posthumous*, ed. Samuel French Morse (New York: Alfred A. Knopf, 1969), p. 161 (hereafter cited as *OP*).

3. Frank Kermode has brilliantly investigated this subject in his *Romantic Image* (London: Routledge & Kegan Paul, 1957; New York: Chilmark Press, n.d.).

4. *Shelley's Prose, or The Trumpet of a Prophecy*, ed. David Lee Clark (Albuquerque: University of New Mexico Press, 1954), pp. 174, 189.

5. *Biographia Literaria*, ed. J. Shawcross, 2 vols. (London: Oxford University Press, 1954), 1:202.

6. *The Letters of John Keats 1814-1821*, ed. Hyder Edward Rollins (Cambridge: Harvard University Press, 1958), 1:186. Keats wrote "existince" for existence.

7. On negative capability see Keats' letter of 21, 27 December 1817 (Rollins, 1:193) and commentaries by Walter Jackson Bate, *John Keats* (Cambridge: Harvard University Press, 1963), pp. 233-63, and George Bornstein, "Keats's Concept of the Ethereal," *Keats-Shelley Journal* 18 (1969): 97-106.

8. *Biographia Literaria*, ed. Shawcross, 2:11.

9. M. H. Abrams, "Structure and Style in the Greater Romantic Lyric," in *From Sensibility to Romanticism: Essays Presented to Frederick A. Pottle*, ed. Frederick W. Hilles and Harold Bloom (New York: Oxford University Press, 1965), p. 528.

10. Robert Langbaum, *The Poetry of Experience: The Dramatic Monologue in Modern Literary Tradition* (New York: W. W. Norton & Co., 1963); see especially chapter 1. Langbaum's book first appeared in 1957.

11. See Langbaum, p. 182, on the gratuitous element.

12. See Harold Bloom's "The Internalization of Quest Romance." The essay originally appeared in *The Yale Review* 58 (summer 1969): 526-36, and is reprinted in Bloom's *Romanticism and Consciousness: Essays in Criticism* (New York: W. W. Norton & Co., 1970), pp. 3-24, and *The Ringers in the Tower: Studies in Romantic Tradition* (Chicago: University of Chicago Press, 1971), pp. 13-35.

13. Bloom, *Romanticism and Consciousness*, p. 17.

14. M. H. Abrams, *Natural Supernaturalism: Tradition and Revolution in Romantic Literature* (New York: W. W. Norton & Co., 1971), pp. 13-14.

15. *The Variorum Edition of the Poems of W. B. Yeats*, ed. Peter Allt and Russell K. Alspach (New York: Macmillan Co., 1957), p. 847 (hereafter cited as *VP*).

16. *Letters of Wallace Stevens*, ed. Holly Stevens (New York: Alfred A. Knopf, 1970), p. 831.

17. *Defence of Poetry*, in *Shelley's Prose*, ed. Clark, p. 287.

18. "The Drunken Boat: The Revolutionary Element in Romanticism," in *Romanticism Reconsidered*, ed. Northrop Frye (New York and London: Columbia University Press, 1963), pp. 16-17. For a placing of these notions of imagery in a fuller context, see Frye's chapter on "The Romantic Myth" in *A Study of English Romanticism* (New York: Random House, 1968).

19. Frye, *Romanticism Reconsidered*, p. 24.

20. See, for example, Carlos Baker, *Shelley's Major Poetry: The Fabric of a Vision* (New York: Russell & Russell, 1961), p. 112, or Earl Wasserman's somewhat different view in *Shelley: A Critical Reading* (Baltimore and London: Johns Hopkins Press, 1971), pp. 255-57.

21. Wasserman, *Shelley: A Critical Reading*, chap. 1.

22. *The Letters of Percy Bysshe Shelley*, ed. Frederick L. Jones (Oxford: At the Clarendon Press, 1964), 2:310.

23. Italics mine. "Preface to . . . *Lyrical Ballads*," in *The Poetical Works of William Wordsworth*, ed. E. de Selincourt (Oxford: At the Clarendon Press, 1944), 2:400-401.

24. See C. K. Stead, *The New Poetic: Yeats to Eliot* (Harmondsworth, England: Penguin Books, 1967), chap. 2 and 3, passim.

25. T. S. Eliot, "Andrew Marvell," in *Selected Essays* (New York: Harcourt, Brace & World, 1964), p. 262.

26. I. A. Richards, *Principles of Literary Criticism* (New York: Harcourt, Brace & Co., n.d.), p. 250. The book was first published in 1925.

27. Eliot thus makes a sort of bridge between the anti-romanticism of New Humanists like Irving Babbitt and that of the New Critics. His relation to Babbitt is discussed in chapter 3.

28. Cleanth Brooks, *Modern Poetry and the Tradition* (Chapel Hill: University of North Carolina Press, 1939), p. 216.

29. F. R. Leavis, *Revaluation* (London: Chatto & Windus, 1936; 4th imp. 1956), pp. 53, 58, and 61, respectively.

30. Brooks, p. viii.

31. Richard Harter Fogle, "Romantic Bards and Metaphysical Reviewers," *ELH* 12 (1945): 221-50. Two other good early defenses are Frederick A. Pottle's "The Case of Shelley," *PMLA* 67 (1952): 589-608, reprinted with revisions in *English Romantic Poets: Modern Essays in Criticism*, ed. M. H. Abrams (New York: Oxford University Press, 1960), pp. 289-306, and C. S. Lewis' "Shelley, Dryden, and Mr. Eliot," in *Rehabilitations and Other Essays* (London: Oxford University Press, 1939), pp. 3-34, also reprinted in the Abrams volume, pp. 247-67. See, too, Richard Foster's argument that, for all its hostility, New Criticism actually continues a romantic viewpoint and sensibility in *The New Romantics: A Reappraisal of the New Criticism* (Bloomington: Indiana University Press, 1962).

32. Cleanth Brooks, *Modern Poetry and the Tradition* (New York: Oxford University Press, 1965), p. xiv.

33. Brooks, 1965, p. xvi. Compare the different and more satisfying context that Geoffrey Hartman elaborates for some of the same insights in *Wordsworth's Poetry 1787-1814* (New Haven and London: Yale University Press, 1964).

34. *Autobiographies* (London: Macmillan, 1966), p. 87.

35. Leavis, pp. 252-53.

36. Allen Tate, "Yeats's Romanticism: Notes and Suggestions," *The Southern Review* 7 (winter 1942): 600.

37. J. Hillis Miller, *Poets of Reality* (New York: Atheneum, 1969), p. 1. Originally published by Harvard University Press, 1965.

38. Miller, p. 2.

39. Monroe K. Spears, *Dionysus and the City: Modernism in Twentieth-Century Poets* (New York: Oxford University Press, 1971), p. 15.

40. Spears, pp. 23, 34.

41. See Brooks' "Retrospective Introduction" to *Modern Poetry and the Tradition* (1965), pp. xiv-xv.

42. Spears, p. 17, and Edmund Wilson, *Axel's Castle: A Study in the Imaginative Literature of 1870-1930* (New York: Charles Scribner's Sons, n.d.), p. 25. Wilson's book first appeared in 1931.

43. On one occasion (in 1947), even Frye tried to dissociate Blake from romanticism; see *Fearful Symmetry: A Study of William Blake* (Princeton: Princeton University Press, 1969), p. 167; in general, however, a postwar revision of the term *romanticism* has made Blake seem a central figure.

44. Spears, p. 18.

45. Spears, p. 18.

46. Spears, p. 18.

47. Kermode, p. 166.

48. Kermode, p. 166.

49. Herbert Read's influential *The True Voice of Feeling: Studies in English Romantic Poetry* (London: Faber & Faber, 1953) sees organic form as "the specifically romantic principle" and postulates a tradition from Coleridge to Eliot based on "expression conceived as direct communication by precise symbolic means of the configuration of perception and feeling"; the volume also reprints a revision of Read's earlier defense of Shelley

against Eliot. F. L. Lucas' *Decline and Fall of the Romantic Ideal* (Cambridge: Cambridge University Press, 1936) bases continuity on liberation of "less conscious" levels of mind; John Heath-Stubbs' *The Darkling Plain: A Study of the Later Fortunes of Romanticism from George Darley to W. B. Yeats* (London: Eyre and Spottiswoode, 1950) views poetry "as a species of mythology or significant dream"; and John Bayley's *The Romantic Survival: A Study in Poetic Evolution* (London: Constable, 1957) first sets up "The Romantic Dilemmas" and then explores them in Yeats, Auden, and Thomas. James Benziger's *Images of Eternity: Studies in the Poetry of Religious Vision from Wordsworth to T. S. Eliot* (Carbondale: Southern Illinois University Press, 1962) emphasizes "the transcendentalizing imagination." Of books devoted almost wholly to modern poetry, C. K. Stead's *The New Poetic: Yeats to Eliot* (London: Hutchinson, 1964) sees moderns as trying to reunite the didactic-prophetic and purely aesthetic offshoots of romanticism, while Daniel Hoffman's *Barbarous Knowledge: Myth in the Poetry of Yeats, Graves, and Muir* (New York and London: Oxford University Press, 1967) sees its three poets as using the romantic strategy of countering scientific materialism by myth.

50. Stephen Spender, *The Struggle of the Modern* (Berkeley and Los Angeles: University of California Press, 1963; 1965 ed.), p. 48. Compare his earlier (p. 23) statement: "It is in the contradiction between an eighteenth-century, almost classical critical awareness and artistic self-consciousness, and this trust in the miracle-producing resources of the individual imagination, to which we owe the great achievements of modern art."

51. Spender, pp. 47 and 49, respectively.

52. Spender, p. 133.

53. Spender, p. 136.

54. Frye, *Fearful Symmetry*, p. 426.

55. *The Sacred Wood* (New York: Barnes & Noble, 1960), p. 157.

56. Harold Bloom, *The Visionary Company: A Reading of English Romantic Poetry* (Garden City, N.Y.: Doubleday & Co., 1961), p. xv. Cf. the epigraph to *The Anxiety of Influence: A Theory of Poetry* (New York: Oxford University Press, 1973).

57. Bloom, *Ringers in the Tower*, p. xi.

58. Kermode, pp. 2 and vii.

59. Kermode, p. 57.

60. Kermode, p. 163.

61. More recently, he has continued calling attention to the links between romantic and modern work in *The Modern Spirit: Essays on the Continuity of Nineteenth- and Twentieth-Century Literature* (New York: Oxford University Press, 1970), which includes an illuminating discussion of New Critical limitations in "The Function of Criticism Once More," but as a whole the earlier book bears more directly on my argument.

62. Langbaum, p. 35.

63. Langbaum, p. 47.

64. Langbaum, p. 79.

1. W. B. Yeats, *Memoirs,* ed. Denis Donoghue (London: Macmillan, 1972), pp. 19, 84.

2. See particularly Harold Bloom, *Yeats* (New York: Oxford University Press, 1970); George Bornstein, *Yeats and Shelley* (Chicago: University of Chicago Press, 1970); and Dwight Eddins, *Yeats: The Nineteenth Century Matrix* (University, Ala.: University of Alabama Press, 1971). There are two earlier full-length studies of the relation to Blake: Margaret Rudd, *Divided Image: A Study of William Blake and W. B. Yeats* (London: Routledge & Kegan Paul, 1953) and Hazard Adams, *Blake and Yeats: The Contrary Vision* (Ithaca: Cornell University Press, 1956). Frank Kermode's *Romantic Image* (London: Routledge & Kegan Paul, 1957; New York: Chilmark Press, n.d.) centers on Yeats.

3. In this and following chapters, dates in parentheses after titles indicate year of first publication unless specified otherwise.

4. *The Oxford Book of Modern Verse 1892-1935* (Oxford: At the Clarendon Press, 1936), pp. xxvi-xxvii. The quotation in the next paragraph is from p. xxix.

5. *Essays and Introductions* (New York: Macmillan Co., 1961), pp. 404-5 (hereafter cited as *E&I*).

6. *E&I* 405. Cf. *Explorations* (New York: Macmillan Co., 1963), p. 373, for a more confident view of them.

7. *The Necessary Angel: Essays on Reality and the Imagination* (New York: Alfred A. Knopf, 1951), p. 36.

8. *E&I* 407. Yeats repeats the remark in *Autobiographies* (London: Macmillan, 1966), p. 358 (hereafter cited as *Auto*).

9. *The Variorum Edition of the Poems of W. B. Yeats,* ed. Peter Allt and Russell K. Alspach (New York: Macmillan Co., 1957), p. 576 (hereafter cited as *VP*).

10. Compare the "rag-and-bone shop of the heart" in "The Circus Animals' Desertion." (*VP* 630)

11. *Uncollected Prose by W. B. Yeats,* ed. John P. Frayne (New York: Columbia University Press, 1970), 1:183 (hereafter cited as *Uncoll*).

12. Yeats provided a more scathing synopsis of the development from Elizabethan to romantic and then to modern in his little poem "Three Movements" (1932):

> Shakespearean fish swam the sea, far away from land;
> Romantic fish swam in nets coming to the hand;
> What are all those fish that lie gasping on the strand?
>
> (*VP* 485)

13. *J. B. Yeats: Letters to His Son W. B. Yeats and Others 1869-1922,* ed. Joseph Hone (London: Faber & Faber, 1944), p. 128. The elder Yeats thought his son's distinction a "splendid sentence."

14. Denis Donoghue, *William Butler Yeats* (New York: Viking Press, 1971), p. 77.

15. M. H. Abrams, *Natural Supernaturalism: Tradition and Revolution in Romantic Literature* (New York: W. W. Norton & Co., 1971), p. 47.

16. Even in the anti-Shelleyan mood of his late essay on *Prometheus Unbound* Yeats conceded that, in contrast to Blake's mysticism, "Shelley's art shows that he was an unconverted man though certainly a visionary." (*E&I* 423)

17. *The Poems of Arthur Henry Hallam*, ed. Richard Le Gallienne (New York: Macmillan & Co.; London: Elkin Mathews & John Lane, 1893), p. 94. In his generally approving review of this volume (*The Speaker*, 22 July 1893, p. 81) Yeats drew a direct line from Shelley to the aesthetic movement: "Writing long before the days of Rossetti and Swinburne, Arthur Hallam explained the principles of the aesthetic movement, claimed Tennyson as its living representative, and traced its origin to Keats and Shelley, who, unlike Wordsworth, made beauty the beginning and end of all things in art." I have discussed Yeats' relation to Hallam and Browning as critics of Shelley more fully in *Yeats and Shelley*, pp. 31-41.

18. *Shelley's Prose, or the Trumpet of a Prophecy*, ed. David Lee Clark (Albuquerque: University of New Mexico Press, 1954), p. 189.

19. *The Letters of W. B. Yeats*, ed. Allan Wade (London: Rupert Hart-Davis, 1954), p. 469 (hereafter cited as *Letters*, followed by Arabic numerals indicating page number).

20. *E&I* 296. Cf. *The Variorum Edition of the Plays of W. B. Yeats*, ed. Russell K. Alspach (New York: Macmillan Co., 1966), pp. 1295-96 (hereafter cited as *VPlays*).

21. *A Vision* (New York: Macmillan Co., 1961), p. 193 (hereafter cited as *Vision*).

22. "Introduction" to *Poems of William Blake*, ed. W. B. Yeats (Cambridge: Harvard University Press, 1969), p. xxiii. The subsequent quotation is from p. xvii.

23. In his view, mysticism made for greater symbolic coherence: "The chief difference between the metaphors of poetry and the symbols of mysticism is that the latter are woven together into a complete system." *The Works of William Blake: Poetic, Symbolic, and Critical*, ed. Edwin John Ellis and William Butler Yeats, 3 vols. (London: Bernard Quaritch, 1893), 1:238 (hereafter cited as *Ellis-Yeats*).

24. That implication may underlie a remark in "Symbolism in Painting" (1898), which is a reworking of Yeats' preface to W. T. Horton's *A Book of Images*: "The systematic mystic is not the greatest of artists, because his imagination is too great to be bounded by a picture or a song, and because only imperfection in a mirror of perfection, or perfection in a mirror of imperfection, delights our frailty." Extensive quotation from Blake follows that remark. (*E&I* 150)

25. *Vision* 142. All quotations in these paragraphs come from Yeats' discussion of phases 16 and 17.

26. *E&I* 347. Cf. a similar remark in *Auto* 490: "Hallam argued that poetry was the impression on the senses of certain very sensitive men. It was such with the pure artists, Keats and Shelley, but not so with the impure artists who, like Wordsworth, mixed up popular morality with

their work." By that time, Yeats had begun to fear that such purity would cut art off from the social order.

27. *Mythologies* (London: Macmillan & Co., 1962), p. 329.

28. Harold Bloom first noticed this parallel, in *Yeats*, p. 341.

29. *Uncoll* 270-71; *Letters* 548.

30. P. 512, from *The Bride of Abydos*, 2:ii.

31. *Auto* 470; cf. *Mythologies*, p. 334.

32. The twin charges of didactic moralism and inability to express detailed characters surface again in the account of Wordsworth in *A Vision*, p. 134.

33. Bloom, *Yeats*, p. 184.

34. *Auto* 313; *E&I* 222.

35. *Pages From a Diary Written in Nineteen Hundred and Thirty*, in *Explorations*, pp. 298-339, passim.

36. Compare, for example, Coleridge: "In looking at objects of Nature while I am thinking, as at yonder moon dim-glimmering thro' the dewy window-pane, I seem rather to be seeking, as it were *asking*, a symbolical language for something within me that already and forever exists. . . ." in *The Notebooks of Samuel Taylor Coleridge*, ed. Kathleen Coburn (New York: Bollingen Foundation, Pantheon Books, 1961) 2:2546.

37. Bloom, *Yeats*, p. 382; Richard Ellmann, *The Identity of Yeats* (New York: Oxford University Press, 1964), p. 3.

38. In *W. B. Yeats: The Later Poetry* (Berkeley and Los Angeles: University of California Press, 1966), Thomas Parkinson reprints a manuscript (p. 146) showing that Yeats at one time thought of combining "The Choice" and the current final stanza under the subtitle "The last romantics." Consideration of such a subtitle suggests both that Yeats saw a strong connection between the two stanzas and that the opening line of the last one was meant more than casually.

39. *VP* 480. Cf. his note to *The Winding Stair*: "In this book and elsewhere I have used towers, and one tower in particular, as symbols and have compared their winding stairs to the philosophical gyres, but it is hardly necessary to interpret what comes from the main track of thought and expression. Shelley uses towers constantly as symbols. . . ." (*VP* 831) Yeats had traced Shelley's use of towers in "The Philosophy of Shelley's Poetry."

40. I have already given my views on Yeats' early romanticism in *Yeats and Shelley*; Harold Bloom uses a different approach to arrive at many similar and some quite different views in his *Yeats*. The two books are in part complementary.

41. M. H. Abrams, "Structure and Style in the Greater Romantic Lyric," in *From Sensibility to Romanticism: Essays Presented to Frederick A. Pottle*, ed. Frederick W. Hilles and Harold Bloom (New York: Oxford University Press, 1965), p. 528.

42. Compare "pictures of the mind" in "In Memory of Eva Gore-Booth and Con Markiewicz."

43. Abrams, "Structure and Style in the Greater Romantic Lyric," p. 532.

44. A. Norman Jeffares has even suggested a possible echo in "The Tower" of Blake on bodily decay; see his *A Commentary on the Collected Poems of W. B. Yeats* (Stanford: Stanford University Press, 1968), p. 258.

45. Horton's contemplation of an image links this poem to the more recondite "Phases of the Moon" (1919), where the creatures of the full moon, or phase 15, fix the mind's eye "upon images that once were thought." (*VP* 375)

46. In *The English Review*, August 1918, and *The Little Review*, September 1918; see the collation in *VP*, pp. 327-28.

47. It moves out-in-out, with a parallel present-past-present pattern.

48. See Jon Stallworthy, *Between the Lines: Yeats's Poetry in the Making* (Oxford: At the Clarendon Press, 1963), p. 17.

49. This phrase comes from Yeats' own note to "The Second Coming," *VP* 825.

50. Bloom, *Yeats*, p. 320.

51. Margaret Rudd first noticed this in her *Divided Image*, p. 119. There is an interesting discussion in Bloom, *Yeats*, p. 319.

52. Bornstein, *Yeats and Shelley*, pp. 195-98.

53. *VP* 425. See *VP* 827 for Yeats' note.

54. Yeats' prose draft for the poem began: "Describe house in first stanza." Parkinson has a valuable discussion of the evolution of the poem, in *W. B. Yeats: The Later Poetry*, pp. 80-81, followed by a longer one of "Among School Children."

55. Jeffares compares Pythagoras' use of a swallow image; see *Commentary*, p. 344.

56. See Stallworthy, p. 38 f.

57. *Coleridge: Poetical Works*, ed. Ernest Hartley Coleridge (London: Oxford University Press, 1969), p. 148. This parallel was first noticed by C. G. Martin, "A Coleridge Reminiscence in Yeats's 'A Prayer For My Daughter,' " *Notes and Queries*, n.s. 12 (July 1965): 258-60.

58. John Unterecker, *A Reader's Guide to William Butler Yeats* (New York: Noonday Press, 1959), p. 191.

59. Parkinson, *W. B. Yeats: The Later Poetry*, p. 105.

60. Kermode, p. 83 f.

61. Yeats' later revision emphasized the danger of too little rather than too much mental control: "That hurry from unmeasured mind."

62. Louis MacNeice, *The Poetry of W. B. Yeats* (New York: Oxford University Press, 1941; 1969 ed.), pp. 69-71.

63. MacNeice, p. 21.

64. The best discussion of magical associations is by Allen Grossman, in chapter 6 of his *Poetic Knowledge in the Early Yeats: A Study of the Wind among the Reeds* (Charlottesville: University Press of Virginia, 1969).

65. I have adapted this phrase from Harold Bloom.

66. See Earl Wasserman, *The Finer Tone: Keats's Major Poems* (Baltimore: Johns Hopkins Press, 1953), chapter 3.

67. Yeats' note identifies the axle-tree with the Irish Tree of Life, otherwise represented as a hazel.

68. *The Poetry and Prose of William Blake,* ed. David V. Erdman and Harold Bloom (Garden City, N.Y.: Doubleday & Co., 1965), p. 554. I have normalized spelling and capitalization.

69. Shelley's Preface to *Alastor,* in *The Complete Poetical Works of Percy Bysshe Shelley,* ed. Thomas Hutchinson (London: Oxford University Press, 1961), p. 14.

70. For a more detailed treatment of Shelleyan elements in *The Shadowy Waters* see Bornstein, *Yeats and Shelley,* pp. 156-62, and for *The King's Threshold* and Shelley's *Defence,* pp. 64-66.

71. Unpublished letter, quoted by A. Norman Jeffares in *W. B. Yeats: Man and Poet* (London: Routledge & Kegan Paul, corrected ed. 1962), p. 167.

72. Yeats' reaction against Blake was often in Blakean terms. Thus, although Blakean elements certainly composed the mythology he discarded in "A Coat" (1914), even that poem may be based on a passage in Blake's "Public Address." See Robert F. Gleckner, "Blake and Yeats," *Notes and Queries,* n.s. 2 (January 1955): 38.

73. *Oxford Book of Modern Verse,* p. xxxvi.

74. See *Alastor,* lines 275-90.

75. Bloom, *Yeats,* p. 313.

76. Yeats' list is reprinted by Curtis Bradford, "The Order of Yeats's Last Poems," *MLN* 76 (June 1961): 515-16. After "The Circus Animals' Desertion" came "Politics" as an envoy of *sprezzatura* and then two plays (*The Death of Cuchulain* and *Purgatory*). This follows the order of the Cuala Press's *Last Poems and Two Plays.*

77. Stallworthy, pp. 121, 94.

78. For the echo of "London" see Stallworthy, p. 117.

79. *Hellas,* line 148; *Blake,* ed. Bloom and Erdman, pp. 157 and 18.

80. See Ernest Schanzer, " 'Sailing to Byzantium', Keats, and Andersen," *English Studies* 41 (December 1960): 376-80.

81. *Blake,* ed. Bloom and Erdman, p. 126.

82. See Bornstein, *Yeats and Shelley,* p. 193 f., for a discussion of the two passages in a different context.

83. In their final arrangement. Yeats wrote "Meru" before most of the others.

84. Bloom, *Yeats,* p. 419. Compare, too, Stevens' "Man and Bottle," discussed in chapter 1. Jeffares, *Commentary,* p. 434, thinks that, like Rocky Face of "The Gyres," the caverned hermits derive from Shelley's Ahasuerus.

85. For Yeats' own commentary on the passage see *Letters* 789-90; Ellmann has an interesting commentary in *The Identity of Yeats,* pp. 268-69.

86. Ms. quoted by Ellmann, *The Identity of Yeats,* p. 270.

87. *Defence of Poetry,* in *Shelley's Prose,* ed. Clark, p. 277.

88. *Letters* 788. The poem was then called "Wisdom."

89. Yeats mentioned "Ode on a Grecian Urn" at least five times, three

of them in connection with the "little town," which he twice associated with Rapallo (*Letters* 738; *Vision* 3).

90. *Letters on Poetry from W. B. Yeats to Dorothy Wellesley* (London: Oxford University Press, 1964), p. 8.

91. Curtis Bradford, *Yeats at Work* (Carbondale: Southern Illinois University Press, 1965), p. 160.

NOTES TO CHAPTER 3

1. T. S. Eliot, "The Poetry of W. B. Yeats," First Annual Yeats Lecture, delivered to the Friends of the Irish Academy at the Abbey Theatre, June 1940, *The Southern Review* 7 (winter 1942): 442-54, as reprinted in *The Permanence of Yeats*, ed. James Hall and Martin Steinmann (New York: Collier Books, Macmillan Co., 1961), p. 296. Compare Eliot's 1953 remark: "[Yeats] was a late developer; when he emerged as a great modern poet, about 1917, we had already reached a point such that he appeared not as a precursor but as an elder and venerated contemporary," in *To Criticize the Critic* (New York: Farrar, Straus, & Giroux, 1965), p. 58 (hereafter cited as *TCC*).

2. Hall and Steinmann, p. 297.

3. See *Selected Essays* (New York: Harcourt, Brace & World, 1964), p. 252 (hereafter cited as *SE*); *After Strange Gods: A Primer of Modern Heresy* (New York: Harcourt, Brace & Co., 1934), p. 50 (hereafter cited as *ASG*); and the 1947 interview used by Richard Ellmann in *Eminent Domain: Yeats among Wilde, Joyce, Pound, Eliot and Auden* (New York: Oxford University Press, 1967), p. 90.

4. All quotations are from the 1964 edition (London: Faber & Faber) (hereafter cited as *UPUC*).

5. According to Valerie Eliot, he told her orally of his early imitation of FitzGerald: "At about fourteen he wrote 'some very gloomy quatrains in the form of the *Rubaiyat*' which had 'captured my imagination.' These he showed to no one and presumed he destroyed." See her "Note" to T. S. Eliot, *Poems Written in Early Youth* (New York: Farrar, Straus, & Giroux, 1967), p. v (hereafter cited as *PWEY*).

6. *On Poetry and Poets* (New York: Noonday Press, Farrar, Straus, & Giroux, 1961), pp. 223-24 (hereafter cited as *OPP*).

7. The only surviving copy of the graduation poem is a typescript at King's College, Cambridge; see *PWEY*, p. 34. A slightly revised form of "If Time and Space" later appeared in *The Harvard Advocate* 83 (3 June 1907): 96.

8. The lines, "We go; as lightning-winged clouds that fly/After a summer tempest," seem to owe something to the phrasing of Shelley's "Ode to the West Wind."

9. She was. As Eliot noted to John Hayward, the day school "was dissolved through lack of pupils a few years later." (*PWEY* 34) Its successor was the still-flourishing St. Louis Country Day School.

10. *Criterion* 9 (January 1930): 357, in a review of Peter Quennell's

Baudelaire and the Symbolists. Herbert Howarth discusses the impact of Symons on Eliot in *Notes on Some Figures behind T. S. Eliot* (Boston: Houghton Mifflin Co., 1964), p. 103 f. (Howarth's book is, of course, indispensable for its treatment of Eliot's biography and milieu.) Eliot designated Symons an "imperfect" critic in *The Sacred Wood.*

11. They were published in the issues for 12 November 1909, 12 January 1910, and 26 January 1910.

12. There is a list of Eliot's courses for 1909-10 in Howarth, pp. 126-27.

13. London: Faber & Faber, 1928, p. viii.

14. "What Dante Means to Me" (1950), in *TCC* 125.

15. Howarth, pp. 136-37.

16. He mentions the projected book complete with title in *The New Laokoon: An Essay on the Confusion of the Arts* (Boston: Houghton Mifflin Co., 1910), p. xiv. There are illuminating discussions of Eliot and Babbitt in Howarth's encyclopedic work and in John D. Margolis' more tightly focused *T. S. Eliot's Intellectual Development, 1922-1939* (Chicago: University of Chicago Press, 1972). I am indebted to both.

17. Babbitt, *Rousseau and Romanticism* (Boston and New York: Houghton Mifflin Co., 1919), p. 237; Eliot, *The Sacred Wood* (New York: Barnes & Noble, 1960), p. ix (hereafter cited as *SW*). Compare Wordsworth's "Preface to the Second Edition" of *Lyrical Ballads* in *The Poetical Works of William Wordsworth*, ed. E. de Selincourt (Oxford: At the Clarendon Press, 1944), 2:400-401, and Eliot's "Tradition and the Individual Talent." (*SW* 58)

18. Babbitt, p. 357; Eliot, *SE* 227. The remainder of the references to Babbitt in this paragraph are from pp. 391 and 287, respectively.

19. Margolis discusses it in *T. S. Eliot's Intellectual Development*, pp. 9-12, and generously made his own copy available to me.

20. Cf. Babbitt, p. 4.

21. Cf. Babbitt, p. 100.

22. "One of the most corrupting, degrading, and badly-paid means of livelihood that a writing man can ply." Quoted by Donald Gallup, "T. S. Eliot & Ezra Pound: Collaborators in Letters," *Atlantic* 225 (January 1970): 54.

23. Compare *UPUC* 29; *OPP* 117, 181, 204. Except for *UPUC*, which belongs to a middle period, these are all relatively late statements.

24. "Observations," *Egoist* 5 (May 1918): 69.

25. See, for example, *SE* 252 and 262; *UPUC* 150 and 152.

26. C. K. Stead, *The New Poetic: Yeats to Eliot* (Harmondsworth, England: Penguin Books, 1967), chap. 3.

27. Robert Langbaum, *The Poetry of Experience: The Dramatic Monologue in Modern Literary Tradition* (New York: W. W. Norton & Co., 1963), p. 233; Frank Kermode, *Romantic Image* (New York: Chilmark Press, n.d.), pp. 43-44, passim; J. Hillis Miller, *Poets of Reality* (New York: Atheneum, 1969), p. 149; and Stead, pp. 190-92.

28. I stress these points because they have been ignored too often by many of Eliot's admirers, some of whom are discussed in chapter 1 along with some honorable exceptions (see also the preceding note). To anyone

who has studied romanticism more impartially, the history of Eliot scholarship is depressing. There are signs of recent improvement.

29. Yeats, *Essays and Introductions* (New York: Macmillan Co., 1961), p. 66.

30. George Wyndham, *Essays in Romantic Literature* (London: Macmillan and Co., 1919), p. 34.

31. Wyndham, p. 41.

32. Ernest J. Lovell, "The Heretic in the Sacred Wood; or, the Naked Man, the Tired Man, and the Romantic Aristocrat: William Blake, T. S. Eliot, and George Wyndham," in *Romantic and Victorian: Studies in Memory of W. H. Marshall*, ed. W. Paul Elledge and Richard L. Hoffman (Rutherford, Madison, and Teaneck, N.J.: Fairleigh Dickinson University Press, 1971), p. 89.

33. Compare, for example, the praise of Whibley for escaping (*SW* 34) or the remarks on escape at the end of "Tradition and the Individual Talent." (*SW* 58)

34. Wordsworth, "Preface" in *Works*, ed. E. de Selincourt, 2:400-401.

35. After his theory of composition, Eliot spoke most often of Wordsworth's revolution in poetic diction, which he saw as explicitly parallel to his own. (*OPP* 28) He considered Wordsworth's theories of diction as intimately linked to his revolutionary faith and social theories. (*UPUC* 73-74) Elsewhere, he principally insisted that Wordsworth, like Yeats and himself, was not a mystic, saw him as first to annex new authority for poetry, and admired *The Prelude*. While in 1917 he had contrasted Wordsworth unfavorably with Donne in use of nature, he later came to respect Wordsworth's relation to nature. Marion Montgomery has two essays on Eliot and Wordsworth in *The Reflective Journey toward Order: Essays on Dante, Wordsworth, Eliot, and Others* (Athens: University of Georgia Press, 1973), which also includes "Around the Prickly Pear: Eliot on Coleridge on Sir John Davies."

36. Bernard Bergonzi, *T. S. Eliot* (New York: Collier Books, Macmillan Co., 1972), p. 72. Cf. Stead, p. 126 f.

37. Shelley, *Defence of Poetry* in *Shelley's Prose, or the Trumpet of a Prophecy*, ed. David Lee Clark (Albuquerque: University of New Mexico Press, 1954), p. 287.

38. The most extended treatments of Wordsworth and Coleridge, Shelley and Keats appear in the lectures on those poets in *UPUC*, and on Byron in the essay "Byron" reprinted in *SE*. All these are discussed below, along with his second review of Blake.

The comic "Five-finger Exercises" begins with a glance at Blake and inserts a phrase from Keats ("palate fine") in poem IV.

39. *Athenaeum* 4685 (13 February 1920): 208.

40. The reader may draw his own conclusions about Eliot's repeated use of the word "naked" here. "The Naked Man" was the original title of the review. Eliot's intense adolescent encounter with the romantics coincided with the awakening of sexuality, as we have seen.

41. See the letters reprinted in T. S. Eliot, *The Waste Land: A Facsimile*

and Transcript, ed. Valerie Eliot (New York: Harcourt, Brace Jovanovich, 1971), p. xxf., and those described in Lovell, "The Heretic in the Sacred Wood," p. 86.

42. "The Romantic Generation, If It Existed," *Athenaeum* 4655 (13 July 1919): 616.

43. *The Tyro* 1 (spring 1921): 4.

44. "Ulysses, Order, and Myth," *The Dial* 75 (November 1923): 482. Only once in those early years did Eliot waver in his anti-romanticism. In a letter to *TLS* (28 October 1920) he criticized Babbitt and Pierre Lasserre for two errors—not differentiating the different sense of *romanticism* when applied to epochs and to individuals, and not supporting the exclusiveness of the labels *romantic* and *classic* by examination of particular texts. Partly under the compulsion of admitting that his admired Charles Maurras was in some sense romantic, he proposed that perhaps the terms should be used as little as possible. It was a momentary aberration.

45. *The Nation & Athenaeum* 41 (17 September 1927): 779.

46. Eliot ended the review with a non sequitur that makes sense mostly as an implicit self-warning: "The poet also knows that it is no good, in writing poetry, to try to be anything but a poet."

47. *Adelphi* 1 (September 1923): 269-77.

48. The version of the essays in *SE* deletes a relevant passage from the *Criterion* form (2 [October 1923]: 39): "So important it [the sense of fact] seems to me, that I am inclined to make one distinction between Classicism and Romanticism of this, that the romantic is deficient or undeveloped in his ability to distinguish between fact and fancy, whereas the classicist, or adult mind, is thoroughly realist—without illusions, without day-dreams, without hope, without bitterness, and with an abundant resignation." Margolis, *T. S. Eliot's Intellectual Development*, pp. 52 f., gives a running description of the exchanges in the two journals. See *SE* 259, "Andrew Marvell," for another discussion by Eliot of "the effort to construct a dream-world" in nineteenth-century English poetry.

49. Similarly, Eliot's asking "why have principles, when one has the inner voice?" (*SE* 17) would be the counterpart of an opponent's asking "Why think or feel, when one has outside authority?" Eliot's lapses have been too influential to pass over in silence.

50. "More About Romanticism," *Adelphi* 1 (December 1923): 567.

51. "Mr. Middleton Murry's Synthesis," *Monthly Criterion* 6 (October 1927): 344. Cf. *UPUC* 128.

52. "Essays on Style and Order," in *For Lancelot Andrewes* (London: Faber and Gwyer, 1928), p. ix. Cf. *TCC* 15.

53. Victor Brombert, "T. S. Eliot and the Romantic Heresy," *Yale French Studies* 13 (spring-summer 1954): 3-16.

54. Bergonzi, p. 126.

55. *TCC* 138. Now that his anti-romantic fit had passed, Eliot generously continued: "differing from myself chiefly in being immensely more learned, more industrious, and endowed with a more powerful and subtle mind."

56. Cf. *UPUC* 156, the close of the Norton lectures, for a gently ironic identification with Coleridge.

57. *OPP* 115. In his 1934 essay "Shakespearian Criticism, I. From Dryden to Coleridge," *A Companion to Shakespeare Studies,* ed. Harley Granville-Barker and G. B. Harrison (Cambridge: At the University Press, 1955), p. 305, Eliot called Coleridge "perhaps the greatest single figure in Shakespeare criticism down to the present day."

58. As quoted by Eliot, *SE* 256-57, from chapter 14 of *Biographia Literaria.* The passage in ellipsis reads: "first put in action by the will and understanding, and retained under their irremissive, though gentle and unnoticed, controul *(laxis effertur habenis).*" For Eliot, imagination in Coleridge's sense meant a period of lack of control, which needed to be hedged round by restraints. This emphasis accords with his overall stance toward romanticism.

59. Coleridge, *Shakespearean Criticism,* ed. Thomas Middleton Raysor (London: Everyman's Library, Dent, 1964), 1:188-89.

60. In the same essay he also barred the door to Yeats ("outside of the tradition altogether"), Landor, Tennyson, Browning, and Hardy. See *SE* 252.

61. "The Imagination then I consider either as primary, or secondary. The Primary Imagination I hold to be the living power and prime agent of all human perception, and as a repetition in the finite mind of the eternal act of creation in the infinite I AM. The Secondary Imagination I consider as an echo of the former, co-existing with the conscious will, yet still as identical with the primary in the *kind* of its agency, and differing only in *degree,* and in the *mode* of its operation. It dissolves, diffuses, dissipates, in order to recreate; or where this process is rendered impossible, yet still at all events it struggles to idealise and to unify. It is essentially *vital,* even as all objects *(as* objects) are essentially fixed and dead.

FANCY, on the other hand, has no other counters to play with, but fixities and definites. The fancy is indeed no other than a mode of memory emancipated from the order of time and space; while it is blended with, and modified by that empirical phenomenon of the will, which we express by the word Choice. But equally with the ordinary memory the Fancy must receive all its materials ready made from the law of association." As quoted by Eliot, *UPUC* 76-77.

62. In "Coleridge and Wordsworth," *UPUC* 78, he again discussed Lowes' *Road to Xanadu,* which he used to support his particular claims. When he confronted as imaginative a poem as "Kubla Khan," he concluded that imagery from Coleridge's reading had sunk down into his feeling but "is not *used*: the poem has not been written." It is an illuminating failure of apprehension by Eliot. (*UPUC* 146)

63. He considered that "Lowes showed, once and for all, that poetic originality is largely an original way of assembling the most disparate and unlikely material to make a new whole." (*OPP* 119) The notion of assembly implies fixities and definites.

64. "Ezra Pound: His Metric and Poetry," reprinted in *TCC* 169, 170; *SW* 147. S. Viswanathan has written a useful survey, "Eliot and Shelley: A Sketch of Shifts in Attitude," *Ariel: A Review of International English Literature* 2 (January 1971): 58-67.

65. P. 92. C. S. Lewis, in "Shelley, Dryden, and Mr. Eliot" (1939), reprinted in *English Romantic Poets: Modern Essays in Criticism,* ed. M. H. Abrams (New York: Oxford University Press, 1960), p. 255, suggests that the lines from *Epipsychidion* "may well derive from *Purgatorio* xv. 49."

66. *TCC* 130, 132. Eliot had just finished a discussion of Dantesque imitation in *Little Gidding.* Cf. *UPUC* 90.

67. Eliot had granted an oblique pardon to Byron as early as *The Sacred Wood,* which carried a line from *Beppo* (stanza 43)—"I also like to dine on becaficas"—as its unidentified second epigraph.

68. *Notes towards the Definition of Culture* (London: Faber & Faber, 1963), p. 112.

69. T. S. Eliot, *Collected Poems 1909-1962* (New York: Harcourt, Brace & World, 1963), p. 3. Subsequent quotations from Eliot's poetry are from this edition and will be identified by page numbers inside parentheses within the text; in extended discussions of lyrics, only page numbers for the first quotation will be given.

70. "Preface" to *Anabasis: a Poem by St.-John Perse* (New York: Harcourt, Brace Jovanovich, 1949), p. 10. The preface is dated 1930.

71. In *Biographia Literaria,* chapter 1, Coleridge says he learned from his schoolmaster Rev. James Bowyer that "Poetry . . . had a logic of its own, as severe as that of science; and more difficult, because more subtle, more complex, and dependent on more, and more fugitive causes."

72. The dramatic apparatus of the poem suggests Eliot's recent reading of Laforgue, which had helped him to cast off his earlier derivative romanticism.

73. Hugh Kenner, *The Invisible Poet: T. S. Eliot* (New York: Harbinger Books, Harcourt, Brace & World, 1959), p. 134.

74. Kenner, pp. 40-41, 128.

75. So do those of Pound, discussed in my forthcoming monograph on *The Post-Romantic Consciousness of Ezra Pound.*

76. "Harold Monro," *Criterion* 11 (July 1932): 590.

77. Grover Smith has noticed this debt in passing, in his *T. S. Eliot's Poetry and Plays: A Study in Sources and Meaning* (Chicago: University of Chicago Press, 1960, emended and expanded ed.), p. 48.

78. *TCC* 130 f; *UPUC* 90.

79. As quoted by Eliot, *TCC* 131-32. It is one of the longest quotations in his prose.

80. *The Waste Land: A Facsimile and Transcript,* pp. 33, 45.

81. *The Complete Poetical Works of Percy Bysshe Shelley,* ed. Thomas Hutchinson (London: Oxford University Press, 1961), p. 514.

82. Stead, pp. 150-51.

83. "Introduction" to *The Oxford Book of Modern Verse* (Oxford: At the Clarendon Press, 1936), p. xxxiv.

84. See, for example, the "acting is suffering/ And suffering is action" speech from *Murder in the Cathedral* (New York: Harcourt, Brace & Co., 1935), p. 21.

85. Compare, too, the corpse in the garden (55), which may have begun to sprout.

86. *Poetical Works,* ed. Hutchinson, p. 242.

87. R. P. Blackmur, *Form and Value in Modern Poetry* (Garden City, N.Y.: Doubleday & Co., 1952), p. 140.

88. *The Waste Land: A Facsimile and Transcript,* p. xxii.

89. See Hugh Kenner, "The Urban Apocalypse," in *Eliot in His Time: Essays on the Occasion of the Fiftieth Anniversary of 'The Waste Land,'* ed. A. Walton Litz (Princeton: Princeton University Press, 1973), pp. 23-49.

90. *Selected Letters of Ezra Pound, 1907-1941,* ed. D. D. Paige (London: Faber & Faber, 1951), p. 92.

91. *The Waste Land: A Facsimile and Transcript,* p. 119.

92. The same conjunction of anti-romanticism and anti-Semitism occurs in Eliot's admired Maurras.

93. Bergonzi, p. 124.

94. I owe this phrase and point to Hugh Kenner, *The Invisible Poet,* p. 249.

95. Bergonzi, p. 136.

96. I am indebted for some of these observations to James Benziger, "The Romantic Tradition: Wordsworth and T. S. Eliot," *Bucknell Review* 8 (1959): 277-86, an earlier version of his remarks in *Images of Eternity: Studies in the Poetry of Religious Vision from Wordsworth to T. S. Eliot* (Carbondale: Southern Illinois University Press, 1962).

97. See book 12, lines 210-15. I have regularized verb forms.

98. *Triumph of Life,* lines 77-79. Cf. *TCC* 128 f., discussed above.

99. The intermediate phrase, referring to a murmuring shell, invokes another favorite romantic symbol.

100. In one of the most advanced commentaries on the poem, C. K. Stead (*The New Poetic,* p. 181) has cited in passing the first ten, descriptive lines to support his contention that "the finest passages in *Four Quartets* . . . are passages which run counter to the planned intention of the poem." He writes, "The lines take life when they are permitted to rest for a moment in the physical world, permitted to express 'the love of created things.' " His remarks form an excellent starting point.

101. William F. Lynch, *Christ and Apollo: The Dimensions of the Literary Imagination* (New York: Sheed & Ward, 1960), reprinted in *T. S. Eliot, "Four Quartets": A Casebook,* ed. Bernard Bergonzi (Nashville and London: Aurora Publishers, 1970), pp. 249-50. Sometimes Eliot consciously deflates the poem's apocalyptic bent, as when he follows "Whirled in a vortex that shall bring/ The world to that destructive fire/ Which burns before the ice-cap reigns" with "That was a way of putting it—not very satisfactory:/ A periphrastic study in a worn-out poetical fashion." (184) But the imagery is too pervasive for more than occasional qualification.

102. "The Mysticism of Blake," *The Nation & Athenaeum* 41 (17 September 1927): 779.

103. John Lehman, "T. S. Eliot Talks about Himself and the Drive to Create," *New York Times Book Review* 103 (29 November 1953): 5; the relevant passage is conveniently reprinted in *T. S. Eliot, "Four Quartets": A Casebook*, ed. Bernard Bergonzi, p. 23.

104. New York: Harcourt, Brace & Co., 1950, p. 181. Eliot italicizes the lines, which are from Earth's speech in act 1.

105. *Poetical Works*, ed. Hutchinson, p. 212.

NOTES TO CHAPTER 4

1. *Letters of Wallace Stevens*, ed. Holly Stevens (New York: Alfred A. Knopf, 1970), p. 677 (hereafter cited as *LWS*, followed by Arabic numerals indicating page number).

2. While the term *romantic* and even specific analogies turn up in Stevens scholarship often enough in passing, his relation to his precursors has received surprisingly little precise or systematic study. Among books, Daniel Fuchs' *The Comic Spirit of Wallace Stevens* (Durham, N.C.: Duke University Press, 1963) contains the most useful short survey (pp. 105 f.), while only A. Walton Litz's *Introspective Voyager: The Poetic Development of Wallace Stevens* (New York: Oxford University Press, 1972) makes much use of Stevens' crucial concept of "new romanticism"—see pp. 190-92 for his excellent brief account. The best general articles are Newton Stallknecht, "Absence in Reality: A Study in the Epistemology of The Blue Guitar," *Kenyon Review* 21 (autumn 1959): 545-62, and Harold Bloom's "*Notes toward a Supreme Fiction*: A Commentary," reprinted in *Wallace Stevens: A Collection of Critical Essays*, ed. Marie Borroff (Englewood Cliffs, N.J.: Prentice-Hall, 1963). There are also two dissertations: a published Polish one by Teresa Truszkowska, *Wallace Stevens' Concept of Poetry and the Romantic Tradition* (Kraków: Nakladem Uniwersytetu Jagiellońskiego, 1971) and an unpublished American one by Mary Joan Girlinghouse, "The New Romantic of Wallace Stevens," dissertation, Catholic University of America, 1970, which argues that "there seems to have been no meaningful chronological growth or dialectical progression of the idea" (p. 9) of new romanticism, or of romanticism in general in Stevens, a conclusion I do not share. Joseph N. Riddel, in *The Clairvoyant Eye: The Poetry and Poetics of Wallace Stevens* (Baton Rouge: Louisiana State University Press, 1965) and elsewhere has cautioned against too simple an identification of Stevens with romanticism (even while indicating useful correspondences), but his two chief objections— Stevens' refusal of transcendental idealism and of the subject-object split—seem to me to pertain only to a part of romanticism, not the whole, and I have proposed alternate ways of seeing the distinctions between Stevens and his predecessors. There remain, of course, a host of scattered

essays and remarks by various critics, and I indicate my debts to the chief of these as they become relevant to the argument.

3. Citations in this paragraph will be found in *LWS* 82, 89, 92, 41, 177, and 71, respectively.

4. Citations in this paragraph will be found in *LWS* 26, 46, 87, 72, and 136, respectively.

5. Citations in this paragraph not otherwise identified will be found in *LWS* 29, 110, 147, and 167, respectively. Cf. also *LWS* 148.

6. English 8a, English Literature—From the publication of the Lyrical Ballads to the death of Scott (1798-1832). See *LWS* 33-34.

7. *The Collected Poems of Wallace Stevens* (New York: Alfred A. Knopf, 1968), pp. 35, 203 (hereafter cited as *CP*).

8. Charles Henri Ford, "Verlaine in Hartford: An Interview with Wallace Stevens," *View* 1 (September 1940): 6. Stevens also mentioned Shakespeare and Verlaine.

9. Robert Buttel, *Wallace Stevens: The Making of Harmonium* (Princeton: Princeton University Press, 1967), p. 7.

10. Buttel, p. 10.

11. "Sonnet," *Harvard Monthly* 28 (July 1899): 188.

12. "The Pigeons," *Harvard Advocate* 69 (3 April 1900): 42.

13. Text quoted in Buttel, p. 52.

14. There is an extended discussion of the parallel by Malcolm Bradbury, "An Ironic Romantic: Three Readings in Wallace Stevens" in *American Poetry*, ed. Irvin Ehrenpreis (New York: St. Martin's Press, 1965), pp. 170-71. Lucy Beckett began her recent study, *Wallace Stevens* (Cambridge: Cambridge University Press, 1974), with a general comparison of Stevens' poetic stance to Keats'.

15. As quoted in *Poems by Wallace Stevens*, ed. Samuel French Morse (New York: Vintage Books, Random House, n.d.), p. xvi. A. Walton Litz says that the manuscript version "may date from as early as 1915, although 1918-1919 seems more likely"; see his *Introspective Voyager*, p. 107.

16. *The Necessary Angel: Essays on Reality and the Imagination* (New York: Alfred A. Knopf, 1951), p. 6 (hereafter cited as *NA*).

17. *Opus Posthumous*, ed. Samuel French Morse (New York: Alfred A. Knopf, 1969), p. 49 (hereafter cited as *OP*). Stevens' use of jars and urns has been explored admirably by Patricia Merivale in "Wallace Stevens' 'Jar': The Absurd Detritus of Romantic Myth," *College English* 26 (April 1965): 527-32.

18. Compare these lines from Keats' final stanza:

> While barred clouds bloom the soft-dying day,
> And touch the stubble-plains with rosy hue;
> Then in a wailful choir the small gnats mourn
> Among the river sallows, borne aloft
> Or sinking as the light wind lives or dies;
> And full-grown lambs loud bleat from hilly bourn;

Hedge-crickets sing; and now with treble soft
The red-breast whistles from a garden-croft;
And gathering swallows twitter in the skies.

(*Keats: Poetical Works,* ed. H. W. Garrod [London: Oxford University Press, 1967], p. 219).

19. Helen Hennessy Vendler, *On Extended Wings: Wallace Stevens' Longer Poems* (Cambridge: Harvard University Press, 1969), pp. 47-48; cf. p. 320.

20. J. V. Cunningham propounded the parallel to Wordsworth in "Tradition and Modernity: Wallace Stevens" (1949; rev. ed. 1960), reprinted in *The Achievement of Wallace Stevens,* ed. Ashley Brown and Robert S. Haller (Philadelphia and New York: J. B. Lippincott Co., 1963), pp. 123-40; cf. Daniel Fuchs, *The Comic Spirit of Wallace Stevens,* p. 31, and A. Walton Litz, *Introspective Voyager,* p. 120. Roy Harvey Pearce, *The Continuity of American Poetry* (Princeton: Princeton University Press, 1961), p. 424, sees *Comedian* as "a kind of reply to 'The Waste Land' " as well.

21. Hi Simons, " 'The Comedian as the Letter C': Its Sense and Its Significance" (1940), reprinted in *The Achievement of Wallace Stevens,* p. 98.

22. According to Holly Stevens, "Bits of Remembered Time," *The Southern Review,* n.s. 7 (July 1971): 654. Besides his undergraduate course at Harvard and extensive primary reading in the romantics, Stevens knew a range of secondary works as well. References in his later prose enable us to pinpoint some of them precisely. The unnamed work by I. A. Richards in "The Noble Rider and the Sound of Words" is *Coleridge on Imagination* (New York: Harcourt, Brace & Co., 1935); the quotation on Stevens' p. 18 comes from Richards' p. 220, while the references on pp. 9 and 19 come from Richards' pp. 171 and 230, respectively, and the reference to Richards' remarks on Coleridge's theory of fancy identifies, of course, a main burden of Richards' book. Later in the same essay, Stevens quotes from "Croce's Oxford lecture of 1933," whose full title was *The Defence of Poetry: Variations on the Theme of Shelley* (Oxford: At the Clarendon Press, 1933); the remark that interested Stevens is on pp. 25-26. Stevens' quotation four pages later from the preface to Rochester's *Valentinian,* identified as coming from "*English Association Essays and Studies* 1939" (Oxford: At the Clarendon Press, 1940), appears there as part of V. De Sola Pinto's essay "Realism in English Poetry," which includes lengthy remarks on Wordsworth, Byron, and Crabbe. Elsewhere in *The Necessary Angel* (p. 136) Stevens quotes observations on romanticism from Ernst Cassirer, *Essay on Man* (New Haven: Yale University Press, 1944), pp. 155-56.

Two quotations from works on romanticism occur in *Opus Posthumous.* "A Collect of Philosophy" quotes from Alfred North Whitehead's chapter on "The Romantic Reaction" in *Science and the Modern World.* The review of Marianne Moore, "A Poet that Matters," quotes from A. E. Powell's Crocean *The Romantic Theory of Poetry* (London: Edward Arnold & Co.,

1926), p. 2. In his earlier letters, Stevens cites the chapter on Milton from George Edward Woodberry's *The Torch* (New York: McClure, Phillips & Co., 1905), which also included chapters on Wordsworth and Shelley, and a later footnote by Holly Stevens informs us that Stevens owned a copy of Sidney Colvin's *Letters of John Keats to His Family and Friends* (London and New York: Macmillan, 1891). (*LWS* 90, 110)

23. The *Collected Poems* ordering follows that of the second edition of *Ideas of Order*, which began with a new poem, "Farewell to Florida."

24. *NA* 30, 48, and 120, respectively.

25. Fuchs, p. 111.

26. "Slight transcendence" is an unfortunate phrase. Transcendence, like virginity, exists either totally or not at all. Stevens resisted transcendental or mystical impulses in romanticism, preferring instead those aspects directed toward this world. His "slight" here drastically qualifies the notion of transcendence; he elsewhere denies it completely.

27. The distinction recurs often in Stevens' prose. Compare *NA* 139, *OP* 164 and 169, and *CP* 247 for additional pejorative comments and *OP* 163 and 171, and *CP* 353, for additional positive ones.

28. "Introduction," *Selected Poems by Marianne Moore*, ed. T. S. Eliot (London: Faber & Faber, 1935), p. 9.

29. Michel Benamou, *Wallace Stevens and the Symbolist Imagination* (Princeton: Princeton University Press, 1972), p. 40.

30. *Selected Poems by Marianne Moore*, ed. T. S. Eliot, p. 9.

31. In a letter to T. C. Wilson, the editor who invited Stevens to do the review, he praised Moore as both disintegrator and reintegrator "endeavoring to create a new romantic." (*LWS* 278)

32. As always, Stevens diverges from his romantic model, in ways touched on below. Here we need note only his insistence that modern poets may and do address themselves to an elite. (*NA* 29) Herbert J. Stern rightly contrasts this with broader romantic aims in *Wallace Stevens: Art of Uncertainty* (Ann Arbor: University of Michigan Press, 1966), p. 79; but romanticism also contained the opposite strain, as in the Advertisement or opening adaptation from Dante of Shelley's *Epipsychidion:* "My song, I fear that thou wilt find but few/ Who fitly shall conceive thy reasoning/ Of such hard matter dost thou entertain."

33. I. A. Richards, *Coleridge on Imagination*, p. 83.

34. In *Adagia* Stevens wrote that "the poem is a nature created by the poet." (*OP* 166) For his notion of mundo see the discussion of *Notes toward a Supreme Fiction* concluding this chapter.

35. Vendler, p. 149.

36. *NA* viii, 59, and 136, respectively (italics mine).

37. Adelaide Kirby Morris, *Wallace Stevens: Imagination and Faith* (Princeton: Princeton University Press, 1974), p. 6. Riddel, in *The Clairvoyant Eye*, p. 171, remarks that "In Stevens' secularization of the Fall, the origin of consciousness was the birth of imagination." Morris, on p. 5, speculates that "Stevens' poetic trinity is a transvaluation of the Christian trinity. In his poetic doctrine, God becomes one with the imagination;

Christ becomes the poet-hero, or incarnation of imagination; and the Holy Ghost becomes the active though diffused presence of imagination in human life."

38. Compare, too, these lines from Wordsworth's *Recluse* cited in his preface to *The Excursion*:

> Paradise, and groves
> Elysian, Fortunate Fields—like those of old
> Sought in the Atlantic Main—why should they be
> A history only of departed things,
> Or a mere fiction of what never was?
> For the discerning intellect of Man,
> When wedded to this goodly universe
> In love and holy passion, shall find these
> A simple produce of the common day

with the quoted lines from Stevens and their continuation:

> The sky will be much friendlier then than now,
> A part of labor and a part of pain,
> And next in glory to enduring love,
> Not this dividing and indifferent blue.

39. Several have, in fact, been written. Of the many good discussions of Stevens' imagery, the two most implicitly (and occasionally explicitly) useful for understanding Stevens against romantic norms are Edward Kessler, *Images of Wallace Stevens* (New Brunswick, N.J.: Rutgers University Press, 1972) and Northrop Frye, "The Realistic Oriole: A Study of Wallace Stevens," reprinted in *Wallace Stevens*, ed. Marie Borroff. See also Frank Doggett, *Stevens' Poetry of Thought* (Baltimore: Johns Hopkins Press, 1966).

40. *CP* 83, 222, 401, and 524, respectively.

41. *CP* 65, 70, 134, and 249, respectively.

42. Vendler, p. 6.

43. I transplant Stevens' phrase from *An Ordinary Evening in New Haven*, where he uses it to make a different point. Its specific context—"that the theory/ Of poetry is the theory of life,/ As it is, in the intricate evasions of as"—itself illustrates my point.

44. "Well Moused, Lion," *The Dial* 76 (January 1924): 87. Miss Moore concluded her review by labeling Stevens "a ferocious jungle animal." (91)

45. Quotations in this paragraph come from *LWS* 123, 231, 446, 450, 628, 629, 652, 654, and 656, respectively.

46. James Baird, *The Dome and the Rock: Structure in the Poetry of Wallace Stevens* (Baltimore: Johns Hopkins Press, 1968), p. 162. Baird also has some provocative remarks on Stevens' animal images for imagination; see particularly p. 154.

47. Frank Kermode, *Wallace Stevens* (New York: Evergreen Books, Grove Press, 1961), p. 97.

48. For a rendering of this passage in verse, see "Recitation After Dinner." (*OP* 87)

49. Yeats also gets into Stevens' poetry in the more direct way, particularly in the volume *Auroras of Autumn*. There "Page from a Tale" includes four separate, italicized phrases from "The Lake Isle of Innisfree," a poem Stevens had cited in a letter of 1909 to illustrate his contention that "the cottage has been the youthful ideal of all men." (*LWS* 120) The phrase "deep heart's core"—quoted in "Page from a Tale"—from Innisfree may underlie Stevens' "heart's strong core" four poems later in the volume. (*CP* 426) Several of Stevens' poems include Yeatsian situations, like "There were ghosts that returned to earth to hear his phrases" at the start of the intervening "Large Red Man Reading." (*CP* 423) Such poems characteristically reverse their Yeatsian analogues. For example, Stevens' "Let's see the very thing and nothing else./ Let's see it with the hottest fire of sight./ Burn away everything not part of it to ash" (*CP* 373) reverses Yeats' "Everything that is not God consumed with intellectual fire" ("Blood and the Moon") by wanting to burn up everything that is *not* part of this world rather than everything that *is* part of it. Stevens' pervasive use of towers also seems to owe something to Yeats.

50. *Harvard Advocate* 125 (December 1938): 41.

51. James McMichael has remarked a similar division in his perceptive commentary on this poem in the course of his article "The Wallace Stevens Vulgates," *Southern Review*, n.s. 7 (July 1971): 706 f., which deals not with the romantic analogues to the poem and not so wholly with its mental action but seeks to place it as one of three poems in a spectrum of attitudes toward death.

52. See, among others, Litz, pp. 195-96; Kessler, p. 102; James Baird, "Transvaluation in Stevens' Poetics," *Studies in Honor of John C. Hodges and Alwin Thayer*, ed. Richard B. Davis and John L. Lievsay (Knoxville: University of Tennessee Press, 1961), p. 168; John J. Enck, *Wallace Stevens: Images and Judgments* (Carbondale: Southern Illinois University Press, 1964), p. 110; and Babbette Deutsch, *Poetry in Our Time* (New York: Columbia University Press, 1956), pp. 248-49.

53. Vendler, pp. 14, 15, 17, 24, and 35.

54. Vendler, p. 36.

55. Riddel has an interesting and related discussion of "Prologues to What Is Possible" at the end of his essay "Stevens on Imagination—the Point of Departure," in *The Quest for Imagination: Essays in Twentieth-Century Aesthetic Criticism*, ed. O. B. Hardison, Jr. (Cleveland: Press of Case Western Reserve University, 1971), pp. 79-81.

56. Ronald Sukenick, *Wallace Stevens: Musing the Obscure* (New York: New York University Press, 1967), p. 192.

57. Neither these two poems nor "A Mythology Reflects Its Region" appeared in print during Stevens' lifetime; all were first published in *Opus Posthumous*, 1957. Morse dates their composition as 1953-54 for "The Sail of Ulysses" and tentatively as 1955 for the other two.

58. Vendler, p. 21.

59. See *LWS* 636, where Stevens describes his development from *Notes* to *Credences of Summer* to *The Auroras of Autumn* as movement from an

"imaginative period" to "as close to the ordinary, the commonplace, and the ugly as it is possible for a poet to get."

60. In emphasizing those elements this brief discussion diverges from the many full-scale expositions of *Notes,* of which I have found particularly helpful those in Riddel, pp. 165-85; Doggett, pp. 98-119; Vendler, pp. 168-205; and Bloom (in *Wallace Stevens,* ed. Borroff), pp. 76-95.

61. Riddel, pp. 173-74.

62. Cf. *LWS* 303: "Poetry is like anything else; it cannot be made suddenly to drop all its rags and stand out naked, fully disclosed."

63. Stevens here uses "pleasure" in its special romantic and post-romantic sense, which has been explored by Lionel Trilling in his essay "The Fate of Pleasure" (1963), collected in *Beyond Culture: Essays on Literature and Learning* (New York: Viking Press, 1968), pp. 57-87. Trilling writes (p. 60): "[Wordsworth] speaks of 'the grand *elementary* principle of pleasure,' which is to say, pleasure not as mere charm or amenity but as the object of an instinct, of what Freud . . . was later to call a *drive.*"

64. Bloom, in *Wallace Stevens,* ed. Borroff, p. 94.

65. Vendler, pp. 198, 200.

66. Doggett, p. 119.

67. Cf. *NA* 57-58: "It is the *mundo* of the imagination in which the imaginative man delights and not the gaunt world of the reason."

68. Shelley has a similar usage in Panthea's speech from *Prometheus Unbound* (IV:236-38) describing the great sphere "solid as crystal" through which music and light (including green light) flow and in which other spheres revolve and the Spirit of Earth sleeps. I am grateful to Ms. Sheryl Pearson for calling this parallel to my attention.

Index

Italicized page numbers indicate detailed discussion of literary works.

Index

GEORGE BORNSTEIN has taught at M.I.T. and
Rutgers and is professor of English at the
University of Michigan. He is the author of
Yeats and Shelley (published by the University
of Chicago Press), coauthor of *British Periodicals
of the 18th and 19th Centuries*
and *Two Centuries of British Periodicals,*
and editor of *Romantic and Modern:
Revaluations of Literary Tradition.*

Library of Congress Cataloging in Publication Data

Bornstein, George.
    Transformations of romanticism in Yeats, Eliot, and
Stevens.

    Includes index.
    1. Yeats, William Butler, 1865–1939—Criticism and
interpretation.   2.   Eliot, Thomas Stearns, 1888–1965—
Criticism and interpretation.   3.   Stevens, Wallace, 1879–
1955—Criticism and interpretation.   4.   Romanticism—
England.   I.   Title.
PS324.B69   821'.9'120914   75-43241
ISBN 0-226-06643-6